# Memoirs of Theobald Wolfe Tone

You are holding a reproduction of an original work that is in the public domain in the United States of America, and possibly other countries. You may freely copy and distribute this work as no entity (individual or corporate) has a copyright on the body of the work. This book may contain prior copyright references, and library stamps (as most of these works were scanned from library copies). These have been scanned and retained as part of the historical artifact.

This book may have occasional imperfections such as missing or blurred pages, poor pictures, errant marks, etc. that were either part of the original artifact, or were introduced by the scanning process. We believe this work is culturally important, and despite the imperfections, have elected to bring it back into print as part of our continuing commitment to the preservation of printed works worldwide. We appreciate your understanding of the imperfections in the preservation process, and hope you enjoy this valuable book.

THEOBALD WOLFE TONE.

Drawn on Stone by C. Hullmandel, from a Portrait by Catherine Sampson Tone.

Published March 20th 1827, by Henry Colburn, London.

Printed by C. Hullmandel.

# MEMOIRS

OF

## THEOBALD WOLFE TONE.

WRITTEN BY HIMSELF.

COMPRISING

A COMPLETE JOURNAL OF HIS NEGOTIATIONS
TO PROCURE THE AID OF THE FRENCH FOR THE
LIBERATION OF IRELAND.

WITH

SELECTIONS FROM HIS DIARY

WHILST AGENT TO THE IRISH CATHOLICS.

EDITED BY HIS SON,

WILLIAM THEOBALD WOLFE TONE.

Victrix causa Diis placuit, sed victa Catoni.
PHARSALIA, lib. i. v. 128.

IN TWO VOLUMES.

VOL. I.

LONDON:
HENRY COLBURN, 8, NEW BURLINGTON STREET.
1827.

LONDON:
PRINTED BY S. AND R. BENTLEY, DORSET STREET.

## PREFACE.

THE present Work is laid before the Public as presenting, in the first place, a most curious and characteristic piece of auto-biography; and, in the second, as calculated to administer, in no slight degree, to that intense interest which is now almost universally felt throughout this Empire, on the subject of the affairs of Ireland. The eventful, though brief life of TONE, and the important scenes wherein he was so prominent an actor, cannot fail to arrest with irresistible force both the attention and the sympathies of the reader; who, whatever may be his political creed, must, if he has one spark of generous feeling, frequently find it kindled as he peruses the melancholy narrative.

For the publication of these documents we are originally indebted to the Author's son, (whose early years were spent in the service of the Emperor Napoleon,) and under whose eye they have been collected and printed in the United States. The present

Edition comprises every thing of interest in the American volumes which can fairly be included under its title.

The Editor introduces the fruits of his labour by stating, that he owes some account of the motives which have engaged him to delay the appearance of the Work until the present day, and to produce it now. But we will leave him to speak for himself.

"These Memoirs were never destined for the Public; they were written for one or two friends, now no more, and for his family, of which my mother and myself are the sole survivors. His pen, which always flowed with light and easy grace, was, of course, allowed to run in these careless memorandums with the utmost effusion and *abandon* of soul; they exhibit his passing feelings on every occasion, and are sometimes as severe on the failings and weaknesses of his own party, and of those to whom he was most warmly and sincerely attached, (and for whom he sacrificed the brilliant prospects of his youth, and, at length, his life,) as on their adversaries. Of course, while the interests in which he was engaged were yet alive, numbers, and some of them unsuspected at the time, might have been dangerously compromised, or seriously hurt, by this publication. In his latter days, when he anticipated, with the deepest despondency, the probable failure of his hopes, he used sometimes to exclaim, ' Thank God! no man has ever been compromised by me.' Young as I was at the time, I was brought up by my surviving parent in all the principles and feelings of my father.

But now, one quarter of a century is more than elapsed, and repeated revolutions have altered the political face of the world. The founder of the United Irish Society, the first of his countrymen who called on the people to unite, without discrimination of faith, for the independence of their country, has sealed with his blood the principles which he professed. His contemporaries, the men with whom he thought and acted, are mostly sunk in the grave; those who survive are either retired from public life or engaged in different pursuits; the very Government against which he struggled exists no more; and the country whose liberty he sought to establish has lost even that shadow of a national administration, and has sunk into a province of England. I cannot think that the publication of these Memoirs, at the present day, can injure the prospects or endanger the peace of any living being. His few surviving friends, and even his opponents, can only look on these relics with feelings of fond recollection for one of the most amiable, affectionate, and gentle-hearted of men—a man of the purest and sincerest principles and patriotism, (whatever may be deemed, according to the reader's opinions, of the *soundness* of his views,) and of the most splendid talents:—it is, besides, a tribute which I owe to his memory, and a sacred duty;—believing, as I do, that, in the eyes of impartial and uninterested posterity, they will be honourable to his character; that they throw a most interesting light on the political situation and history of Ireland; and that even yet, and in its present state, the views which they contain may be of some use to that country for which he died, and for which, though an exile from my infancy, I must ever feel the interest due to my native land.

Another motive which has determined me to bring out this work at present, is the late publication of some fragments of it in the New Monthly Magazine—a publication entirely unexpected by me, as I have never had any acquaintance or correspondence with the Editors of that journal. As I possess, and now republish, the original manuscript from whence the fragments were taken, I must do those gentlemen the justice to give my testimony in favour of their accuracy, (with the exception of a few trifling mistakes, very pardonable at such a distance of time, and which shall be rectified in the present work,) and to thank them for the liberality of their comments and observations. The character of these comments, and the very appearance of this biographical sketch, convince me that my father's name is not yet quite forgotten, and is still respected, even in the country of his adversaries. The amiability of his personal character secured him, indeed, even during his life-time and amidst all the rancour of political animosity, the rare advantage of preserving the friendship of many valuable and illustrious individuals, who were opposed to him in principles. He scarcely had a personal enemy, unless, perhaps, we except the Chancellor Fitzgibbon (Lord Clare) and the Hon. George Ponsonby, who agreed in this point alone: his spirit could never stoop to the petulant insolence of the one nor to the haughty dulness of the other. But I have never seen his name mentioned in any history of the times without respect and regret. I cannot, therefore, believe that even the most zealous partizans of the British Government would have the weakness, at this time and distance, to feel any objection to the publication of these writings.

Although the character of TONE, and his political principles, will be best developed by himself, yet his son may be allowed to give way to some of his feelings on this subject. His image is yet blended with the recollections of my infancy. To the soundest judgment and most acute penetration in serious business, he joined a simple and unaffected modesty, and the most perfect disinterestedness; no human breast could be more free from the meaner passions—envy, jealousy, avarice, cupidity; and, often oblivious of himself, he delighted in the fame and glory of others. Injuries he easily forgot; kindness, never. Though his constitution was nervous and sensitive to a very high degree, he was naturally of a most cheerful temper, and of a confiding, unsuspicious, and affectionate heart. Indeed, few men have enjoyed so completely the happiness of loving and of being beloved. His wife and family he perfectly adored; and the circle of his intimate friends, of those who were really and devotedly attached to him, comprised men of the most opposite parties and descriptions. His character was tinged with a vein of chivalry and romance; and, lively, polite, and accomplished, his youth was not entirely free from some imprudence and wildness. He was fond of pleasure as well as of glory; but the latter feeling was always in him subservient to principle, and his pleasures were pure, elegant, and of a simple taste, — such as music, literature, field sports; and polite society and conversation, especially that of amiable and accomplished women, with whom he was a universal favourite. His musical and literary taste was of the most cultivated delicacy; and the charms of his conversation, where a natural and national vein of wit and feeling flowed without effort or affectation, were indescribable. But, though formed to be the delight of society, the joys of home and domestic life were his real element. He was the fondest of husbands, of fathers, of sons, of brothers, and of friends. In the privacy of his modest fireside, the liveliest flow of spirits and of feeling was never interrupted by one moment of dulness or of harshness, and it was the happiest of retreats.

His success in the world was astonishing, and owing almost as much to the amiability of his character and his social qualities, as to his extraordinary talents. Obscure in his birth, and struggling with poverty and difficulties, his classical triumphs and acquirements at the University were of the highest order. On entering afterwards into life, he supported his father and numerous family by his sole efforts, and rose not only to independence and fame, but was received as a favourite in the first aristocratic circles, even before he engaged in politics. Amongst the illustrious families and characters with whom he was familiarly acquainted, and who certainly long remembered his name with affection, were the Duke of Leinster, Lord Moira and his noble and princely mother, the Hon. George Knox and Marcus Beresford, Plunkett, Grattan, Curran, Hamilton Rowan, P. Burrowes, Sir Laurence Parsons, Emmett, C. Bushe, Whitley Stokes, &c. I have already observed that, however opposed to many of them in politics, and when he was become a marked leader and most obnoxious to the government, he preserved their affection; and when, after Jackson's trial, he lay under a kind of proscription, they gave him noble and generous proofs of it.

His success in politics was no less wonderful. When he wrote his first pamphlet in favour of the Catholics, (the Northern Whig,) he was not acquainted with a single individual of that religion—so complete at that period was the distinction marked in society between the several sects. In a few months, he was the prime mover of their councils and accomplished the union between them and the Dissenters of the North.

His political principles will of course be blamed or approved, according to those of the reader. During his lifetime, some regarded him as a fanatical democrat and furious demagogue, whilst others in his own party accused him of haughtiness in his manner and of aristocratical prejudices. The fact is, that, though he preferred in theory a republican form of government, his main object was to procure the independence of his country under a liberal administration, whatever might be its form or name. His tastes and habits were rather aristocratical for the society with which he was sometimes obliged to mingle. I believe that, in reading these memoirs, many people will be surprized at (and some perhaps will blame) the moderation of his views. (The persecutions of the Government drove him much farther than he purposed at first.) But, from their fair and impartial perusal none can possibly rise without being convinced of his purity and patriotism, whatever they may deem of his wisdom and foresight. No man who ever engaged so deeply and earnestly in so great a cause was influenced so little by any motives of personal ambition, or so disinterestedly devoted to what he thought the interest of his country.

In opening these pages, it should also be remembered, that the situation and political organization of Ireland at that period were totally different both from what they had been before and from what they have fallen to since. She then possessed a separate government, and a national legislature nominally independent;—my father never considered himself as an Englishman, nor as a subject of Great Britain; but as a native and subject of the kingdom of Ireland, most zealously and passionately devoted to the rights, the liberties, and glory of his country.

At the epoch of the American war (1782), whilst England was exhausted by that fruitless contest, the unguarded state of Ireland, the efforts of the patriots in the legislature, and the simultaneous and formidable rising of the volunteers, had wrung from the British Government the reluctant acknowledgment of its independence. This period was brief and glorious. With the first dawn of liberty, the country took a new spring and began to flourish by her natural resources—the spirit of her people reviving with her commerce, industry, and manufactures. But this dawn was soon overcast by the corruption of her government and the bigoted intolerance of the ruling Protestant ascendancy; the former caried to the most open profligacy, and the latter to the most besotted blindness. My object is not to write a history, nor to anticipate what my father has urged with such force and eloquence in the following works and memoirs; but, had the Irish legislature, who recovered their independent rights, had the liberality to emancipate their Catholic brethren and allow them to participate in the benefits of free and equal citizenship, and had the volunteers admitted them into their ranks, England would never have recovered the power which she had lost. It would be a curious, but at this day a very vain, speculation, to calculate what those two independent but allied kingdoms might have risen to, cultivating their separate means under one sovereign and with one interest.

This wakening of the spirit of liberty roused, however, from their long slumber of slavery, the oppressed and degraded Catholics; who, by a strange anomaly, forming the original population of the country and the mass of the people, were at that period, and are still in some respects, aliens in their native land. My father was the first Protestant who engaged in their cause to its whole length, and experienced the greatest difficulty, in the beginning, to rouse them, if not to a sense of their wrongs, at least to the spirit of expressing them.*

But these efforts, by which the whole island began shortly to heave to her foundations, alarmed the jealousy of the members of that party which monopolized all the power and property of the country. They sacrificed its prosperity, honour, and independence, to secure the support of England; and the British ministry, with patient discretion, awaited the result; they gave all their means and aid to strengthen the Irish administration, and allowed it to render itself as odious as possible, and to destroy, in the hearts of the people, by its cruelty and insolence, all affection for their national Government. No other arms but those of corruption were used by England against the independence of Ireland, for its own administration took on itself all the task of reducing the people to slavery. (The distant King and Parliament of England were often solicited as mediators by the oppressed and miserable Irish.) It

* It is a remarkable fact, that most of the leaders of the United Irishmen who perished in the civil wars were Protestants:—Tone, Emmett, Russel, Lord Edward Fitzgerald, &c. Of the twenty prisoners in Fort George, four only were Catholics.

was this Government and this party, against which the animosity and attacks of my father were directed; it was the *Irish* Government which he sought to overturn, by uniting the divided factions of the people. His resentment against England was a secondary and incidental passion; it arose from her support of those abuses. He long endeavoured by legal and constitutional means, and even by soliciting the British Monarch and Government, to effect a reform; nor was it till all his hopes proved fruitless from that quarter, that he determined on attempting, by any means, the separation of the two countries.

As for the Irish administration, England reaped the fruits of her policy. It became so corrupt and so infamous, that it could no longer stand; and finally, its members bartered the existence of their country as a nation for paltry personal compensations to themselves. It was the cheapest bargain England ever drove. Was it the wisest? Instead of using her influence to reorganize that wretched government—to give it strength and popularity—by emancipating the people and attaching them to their institutions, she chose to absorb Ireland in her own sphere and efface it from the list of nations. But that execrable administration, in disappearing from existence, left behind it, as a pernicious legacy, all its abuses, confirmed and rooted in the soil, and now supported by the direct and open authority of the British monarch, laws, parliament, and constitution.

The union and incorporation of the two countries was but nominal, and the mass of the Irish population participated neither in the benefits nor privileges of the British institution.

This was a wretched and narrow policy. Instead of encouraging, by every means in its power, the industry and the mental and physical resources of Ireland, and thus adding to the general mass of wealth and information of the whole empire, a petty jealousy of her competition with the trade and manufactures of England has always engaged the Government of the latter country to keep down and crush, in every possible way, the natural spring and spirit of the Irish.

Whether England has gained much by the Union, time will show. The ministry has gained a clear reinforcement of 100 votes in Parliament; for no Irishman will ever consider himself as an Englishman, and whilst his own country is miserable and enslaved, what earthly motive but his own interest can influence him in questions which regard merely the liberties or interests of England? The people show no symptoms of attachment or loyalty to their new masters:—and for what should they be loyal? For six hundred years of slavery, misrule, and persecution! Ireland must be guarded at the same expense and with the same care as formerly, and is rather a heavy clog on the powers and means of Great Britain than a support and an addition to them. Nor is it absolutely impossible that, if some ambitious and unprincipled monarch hereafter should mount the throne, he may find in the Irish Catholics, of whom the mass will be brutalized by misgovernment, and rendered ignorant and ferocious, very proper instruments for his designs. They have no reason to admire nor to be attached to the British constitution, and would follow the call of Satan himself, were he to cheer them on to revenge—and who could blame them?

But I must not lose myself in dissertations which do not concern my subject,—for in my father's time no one dreamed of that Union; and his most violent adversaries, the most furious upholders of the Protestant ascendancy, would have been indignant at such a suggestion. Had it been prematurely proposed, they would, perhaps, have joined with their adversaries rather than have listened to it. The only conclusion which I wish to draw from these premises is, that England, by dissolving that Irish government, *has fully confirmed the charges adduced against it, and my father's opinion of it;* and till the abuses which it supported, and which have survived its fall, are corrected,—till that monopoly is removed by which all the rights and powers of citizenship and sovereignty are usurped by a favoured minority, whilst the remainder of the population groans in slavery,—Ireland, either under a separate and national administration, or as a province of Great Britain, will ever remain in an unnatural state of anarchy and misery, unable to cultivate her resources either for her own benefit or even for that of her masters.

The only liberties which I have taken with the following Memoirs, in preparing them for the public, were to suppress a few passages relative to family affairs (which concern nobody), and the account of some early amours, which my father, though a little wild in his youth, was too much of a gentleman to have allowed to appear, and which it would ill become his son to revive at this day."

# MEMOIRS

OF

# THEOBALD WOLFE TONE.

As I shall embark in a business, within a few days,* the event of which is uncertain, I take the opportunity of a vacant hour to throw on paper a few memorandums relative to myself and my family, which may amuse my boys, for whom I write them, in case they should hereafter fall into their hands.

I was born in the city of Dublin, on the 20th of June, 1763. My grandfather was a respectable farmer near Naas, in the county of Kildare. Being killed by a fall off a stack of his own corn, in the year 1766, his property, being freehold leases, descended to my father, his eldest son, who was at

* This Narrative was commenced at Paris in the month of August, 1796.

that time in successful business as a coachmaker. He set, in consequence, the lands which came thus into his possession, to his youngest brother, which eventually was the cause of much litigation between them, and ended in a decree of the Court of Chancery that utterly ruined my father; but of that hereafter. My mother, whose name was Lamport, was the daughter of a captain of a vessel in the West India trade, who, by many anecdotes which she has told me of him, was a great original; she had a brother who was an excellent seaman, and served as first lieutenant on board the Buckingham, commanded by Admiral Tyrrel, a distinguished officer in the British service.

I was their eldest son; but, before I come to my history, I must say a few words of my brothers. William, who was born in August, 1764, was intended for business, and was, in consequence, bound apprentice, at the age of fourteen, to an eminent bookseller. With him he read over all the voyages he could find, with which and some military history, he heated an imagination naturally warm and enthusiastic so much, that, at the age of sixteen, he ran off to London, and entered as a volunteer in the East India Company's service; but his first essay was very unlucky; for, instead of finding his way out to India, he was stopped at the Island of St. Helena, on which barren rock he remained in garrison for six years, when, his time being expired, he returned to Europe. It is highly to his honour, that, though he entered into such execrable society as the troops in the Company's service must be supposed to be, and at such an early age, he passed through them without being affected by the contagion of their manners or their principles. He even found means, in that degraded situation and remote spot, to cultivate his mind to a certain degree, so that I was much surprised, at our meeting in London, after a separation of, I believe, eight years, to find him with the manners of a gentleman and a considerable acquaintance with the best parts of English literature: he had a natural turn for poetry, which he had much improved, and I have among my papers a volume of his poems, all of them pretty, and some of them elegant. He was a handsome, well-made lad, with a very good address, and extremely well received among the women, whom he loved to excess. He was as brave as Cæsar, and loved the army. It was impossible for two men to entertain a more sincere, and, I may say, enthusiastic affection for each other, than he and I; and, at this hour, there is scarcely any thing on earth I regret so much as our separation. Having remained in Europe for three or four years, my father being, as I have above alluded to, utterly ruined by a lawsuit with his brother, Will took the resolution to try his fortune once more in India, from which (my own affairs being nearly desperate,) I did not attempt to dissuade him. In consequence, he re-entered the Company's service in the beginning of the year 1792, and arrived at Madras towards the end of the same year. With an advantageous figure, a good address, and the talents I have described, he recommended himself so far to the colonel of the battalion in which he served, that he gave him his discharge, with letters to his friends at Calcutta, and a small military command, which defrayed the expense of his voyage and procured him a gratification from the Company of £50. sterling for his good behaviour, on his arrival. The service he performed was quelling, at some hazard, a dangerous mutiny which arose among the black troops who were under his command, and had formed a scheme to run away with the ship. He had the good fortune to recommend himself so far to the persons at Calcutta to whom he had brought letters, that they introduced him, with strong recommendations, to a Mr. Marigny, a French officer, second in command in the army of the Nizam, who was then at Calcutta, purchasing military stores for that prince. Marigny, in consequence, gave him a commission in the Nizam's service, and promised him the command of a battalion of artillery, (the service to which he was attached,) as soon as they should arrive at the army. The stores, &c. being purchased, Will marched with the first division, of which he had the command, and arrived safely at the Nizam's camp. After some time, Marigny followed him, but, by an unforeseen accident, all my brother's expectations were blown up. A quarrel took place between Marigny and the Frenchman first in command, in which my brother, with an honourable indiscretion, engaged on the side of his friend. The consequence was, that Marigny was put in irons, as would have been Will also, if he had not applied for protection as a British subject to the English resident at the Nizam's court. This circumstance, together with the breaking out of the war between England and France, utterly put an end to all prospects of his advancement, as all the European officers in the Nizam's service were French, and he determined, in consequence, to return to Calcutta. On his journey, having travelled four hundred miles, and having yet two hundred to travel, he alighted off his horse, and went to shoot in a jungle, or thick wood, by the road side; on his return, he found his servant and horses in the hands of five ruffians who were plundering his baggage; he immediately ran up and fired on them, by which he shot one of them in the belly; another returned the fire with one of his own pistols, which they had seized, and shot him through the foot; they then made off with their booty, and, in this condition, my brother had to travel two hundred miles in that burning climate, at the commencement too of the rainy season, badly wounded, and without resources; his courage, however, and a good constitution, supported him, and he arrived at length at Calcutta, where he got speedily cured. His friends there had not forgotten him, and after some time, an opportunity offering of Major Palmer going up to Poonah as Resident at the court of the Paishwa of the Mahrattahs, they procured him strong recommendations to that court, and he set off with Major Palmer in high health and spirits, with expectations of the command at least of a battalion of artillery. Such is the substance of the last letter which I received from him. Since that time, I am utterly ignorant of his fate. I hope and trust the best respecting him; he has a good constitution, unshaken courage, a fluent address, and his variety of adventures must, by this time, have sufficiently matured his mind and given him experience. I look, therefore, with confidence to our meeting again, and the hour of that meeting will be one of the happiest of my life.

My second brother, Matthew, was of a temper very different from that of William; with less fire, he was much more solid; he spoke little, but thought a great deal; in the family we called him the Spectator, from his short face and his silence; but though he had not Will's volubility, and could not, like him, make a great display with frequently little substance, —and though his manner was reserved and phlegmatic, so as to be frequently absent in company, he had a rambling, enthusiastic spirit, stronger than any of us. He loved travelling and adventures for their own sakes. In consequence, before he was twenty-five, he had visited England twice or three times, and had spent twelve months in America, and as much in the West Indies. On his return from this last place, he mentioned to me his determination to pass over to France, and enter as a volunteer in the service of the Republic, in which I encouraged and assisted him. This was in the month of August, 1794. In consequence, he crossed over to Hamburgh, whence he passed to Dunkirk, and presenting himself as an Irishman desirous of the honour of serving in the French armies, was immediately thrown into prison on suspicion. There he remained until May, 1795, when he was discharged by the order of the Committee of Public Safety, and going on to Havre de Grace, he took his passage to America, where he arrived in safety, for the second time, about Christmas, at which time I was actually at New York, waiting for my passage to France; so that we were together in America, without knowing of each other, a circumstance which I regret most exceedingly, as, in the present situation of my affairs, it is at least possible that we may never meet again; but I am not of a very desponding temper. The variety of adventures we have both gone through, and the escapes we have had in circumstances of great peril, have made me a kind of fatalist, and therefore I look with confidence to the day (and, I hope, not a very remote one,) when the whole of my family shall be reunited and happy, by which time I think the spirit of adventure will, or at least ought to be, pretty well laid in all of us. My brother Matthew, like Will, is something of a poet, and has written some trifles in the burlesque style, that are not ill done. He is a brave lad, and I love him most sincerely. His age, at the time I write this, is about 26 or 27 years. Matthew is a sincere and ardent republican, and capable, as I think, of sacrificing every thing to his principles. I know not what effect his lying so long in a French prison may have had upon him, but, if I do not deceive myself, it has made no change in his sentiments. He is more temperate in all respects than William or myself, for we have both a strong attachment to pleasures and amusements, and a dash of coxcombry, from which he is totally free; and perhaps a little, at least, of the latter foible would be of no prejudice to him, nor render him less agreeable.

My third brother, Arthur, is much younger than any of us, being born about the year 1782; of course he is now fourteen years of age. If I can judge, when he grows up, he will resemble William exactly in mind and person. He is a fine, smart boy, as idle as possible, (which we have all been, without exception) with very quick parts, and as stout as a lion. My father was bent on making him an attorney, for which no boy on earth was ever so unfitted. He wished himself, having the true vagrant turn of the family, to go to sea; his father was obstinate, so was he, and the boy was in a fair way to be lost, when I prevailed, with some difficulty, on his father to consent to his going at least one voyage. In consequence, he sailed with a Captain Meyler to Portugal, being then about twelve years of age. On his return, he liked the sea so well that he was bound regularly apprentice to Captain Meyler, under whom he made a voyage to London and a second voyage to Portugal. On his return from this last trip, in June, 1795, he found me at Belfast on my departure for America, and he determined to accompany me. I was extremely happy to have him with us, and, in consequence, he crossed the Atlantic with me, and remained until I decided on coming to France, when I resolved to dispatch him to Ireland, to give notice to my friends there of what I was about. I put him, in consequence, on board the Susannah, Captain Baird, at Philadelphia, on the 10th December, 1795, since which time, from circumstances, it has been impossible for me to have heard of him; but I rely, with confidence, that he has arrived safe, and discharged his commission with ability and discretion.

My sister, whose name is Mary, is a fine young woman; she has all the peculiarity of our disposition, with all the delicacy of her own sex. If she were a man, she would be exactly like one of us; and, as it is, being brought up amongst boys, (for we never had but one more sister, who died a child,) she has contracted a masculine habit of thinking, without, however, in any degree, derogating from that feminine softness of manner which is suited to her sex and age. When I was driven into exile in America, as I shall relate hereafter, she determined to share my fortunes, and in consequence she also, like the rest of us, has made her voyage across the Atlantic.

My father and mother were pretty much like other people; but from this short sketch, with what I have to add concerning myself, I think it will appear that their children were not at all like other people, but have had, every one of them, a wild spirit of adventure, which, though sometimes found in an individual, rarely pervades a whole family, including even the females!—For my brother William has visited Europe, Asia, and Africa, before he was thirty years of age; Matthew has been in America twice, in the West Indies once, not to mention several trips to England, and his voyage and imprisonment in France, and all this before he was twenty-seven. Arthur, at the age of fourteen, has been once in England, twice in Portugal, and has twice crossed the Atlantic, going to and returning from America. My sister Mary crossed the same ocean, and I hope will soon do the same on her return. I do not here speak of my wife and our little boys and girl, the eldest of which latter was about eight, and the youngest two years old when we sailed for America: and, by all I can see, it is by no means certain that our voyages are yet entirely finished.

I come now to myself. I was, as I have said, the eldest child of my parents, and a very great favourite. I was sent at the age of eight or nine to an excellent English school, kept by Sisson Darling, a man to whose kindness and affection I was much indebted, and who took more than common pains with me. I respect him yet. I was very idle, and it was only the fear of shame which could induce me to exertion; nevertheless, at the approach of our public examinations, which were held quarterly, and at which all our parents and friends attended, I used to labour for some time, and generally with success, as I have obtained six or seven premiums in different branches at one examination, for mathematics, arithmetic, reading, spelling, recitation, use of the globes, &c. In two branches I always failed,—writing and the catechism, to which last I could never bring myself to apply. Having continued with Mr. Darling for about three years, and pretty nearly exhausted the circle of English education, he recommended strongly to my father to put me to a Latin school, and to prepare me for the University, assuring him that I was a fine boy, of uncommon talents, particularly for the mathematics; that it was a thousand pities to throw me away on business, when, by giving me a liberal education, there was a moral certainty I should become a fellow of Trinity College, which was a noble independence, besides the glory of the situation. In these arguments he was supported by the Parson of the Parish, Doctor Jameson, a worthy man, who used to examine me from time to time in the elements of Euclid. My father, who, to do him justice, loved me passionately, and spared no expense on me that his circumstances would afford, was easily persuaded by these authorities. It was determined that I should be a fellow of Dublin College. I was taken from Mr. Darling, from whom I parted with regret, and placed, about the age of twelve, under the care of the Rev. Wm. Craig, a man very different, in all respects, from my late preceptor. As the school was in the same street where we lived, (Stafford-street,) and as I was under my father's eye, I began Latin with ardour, and continued for a year or two with great diligence, when I began Greek, which I found still more to my taste; but, about this time, whether unlucky for me or not the future colour of my life must determine, my father, meeting with an accident of a fall down stairs, by which he was dreadfully wounded in the head, so that he narrowly escaped with life, found, on his recovery, his affairs so deranged in all respects, that he determined on quitting business and retiring to the country; a resolution which he executed accordingly, settling with all his creditors, and placing me with a friend near the school, whom he paid for my diet and lodging, besides allowing me a trifling sum for my pocket. In this manner I became, I may say, my own master before I was sixteen; and as at this time I am not remarkable for my discretion, it may well be judged I was less so then. The superintendence of my father being removed, I began to calculate that, according to the slow rate chalked out for me by Craig, I could very well do the business of the week in three days, or even two, if necessary, and that, consequently, the other three were lawful prize; I therefore resolved to appropriate three days in the week, at least, to my amusements, and the others to school, always keeping in the latter three the day of repetition, which included the business of the whole week, by which arrangement I kept my rank with the other boys of my class. I found no difficulty in convincing half a dozen of my schoolfellows of the justice of this distribution of our time, and by this means we established a regular system of what is called *mitching*; and we contrived, being some of the smartest boys at school, to get an ascendancy over the spirit of the master, so that when we entered the school in a body, after one of our days of relaxation, he did not choose to burn his fingers with any one of us, nor did he once write to my father to inform him of my proceedings, for which he most certainly was highly culpable. I must do myself and my schoolfellows the justice to say, that, though we were abominably idle, we were not vicious; our amusements consisted in walking to the country, in swimming-parties in the sea, and, particularly, in attending all parades, field days, and reviews of the garrison of Dublin in the Phœnix Park. I mention this particularly, because, independent of confirming me in a rooted habit of idleness, which I lament most exceedingly, I trace to the splendid appearance of the troops, and the pomp and parade of military show, the untameable desire which I ever since have had to become a soldier, a desire which has never once quitted me, and which, after sixteen years of various adventures, I am at last at liberty to indulge. Being at this time approaching seventeen years of age, it will not be thought incredible that *woman* began to appear lovely in my eyes, and I very wisely imagined that a red coat and cockade, with a pair of gold epaulets, would aid me considerably in my approaches to the objects of my adoration.

This, combined with the reasons above mentioned, decided me. I began to look on classical learning as nonsense; on a fellowship in Dublin college as a pitiful establishment; and, in short, regarded an ensign in a marching regiment the happiest creature living. The hour when I was to enter the University, which now approached, I looked forward to with horror and disgust. I absented myself more and more from school, to which I preferred attending the recruits on drill at the barracks; so that at length my schoolmaster, who apprehended I should be found insufficient at the examination for entering the college, and that he, of consequence, would come in for his share of the disgrace, thought proper to do what he should have done at least three years before, and wrote my father a full account of my proceedings. This immediately produced a violent dispute: I declared my passion for the army, and my utter dislike to a learned profession; but my father was as obstinate as I, and as he utterly refused to give me any assistance to forward my scheme, I had no resource but to submit or to follow my brother William's example, which latter I was too proud to do. In consequence, I sat down again, with a very bad grace, to pull up my lost time; and at length, after labouring for some time sorely against the grain, entered a pensioner of Trinity College, in February, 1781—being then not quite eighteen years of age: my tutor was the Rev. Matthew Young, the most popular in the University, and one of the first mathematicians in Europe. At first I began to study Logic courageously, but unluckily, at my very first examination, I happened to fall into the hands of an egregious dunce, one Ledwich, who, instead of giving me the premium, which, as best answerer, I undoubtedly merited, awarded it to another, and to me very indifferent judgments. I did not stand in need of this piece of injustice to alienate me once more from my studies. I returned with eagerness to my military plan: I besought my father to equip me as a volunteer, and to suffer me to join the British army in America, where the war still raged. He refused me as before, and in revenge I would not go near the College, nor open a book that was not a military one. In this manner we continued for above a twelvemonth, on very bad terms, as may well be supposed, without either party relaxing an inch from his determination. At length, seeing the war in America drawing to a close, and being beset by some of my friends who surrounded me, particularly Dr. Jameson, whom I have already mentioned, and a Mr. Brown, (who had been submaster at Mr. Darling's academy, and was now become a lawyer,) I submitted a second time, and returned to my studies after an interval of above a year. To punish me for my obstinacy, I was obliged to submit to "drop a class," as it is called in the University, namely, to recommence with the students who had entered a year after me. I continued my studies at College as I had done at school: that is, I idled until the last moment of delay. I then laboured hard for about a fortnight before the public examinations, and always secured good judgments, besides obtaining three premiums in the three last years of my course. During my progress through the University, I was not without adventures. Towards the latter end of the year 1782, I went out as second to a young fellow of my acquaintance, of the name of Foster, who fought with another lad, also of my acquaintance, named Anderson, and had the misfortune to shoot him through the head. The second to Anderson was William Armstrong, my most particular friend, who is now a very respectable clergyman, and settled at Dungannon. As Anderson's friends were outrageous against Foster and me, we were obliged at first to withdraw ourselves, but after some time their passion abated, and I returned to College, whence this adventure was near driving me a second time and for ever. Foster stood his trial and was acquitted; against me there was no prosecution. In this unfortunate business the eldest of us was not more than twenty years of age.

At length, about the beginning of the year 1785, I became acquainted with my wife. She was the daughter of William Witherington, and lived, at that time, in Grafton-street, in the house of her grandfather, a rich old clergyman, of the name of Fanning. I was then a scholar of the house in the University, and every day, after commons, I used to walk under her windows with one or the other of my fellow-students. I soon grew passionately fond of her, and she, also, was struck with me, though certainly my appearance, neither then nor now, was much in my favour; so it was, however, that before we had ever spoken to each other, a mutual affection had commenced between us. She was, at this time, not sixteen years of age, and as beautiful as an angel. She had a brother some years older than herself; and as it was necessary, for my admission to the family, that I should be first acquainted with him, I soon contrived to be introduced to him; and as he played well on the violin, and I was myself a musical man, we grew intimate; the more so, as it may well be supposed I neglected no fair means to recommend myself to him and the rest of the family, with whom I soon became a favourite. My affairs now advanced prosperously; my wife and I grew passionately fond of each other; and, in a short time, I proposed to her to marry me without asking consent of any one, knowing well it would be in vain to expect it: she accepted the proposal as frankly as I made it, and one beautiful morning, in the month of July, we ran off together and were married. I carried her out of town to Maynooth for a few days, and when the first eclat of passion had subsided, we were forgiven on all sides, and settled in lodgings near my wife's grandfather.

I was now, for a very short time, as happy as possible, in the possession of a beautiful creature that I adored, and who every hour grew more and more upon my heart. The scheme of a fellowship, which I never relished, was now abandoned, and it was determined that, when I had taken my degree of Bachelor of Arts, I should go to the Temple, study the law, and be called to the bar. I continued, in consequence, my studies in the University, and obtained my last premium two or three months after I was married. In February, 1786, I commenced Bachelor of Arts, and shortly after resigned my scholarship, and quitted the University. I may observe here, that I made some figure as a scholar; and should have been much more successful if I had not been so inveterately idle, partly owing to my passion for a military life, and partly to the distractions to which my natural dispositions and temperament but too much exposed me. As it was, however, I obtained a scholarship, three premiums, and three medals from the Historical Society, a most admirable institution, of which I had the honour to be Auditor and also to close the session with a speech from the chair, the highest compliment which that society is used to bestow. I look back on my college days with regret, and I preserve, and ever shall, a most sincere affection for the University of Dublin.

But to return. The tranquil and happy life I spent for a short period after my marriage was too good to last. We were obliged to break off all connection with my wife's family, who began to treat us with all possible slight and disrespect. We removed, in consequence, to my father's, who then resided near Clain, in the county of Kildare, and whose circumstances could, at that time, but ill bear such an addition to his family. It is doing him, however, but justice to mention, that he received and treated us with the greatest affection and kindness, and, as far he was able, endeavoured to make us forget the grievous mortifications we had undergone. After an interval of a few months, my wife was brought to bed of a girl, a circumstance which, if possible, increased my love for her a thousand fold; but our tranquillity was again broken in upon by a most terrible event. On the 16th October, 1786, the house was broken open by a gang of robbers, to the number of six, armed with pistols, and having their faces blackened. Having tied the whole family, they proceeded to plunder and demolish every article they could find, even to the unprofitable villainy of breaking the china, looking-glasses, &c. At length, after two hours, a maid-servant, whom they had tied negligently, having made her escape, they took the alarm, and fled with precipitation, leaving the house such a scene of horror and confusion as can hardly be imagined. With regard to myself, it is impossible to conceive what I suffered. As it was early in the night, I happened to be in the court-yard, where I was seized and tied by the gang, who then proceeded to break into the house, leaving a ruffian sentinel over me, with a case of pistols cocked in his hand. In this situation I lay for two hours, and could hear distinctly the devastation which was going on within. I expected death every instant, and can safely and with great truth declare, my apprehensions for my wife had so totally absorbed the whole of my mind, that my own existence was then the least of my concern. When the villains, including my sentry, ran off, I scrambled on my feet with some difficulty, and made my way to a window, where I called, but received no answer. My heart died within me. I proceeded to another and another, but still no answer. It was horrible. I set myself to gnaw the cords with which I was tied, in a transport of agony and rage, for I verily believed that my whole family lay murdered within, when I was relieved from my unspeakable terror and anguish by my wife's voice, which I heard calling on my name at the end of the house. It seems that, as soon as the robbers fled, those within had untied each other with some difficulty, and made their escape through a back window: they had got a considerable distance from the house before, from their fright, they recollected me, of whose fate they were utterly ignorant, as I was of theirs. Under these circumstances, my wife had the courage to return alone, and in the dark, to find me out, not knowing but she might again fall into the hands of the villains from whom she had scarcely escaped, or that I might be lying a lifeless carcase at the threshold. I can imagine no greater effort of courage; but of what is not a woman capable for him she truly loves? She cut the cords which bound me, and at length we joined the rest of the family at a little hamlet within half a mile of the house, whither they had fled for shelter. Of all the adventures wherein I have been hitherto engaged, this, undoubtedly, was the most horrible. It makes me shudder even now to think of it. It was some consolation that none of us sustained any personal injury, except my father, whom one of the villains scarred on the side of the head with a knife: they respected the women, whose danger made my only fear, and one of them had even the humanity to carry our little daughter from her cradle where she lay screaming, and to place her beside my wife on the bed whereon she was tied with my mother and sister. This terrible scene, besides infinitely distressing us by the heavy loss we sustained, and which my father's circumstances could very ill bear, destroyed, in a great degree, our domestic enjoyments. I slept continually with a case of pistols at my pillow, and a mouse could not stir but I was on my feet and through the house from top to bottom. If any one knocked at the door after nightfall, we flew to our arms, and, in this manner, we kept a most painful garrison through the winter. I should observe here, that two of the ruffians being taken in an unsuccessful attempt, within a few days after our robbery, were hanged, and that my father's watch was found on one of them.

At length, when our affairs were again reduced into some little order, my father supplied me with a small sum of money, (which was, however, as much as he could spare,) and I set off for London, leaving my wife and daughter with my father, who treated them, during my absence, with great affection. After a dangerous passage to Liverpool, wherein we ran some risk of being lost, I arrived in London, in January, 1787, and immediately entered my name as a student at law on the books of the Middle Temple; but this I may say was all the progress I ever made in that profession. I had no great affection for study in general, but that of the law I particularly disliked, and to this hour I think it an illiberal profession, both in its principles and practice. I was, likewise, amenable to nobody for my conduct; and, in consequence, after the first month I never opened a law book, nor was I ever three times in Westminster Hall in my life. In addition to the reasons I have mentioned, the extreme uncertainty of my circumstances, which kept me in much uneasiness of mind, disabled me totally from that cool and systematic habit of study which is indispensable for attaining a knowledge of a science so abstruse and difficult as that of the English code. However, one way or another I contrived to make it out. I had chambers in the Temple, (No. 4, Hare Court, on the first floor,) and whatever difficulties I had otherwise to struggle with, contrived always to preserve the appearance of a gentleman, and to maintain my rank with my fellow-students, if I can call myself a student. One resource I derived from the exercise of my talents, such as they were: I wrote several articles for the European Magazine, mostly critical reviews of new publications. My reviews were poor performances enough; however, they were in general as good as those of my brother critics; and in two years I received, I suppose, about £50 sterling for my writings, which was my main object; for, as to literary fame, I had then no great ambition to attain it. I likewise, in conjunction with two of my friends, named Jebb and Radcliff, wrote a burlesque novel, which we called "Belmont Castle," and was intended to ridicule the execrable trash of the Circulating Libraries. It was tolerably well done, particularly Radcliff's part, which was by far the best; yet so it was that we could not find a bookseller who would risk the printing it, though we offered the copyright gratis to several. It was afterwards printed in Dublin, and had some success, though I believe, after all, it was most relished by the authors and their immediate connexions.

At the Temple I became intimate with several young men of situation and respectability, particularly with the Hon. George Knox, son of Lord Northland, with whom I formed a friendship of which I am as proud as of any circumstance in my life. He is a man of inappreciable merit, and loved to a degree of enthusiasm by all who have the happiness to know him. I scarcely know any person whose esteem and approbation I covet so much; and I had, long after the commencement of our acquaintance, when I was in circumstances of peculiar and trying difficulty and deserted by many of my former friends, the unspeakable consolation and support of finding George Knox still the same, and of preserving his esteem unabated. His steady friendship on that occasion I shall mention in its place; it has made an indelible impression of gratitude and affection on my heart. I likewise renewed an old college acquaintance with John Hall, who, by different accessions to his fortune, found himself in possession of about £14,000 sterling a year. He had changed his name twice, for two estates; first to that of Stevenson, and then to Wharton, which is his present name. He was then a member of the

British Parliament, and to his friendship I was indebted for the sum of £150 sterling, at a time when I was under great pecuniary difficulties. Another old college friend I recall with sentiments of sincere affection,—Benjamin Phipps, of Cork. He kept a kind of bachelor's house, with good wine and an excellent collection of books, (*not law books,*) all which were as much at my command as at his. With some oddities, which to me only rendered him more amusing, he had a great fund of information, particularly of political detail, and in his company I spent some of the pleasantest hours which I passed in London.

At length, after I had been at the Temple something better than a year, my brother William, who had returned a few months before from his first expedition to St. Helena, joined me, and we lived together in the greatest amity and affection for about nine months, being the remainder of my stay in London. At this distance of time, now eight years, I feel my heart swell at the recollection of the happy hours we spent together. We were often without a guinea, but that never affected our spirits for a moment, and if ever I felt myself oppressed by some untoward circumstance, I had a never-failing resource and consolation in his friendship, his courage, and the invincible gaiety of his disposition, which nothing could ruffle. With the companionable qualities he possessed, it is no wonder that he recommended himself to Ben. Phipps, so that he was soon, I believe, a greater favourite with him than even I was. They were inseparable. It fills my mind now with a kind of tender melancholy, which is not unpleasing, to recall the many delightful days we three have spent together, and the walks we have taken—sometimes to a review; sometimes to see a ship of war launched; sometimes to visit the Indiamen at Deptford, a favourite expedition with Phipps. Will, besides his natural gaiety, had an inexhaustible fund of pure Irish humour; I was pretty well myself, and Phipps, like the landlord of the Hercules Pillars, was *an excellent third man*. In short, we made it out together admirably. As I foresaw by this time that I should never be Lord Chancellor, and as my mind was naturally active, a scheme occurred to me, to the maturing of which I devoted some time and study; this was a proposal to the minister to establish a colony in one of Cook's newly discovered islands in the South Sea, on a military plan, (for all my ideas ran in that track,) in order to put a bridle on Spain in time of peace, and to annoy her grievously in that quarter in time of war. In arranging this system, which I think even now was a good one for England, I read every book I could find relating to South America, as Ulloa, Anson, Dampierre, Woodes, Rogers, Narborough, and especially the Bucaniers, who were my heroes, and whom I proposed to myself as the archetypes of the future colonists. Many and many a delightful evening did my brother, Phipps, and I, spend in reading, writing, and talking of my project, in which, if it had been adopted, it was our firm resolution to have embarked. At length, when we had reduced it into a regular shape, I drew up a memorial on the subject, which I addressed to Mr. Pitt, and delivered with my own hand to the porter in Downing-street. We waited, I will not say patiently, for about ten days, when I addressed a letter to the minister mentioning my memorial and praying an answer, but this application was as unsuccessful as the former. Mr. Pitt took not the smallest notice of either memorial or letter, and all the benefit we reaped from our scheme was the amusement it afforded us during three months, wherein it was the subject of our constant speculation. I regret the delightful reveries which then occupied my mind. It was my first essay in what I may call politics, and my disappointment made an impression on me that is not yet quite obliterated. In my anger, I made something like a vow that, if ever I had an opportunity, I would make Mr. Pitt sorry, and perhaps fortune may yet enable me to fulfil that resolution. It was about this time I had a very fortunate escape:—my affairs were exceedingly embarrassed, and just at a moment when my mind was harassed and sore with my own vexations, I received a letter from my father, filled with complaints, and a description of the ruin of his circumstances, which I afterwards found was much exaggerated. In a transport of rage, I determined to enlist as a soldier in the India Company's service; to quit Europe for ever, and to leave my wife and child to the mercy of her family, who might, I hoped, be kinder to her when I was removed. My brother combated this resolution by every argument in his power; but, at length, when he saw me determined, declared I should not go alone, and that he would share my fate to the last extremity. In this gloomy state of mind, deserted as we thought by gods and men, we set out together for the India House, in Leadenhall-street, to offer ourselves as volunteers; but on our arrival there, were informed that the season being passed, no more ships would be sent out that year, but that, if we returned about the month of March following, we might be received. The clerk to whom we addressed ourselves seemed not a little surprised at two young fellows of our appearance presenting ourselves on such a business, for we were extremely well-dressed, and Will (who was spokesman for both) had an excellent address. Thus we were stopped; and I believe we were the single instance, since the beginning of the world, of two men absolutely bent on ruining themselves who could not find the means! We returned to my chambers, and, desperate as were our fortunes, could not help laughing to think that India, the great gulf of all undone beings, should be shut against us alone. Had it been the month of March instead of September, we should most infallibly have gone off; and, in that case, I should most probably at this hour be carrying a brown musket on the coast of Coromandel. Providence, however, decreed it otherwise, and reserved me, as I hope, for better things.

I had been now two years at the Temple, and had

kept eight terms;—that is to say, I had dined three days in each term in the common hall. As to law, I knew exactly as much about it as I did of necromancy. It became, however, necessary to think of my return; and, in consequence, I made application, through a friend, to my wife's grandfather, to learn his intentions as to her fortune. He exerted himself so effectually in our behalf, that the old gentleman consented to give 500*l*. immediately, and expressed a wish for my immediate return. In consequence, I packed up directly, and set off, with my brother, for Ireland. We landed at Dublin on the 23d December, and on Christmas-day, 1788, arrived at my father's house at Blackhall, where I had the satisfaction to find all my family in health, except my wife, who was grown delicate, principally from the anxiety of her mind on the uncertainty of her situation. Our little girl was now between two and three years old, and was charming. After remaining a few days at Blackhall, we came up to Dublin, and were received as at first, by my wife's family, in Grafton-street. Mr. Fanning paid me punctually the sum he had promised, and my wife and I both flattered ourselves that all past animosities were forgotten, and that the reconciliation was as sincere on their part as it most assuredly was on ours. I now took lodgings in Clarendon-street, purchased about 100*l*. worth of law books, and determined, in earnest, to begin and study the profession to which I was doomed. In pursuance of this resolution, I commenced Bachelor of Laws in February, 1789, and was called to the bar in due form, in Trinity term following; shortly after which I went my first (the Leinster) circuit, having been previously elected a member of the Bar club. On this circuit, notwithstanding my ignorance, I pretty nearly cleared my expenses; and I cannot doubt, had I continued to apply sedulously to the law, I might have risen to some eminence; but, whether it was my incorrigible habits of idleness, the sincere dislike I had to the profession, (which the little insight I was beginning to get into it did not tend to remove,) or controlling destiny, I know not; but so it was, that I soon got sick and weary of the law. I continued, however, for form's sake, to go to the courts and wear a foolish wig and gown, for a considerable time, and I went the circuit, I believe, in all three times; but as I was, modestly speaking, one of the most ignorant barristers in the four courts, and as I took little, or rather no pains to conceal my contempt and dislike of the profession, and especially as I had neither the means nor the inclination to treat messieurs the attorneys, and to make them drink, (a sacrifice of their respectability which even the most liberal-minded of the profession are obliged to make,) I made, as may be well supposed, no great exhibition at the Irish bar.

I had not been long a counsellor when the *coup de grace* was given to my father's affairs by a decree in Chancery which totally ruined him; this was in the law-suit between him and his brother, who was lieutenant of Grenadiers in the 22d regiment. During the whole of this business I obstinately refused to take any part, not thinking it decent to interfere where the parties were both so nearly allied to me. When, however, my father was totally ruined, I thought it my duty, as it was most certainly my inclination, to assist him, even to distressing myself; a sacrifice which the great pains and expense he had bestowed on my education well merited. I, in consequence, strained every nerve to preserve a remnant of his property; but his affairs were too desperate, and I was myself too poor to relieve him effectually, so that, after one or two unavailing efforts, by which I lost considerably with reference to my means without essentially serving him, we were obliged to submit, and the last of his property, consisting of two houses, one in Stafford-street, and one on Summerhill, were sold, much under their value, to men who took advantage of our necessities, as is always the case. Soon after, he had the good fortune to obtain a place under the paving board, which he yet retains, and which secures him a decent, though moderate, independence.

As the law grew every day more and more disgustful, to which my want of success contributed, though in that respect I never had the injustice to accuse the world of insensibility to my merit, as I well knew the fault was my own;—but being, as I said, more and more weary of a profession for which my temper and habits so utterly disqualified me, I turned my attention to politics, and, as one or two of my friends had written such things with success, determined to try my hand on a pamphlet. Just at this period the *Whig Club* was instituted in Ireland, and the press groaned with publications against them on the part of Government. Two or three defences had likewise appeared, but none of them extraordinary. Under these circumstances, though I was very far from entirely approving the system of the Whig Club, and much less their principles and motives, yet, seeing them at the time the best-constituted political body which the country afforded, and agreeing with most of their positions, though my own private opinions went infinitely farther, I thought I could venture on their defence without violating my own consistency. I therefore sat down, and in a few days finished my first pamphlet, which I entitled " *A Review of the last Session of Parliament.*" To speak candidly of this performance, it was barely above mediocrity, if it rose so high; nevertheless, as it was written evidently on honest principles, and did not censure or flatter one party or the other, without assigning sufficient reason, it had a certain degree of success. The *Northern Whig Club* reprinted and distributed a large impression at their own expense, with an introduction highly complimentary to the author, whom, at that time, they did not even know; and a very short time after, when the production was understood to be mine, they did me the honour to elect me a member of their body, which they notified to me by a very handsome letter, signed by their Secretary, Henry Joy, jun. of Belfast, and to which I returned a suitable answer. But this was not all. The leaders of the Whig Club, conceiving that my talents, such as they were, might be of service to their cause, and not expecting much intractability from a young lawyer who had his fortune to make, sent a brother barrister to compliment me on my performance, and to thank me for the zeal and ability I had shown. I was, in consequence, introduced to George Ponsonby, a distinguished member of the body, and who might be considered as the leader of the Irish opposition; with him, however, I never had any communication further than ordinary civilities. Shortly after, the barrister above-mentioned spoke to me again: he told me the Ponsonbys were a most powerful family in Ireland; that they were much pleased with my exertions, and wished, in consequence, to attach me to them; that I should be employed as counsel on a petition then pending before the House of Commons, which would put a hundred guineas in my pocket, and that I should have professional business put in my way, from time to time, that should produce me at least as much per annum; he added, that they were then, it was true, out of place, but that they would not be always so, and that, on their return to office, their friends when out of power would naturally be first considered; he likewise observed, that they had influence, direct or indirect, over no less than two-and-twenty seats in Parliament; and insinuated pretty plainly that when we were better acquainted, it was highly probable I might come in on one of the first vacancies. All this was highly flattering to me, the more so as my wife's fortune was now nearly exhausted, partly by our inevitable expenses, and partly by my unsuccessful efforts to extricate my father. I did, it was true, not much relish the attaching myself to any great man, or set of men, but I considered, as I have said before, that the principles they advanced were such as I could conscientiously support, *so far as they went*, though mine went much beyond them. I therefore thought there was no dishonour in the proposed connexion, and I was certainly a little dazzled with the prospect of a seat in Parliament, at which my ambition began to expand. I signified, in consequence, my readiness to attach myself to the Whigs, and I was instantly retained in the petition for the borough of Dungarven, on the part of James Carrigee Ponsonby, Esq.

I now looked upon myself as a sort of political character, and began to suppose that the House of Commons, and not the bar, was to be the scene of my future exertions; but in this I reckoned like a sanguine young man. Month after month elapsed without any communication on the part of George Ponsonby, whom I looked upon as most immediately my object. He always spoke to me, when we met by chance, with great civility, but I observed that he never mentioned one word of politics. I therefore at last concluded that he had changed his mind, or that, on a nearer view, he had discovered my want of capacity; in short I gave up all thoughts of the connexion, and determined to trouble myself no more about Ponsonby or the Whigs; and I calculated, that as I had written a pamphlet which they thought had served them, and as they had in consequence employed me professionally in a business which produced me eighty guineas, accounts were balanced on both sides, and all further connexion was at an end. But my mind had now got a turn for politics. I thought I had at last found my element, and I plunged into it with eagerness. A closer examination into the situation of my native country had very considerably extended my views, and, as I was sincerely and honestly attached to her interests, I soon found reason not to regret that the Whigs had not thought me an object worthy their cultivation. I made speedily what was to me a great discovery, though I might have found it in Swift and Molyneux;—namely, that the influence of England was the radical vice of our Government, and consequently that Ireland would never be either free, prosperous, or happy, until she was independent; and, that independence was unattainable whilst the connexion with England existed. In forming this theory, which has ever since unvaryingly directed my political conduct, to which I have sacrificed every thing, and am ready to sacrifice my life if necessary, I was exceedingly assisted by an old friend of mine, Sir Lawrence Parsons, whom I look upon as one of the very *very few* honest men in the Irish House of Commons. It was he who first turned my attention to this great question, but I very soon ran far a-head of my master. It is in fact to him I am indebted for my first comprehensive view of the actual situation of Ireland: what his conduct might be in a crisis, I know not, but I can answer for the truth and justice of his theory. I now began to look on the little politics of the Whig Club with great contempt—their peddling about petty grievances, instead of going to the root of the evil; and I rejoiced that, if I was poor, as I actually was, I had preserved my independence and could speak my sentiments without being responsible to any body but the law.

An occasion soon offered to give vent to my newly received opinions. On the appearance of a rupture with Spain, I wrote a pamphlet to prove that Ireland was not bound by the declaration of war, but might, and ought, as an independent nation, to stipulate for a neutrality. In examining this question, I advanced that of separation, with scarcely any reserve, much less disguise; but the public mind was by no means so far advanced as mine, and my pamphlet made not the smallest impression. The day after it appeared, as I stood *perdue* in the bookseller's shop, listening after my own reputation, Sir Henry Cavendish, a notorious slave of the House of Commons, entered, and throwing my unfortunate pamphlet on the counter in a rage, exclaimed: *Mr. Byrne, if the author of that work is serious, he ought to be hanged.* Sir Henry was succeeded by a Bishop, an *English* Doctor of Divinity, with five or six thousand a year, *laboriously* earned in the church. His lordship's anger was not much less than that of the other personage. *Sir*, said he, *if the principles contained in that abominable work were to spread, do you know that you would have to pay for your coals at the rate of five pounds a ton?* Notwithstanding these criticisms, which I have faithfully quoted against myself, I continue to think my pamphlet a good one; but apparently the publisher, Mr. Byrne, was of a different opinion, for I have every reason to believe that he suppressed the whole impression, *for which his own Gods damn him.*

Shortly after the premature end of my second pamphlet, which I have recorded, and which did not, however, change my opinion on its merit, for *Victrix causa Diis placuit, sed victa Catoni,* we came to an open rupture with my wife's family. It is not my intention to enter upon this subject. One circumstance is sufficient to prove that the breach was not of our seeking, viz. that we had every thing to lose and nothing to gain by a quarrel. * * * * *

About this time it was that I formed an acquaintance with my invaluable friend Russell, a circumstance which I look upon as one of the most fortunate of my life. He is a man whom I love as a brother. I will not here attempt a panegyric on his merits; it is sufficient to say, that to an excellent understanding he joins the purest principles and the best of hearts. I wish I had ability to delineate his character, with justice to his talents and his virtues. He well knows how much I esteem and love him, and I think there is no sacrifice friendship could exact, that we would not with cheerfulness make for each other, to the utmost hazard of life or fortune.

There cannot be imagined a more perfect harmony, I may say identity of sentiment, than exists between us; our regard for each other has never suffered a moment's relaxation from the hour of our first acquaintance, and I am sure it will continue to the end of our lives. I think the better of myself for being an object of esteem to such a man as Russell. I love him and I honour him. I frame no system of happiness for my future life, in which the enjoyment of his society does not constitute a most distinguishing feature, and, if I am ever inclined to murmur at the difficulties wherewith I have so long struggled, I think on the inestimable treasure I possess in the affection of my wife and the friendship of Russell, and acknowledge that all my labours and sufferings are overpaid. I may truly say that, even at this hour, when I am separated from both of them and uncertain whether I may ever be so happy as to see them again, there is no action of my life which has not a remote reference to their opinion, which I equally prize. When I think I have acted well, and that I am likely to succeed in the important business wherein I am engaged, I say often to myself, My dearest love and my friend Russell will be glad of this.

But to return to my history. My acquaintance with Russell commenced by an argument in the gallery of the House of Commons. He was at that time enamoured of the Whigs, but I knew these gentlemen a little better than he, and indeed he did not long remain under the delusion. We were struck with each other, notwithstanding the difference of our opinions, and agreed to dine together next day, in order to discuss the question. We liked each other better the second day than the first, and every succeeding one has increased and confirmed our mutual esteem.

My wife's health continuing still delicate, she was ordered by her physician to bathe in the salt-water. I hired, in consequence, a little box of a house on the sea side, at Irishtown, where we spent the summer of 1790. Russell and I were inseparable, and, as our discussions were mostly political, and our sentiments agreed exactly, we extended our views, and fortified each other in the opinions, to the propagation and establishment of which we have ever since been devoted. I recall with transport the happy days we spent together during that period; the delicious dinners, in the preparation of which my wife, Russell, and myself, were all engaged; our afternoon walks, and the discussions we had as we lay stretched on the grass. It was delightful! Sometimes Russell's venerable father, a veteran of nearly seventy, with the courage of a hero, the serenity of a philosopher, and the piety of a saint, used to visit our little mansion, and that day was a *fête*. My wife doated on the old man, and he loved her like one of his children. I will not attempt, because I am unable, to express the veneration and regard I had for him, and I am sure that, next to his own sons, and scarcely below them, he loved and esteemed me. Russell's brother, John, too, used to visit us; a man of a most warm and affectionate heart, and incontestably of the most companionable talents I ever met. His humour, which was pure and natural, flowed in an inexhaustible stream. He had not the strength of character of my friend Tom, but for the charms of conversation he excelled him and all the world. Sometimes, too, my brother William used to join us for a week, from County Kildare, where he resided with my brother Matthew, who had lately commenced a cotton manufactory at Prosperous, in that county. I have already mentioned the convivial talents he possessed. In short, when the two Russells, my brother, and I, were assembled, it is impossible to conceive a happier society. I know not whether our wit was perfectly classical or not, nor does it signify. If it was not sterling, at least it passed current amongst ourselves. If I may judge, we were none of us destitute of the humour indigenous to the soil of Ireland; for three of us I can answer, they possessed it in an eminent degree; add to this, I was the only one of the four who was not a poet, or at least a maker of verses: so that every day produced a ballad, or some poetical squib, which amused us after dinner; and, as our conversation turned upon no ribaldry nor indecency, my wife and sister never left the table. These were delicious days. The rich and great, who sit down every day to the monotony of a splendid entertainment, can form no idea of the happiness of our frugal meal, nor of the infinite pleasure we found in taking each his part in the preparation and attendance. My wife was the centre and the soul of all. I scarcely know which of us loved her best; her courteous manners, her goodness of heart, her incomparable humour, her never-failing cheerfulness, her affection for me and for our children, rendered her the object of our common admiration and delight. She loved Russell as well as I did. In short, a more interesting society of individuals, connected by purer motives and animated by a more ardent attachment and friendship for each other, cannot be imagined.

During the course of this summer, there were strong appearances of a rupture between England and Spain, relative to Nootka Sound. I had mentioned to Russell my project for a military colony in the South Seas, and, as we had neither of us any thing better to do, we sat down to look over my papers and memorandums regarding that business. After some time, rather to amuse ourselves than with an expectation of its coming to any thing, we enlarged and corrected my original plan, and, having dressed up a handsome memorial on the subject, I sent it enclosed in a letter to the Duke of Richmond, then Master of the Ordnance. I thought I should hear no more about it, but we were not a little surprised when, a few days after, I received an answer from his Grace, in which, after speaking with great civility of the merits of my plan, he informed me such business was out of his department, but that, if I desired it, he would deliver my memorial, and recommend it to the notice of Lord Grenville, Secretary of State for Foreign Affairs, whose business it properly was. I immediately wrote him an answer of acknowledgment, entreating him to support my plan, and by the same post, wrote also to Lord Grenville. In a few days I received answers from them both, informing me that the memorial had been received by Lord Grenville, and should be taken into speedy consideration, when, if any measures were to be adopted in consequence, I might depend on receiving further information. These letters we looked upon as leaving it barely possible that something might be done in the business, though very unlikely; and so indeed it proved; for shortly after, a kind of peace, called a convention, was agreed upon between Spain and England, on which I wrote once more to Lord Grenville, enclosing a second memorial, in order to learn his determination, when I received a very civil answer, praising my plan, &c. and informing me that existing circumstances had rendered it unnecessary, at that time, to put it in execution, but that ministers would keep it in recollection. Thus ended, for the second time, my attempt to colonize in the South Seas, a measure which I still think might be attended with the most beneficial consequences to England. I keep all the papers relating to this business, including the originals of the minister's letters, and I have likewise copied the whole of them in a quarto book, to which I refer for further information. It was singular enough, this correspondence!—continued by two of the King of England's cabinet-ministers at St.

James's, on the one part, and Russell and myself, from my little box at Irishtown, on the other. If the measure I proposed had been adopted, we were both determined on going out with the expedition, in which case, instead of planning revolutions in our own country, we might be now, perhaps, carrying on a privateering war (for which, I think, we have each of us talents,) on the coasts of Spanish America. This adventure is an additional proof of the romantic spirit I have mentioned in the beginning of my memoirs, as a trait in our family; and, indeed, my friend Russell was, in that respect, completely one of ourselves. The minister's refusal did not sweeten us much towards him. I renewed the vow I had once before made, to make him, if I could, repent of it, in which Russell most heartily concurred. Perhaps the minister may yet have reason to wish he had let us go off quietly to the South Seas. I should be glad to have an opportunity to remind him of his old correspondent, and if I find one I will not overlook it. I dare say he has utterly forgotten the circumstance, but I have not. " Every thing, however, is for the best," as Pangloss says, " in this best of all possible worlds:" If I had gone to the Sandwich Islands, in 1790, I should not be to-day *chef de brigade* in the service of the French Republic, not to mention what I may be in my own country, if our expedition thither succeeds.

But to return. Shortly after this disappointment, Russell, who had for two or three years revelled in the ease and dignity of an Ensign's half pay, (amounting to 28*l*. sterling a-year,) which he had earned before he was twenty-one by broiling in the East Indies for five years, was unexpectedly promoted by favour of the commander-in-chief to an Ensigncy on full pay, in the 64th regiment of foot, then quartered in the town of Belfast. He put himself, in consequence, in battle array, and prepared to join. I remember the last day he dined with us in Irishtown, where he came, to use his own quotation, "*all clinquant, all in gold!*" We set him to cook part of the dinner in a very fine suit of laced regimentals. I love to recall those scenes. We parted with the sincerest regret on both sides; he set off for Belfast, and shortly after we returned to town for the winter, my wife's health being perfectly re-established, as she manifested by being, in due time, brought to bed of our eldest boy, whom we called William, after my brother.

This winter I endeavoured to institute a kind of political club, from which I expected great things. It consisted of seven or eight members, (eminent for talents and patriotism, and who had already more or less distinguished themselves by their literary productions,) comprising John Stack, fellow of Trinity college; Dr. Wm. Drennan, author of the celebrated letters signed Orellana; Joseph Pollock, author of the still more justly celebrated letters of Owen Roe O'Neil; Peter Burrowes, a barrister, a man of a most powerful and comprehensive mind;

William Johnson, a lawyer, also of respectable talents; Whitley Stokes, a fellow of Trinity college, a man, the extent and variety of whose knowledge is only to be exceeded by the number and intensity of his virtues; Russell, a corresponding member, and myself. As our political opinions at that time agreed in most essential points, however they may have since differed, and as this little club most certainly comprised a great proportion of information, talents, and integrity, it might naturally be expected that some distinguished publications should be the result; yet, I know not how it was, we did not draw well together; our meetings degenerated into downright ordinary suppers; we became a mere oyster club, and at length a misunderstanding, or rather a rooted dislike to each other, which manifested itself between Drennan and Pollock, (who were completely Cæsar and Pompey with regard to literary empire) joined to the retreat of John Stack to his living in the North, and the little good we saw resulting from our association, induced us to drop off one by one; and thus, after three or four months of sickly existence, our club departed this life, leaving behind it a puny offspring of about a dozen essays on different subjects, all, as may be supposed, tolerable, but not one of any distinguished excellence. I am satisfied either of the members, by devoting a week of his time to a well-chosen subject, would have produced a work of ten times more value than the whole club were able to show from their joint labours during its existence. This experiment satisfied me that men of genius, to be of use, must not be collected in numbers. They do not work well in the aggregate, and, indeed, even in ordinary conversations, I have observed that too many wits spoil the discourse. The dullest entertainment at which I ever remember to have assisted was one formed expressly to bring together nearly twenty persons, every one more or less distinguished for splendid talents or great convivial qualities. We sat and prosed together in great solemnity, endeavouring, by a rapid circulation of the bottle, to animate the discourse; but it would not do, every man was clad in a suit of intellectual armour in which he found himself secure, it is true, but ill at his ease; and we all rejoiced at the moment when we were permitted to run home and get into our *robes de chambre* and slippers. Any two of the men present would have been the delight and entertainment of a well-chosen society, but altogether there was, as Wolsey says, "*too much honour.*"\*

---

\* *Note by the Editor.*—About this time, whilst his ideas on the evils resulting from the connection with Britain were fermenting in his mind, my father wrote a letter to his friend Russell, wherein he expanded upon them, and concluded,— "Such and such men," mentioning his friends and associates in the Club, "think with me." This very innocent paper produced, about two years afterwards, in 1793, a most ridiculous alarm and disturbance. It would not have been noticed, at the time it was written, more than those pamphlets which were published; but then, when the political fever raged at the highest, and when it was already forgotten by himself and his friends, it fell, by some chance or indiscretion, into the hands of the Government. The gentlemen mentioned, many of whom had since

In recording the names of the members of the Club, I find I have strangely omitted that of a man whom, as well for his talents as his principles, I esteem as much as any, far more than most of them, I mean Thomas Addis Emmet, a barrister. He is a man completely after my own heart; of a great and comprehensive mind; of the warmest and sincerest affection for his friends; and of a firm and steady adherence to his principles, to which he has sacrificed much, as I know, and would, I am sure, if necessary, sacrifice his life. His opinions and mine square exactly. In classing the men I most esteem, I would place him beside Russell, at the head of the list; because, with regard to them both, the most ardent feelings of my heart coincide exactly

espoused the part of the Administration, were all summoned before the Secret Committee: for that most illegal tribunal, the Star Chamber of Ireland, assumed the power of examining any suspected individuals on the opinions, as well as the actions, of themselves and of others; putting them on their oath, to answer all their questions, and imprisoning them arbitrarily. On this occasion these gentlemen were charged with being privy not only to a theoretical disquisition, but to a deep conspiracy against the Government, as far back as the year 1791. It is, however, remarkable, that my father was not called before them. Perhaps he was deemed incorrigible.

This letter is alluded to in several parts of his subsequent memoirs, in Curran's life by his son, and in several of Lord Clare's speeches to Parliament. His Lordship never lost an opportunity of alluding to that dangerous production, which disclosed the long meditation of those traitorous and rebellious designs, and it was laid before the British Parliament and Privy Council!

with the most severe decision of my judgment. There are men whom I regard as much as it is possible. I am sure, for example, if there be on earth such a thing as sincere friendship, I feel it for Whitley Stokes, for George Knox, and for Peter Burrowes. They are men whose talents I admire, whose virtues I reverence, and whose persons I love; but the regard which I feel for them, sincere and affectionate as it is, is certainly not of the same species with that which I entertain for Russell and Emmet. Between us there has been, from the very commencement of our acquaintance, a coincidence of sentiment, a harmony of feelings on points which we all conscientiously consider as of the last importance, which binds us in the closest ties to each other. We have unvaryingly been devoted to the pursuit of the same object, by the same means; we have had a fellowship in our labours, a society in our dangers; our hopes, our fears, our wishes, our friends, and our enemies, have been the same. When all this is considered, and the talents and principles of the men taken into the account, it will not be wondered at if I esteem Russell and Emmet as the first of my friends. If ever an opportunity offers, (as circumstances at present seem likely to bring forward,) I think their country will ratify my choice. With regard to Burrowes and Knox, whom I do most sincerely and affectionately love, their political opinions differ fundamentally from mine; and, perhaps, it is for the credit of us all three, that, with such an irreconcilable difference of sentiment, we have all along preserved a mutual regard and esteem for each other; at least, I am sure I feel it particularly honourable to myself, for there are, perhaps, no two men in the world about whose good opinion I am more solicitous. Nor shall I soon forget the steady and unvarying friendship I experienced from them both, when my situation was, to all human appearance, utterly desperate, and when others, with at least as little reason, shunned me as if I had the red spots of the plague out on me—but of that hereafter. With regard to Whitley Stokes, his political opinions approach nearer to mine than those of either Knox or Burrowes. (I mention this, for, in these days of unbounded discussion, politics unfortunately enter into every thing, even into our private friendships.) We, however, differ on many material points, and we differ on principles which do honour to Stokes's heart. With an acute feeling of the degradation of his country, and a just and generous indignation against her oppressors, the tenderness and humanity of his disposition is such, that he recoils from any measures to be attempted for her emancipation which may terminate in blood: in this respect I have not the virtue to imitate him. I must observe, that, with this perhaps extravagant anxiety for the lives of others, I am sure in any cause which satisfied his conscience, no man would be more prodigal of his own life than Whitley Stokes, for he is an enthusiast in his nature, but "what he would highly that would be holily," and I am afraid, in the present state of affairs, that is a thing impossible. I love

Stokes most sincerely. With an excellent and highly cultivated mind, he possesses the distinguishing characteristic of the best and most feeling heart, and I am sure it will not hurt the self-love of any of the friends whose names I have recorded, when I say that, in the full force of the phrase, I look upon Whitley Stokes as the *very best man* I have ever known. Now that I am upon this subject, I must observe that in the choice of my friends I have been all my life extremely fortunate; I hope I am duly sensible of the infinite value of their esteem, and I take the greatest pride in being able to say that I have preserved the esteem even of those from whom I most materially differed on points of the last importance, and on occasions of peculiar difficulty; and this too without any sacrifice of consistency or principle on either side; a circumstance which, however, redounds still more to their credit than to mine. But to return to my history from this long digression, on which however I dwell with affection! Exiled as I am from the inestimable friends I have mentioned, it is a consolation to my soul to dwell upon their merits, and the sincere and animated affection I feel for them. God knows whether we shall ever meet, or if we do, how many of us may survive the contest in which we are, by all appearance, about to embark. If it be my lot, for one, to fall, I leave behind me this small testimony of my regard for them, written under circumstances which, I think, may warrant its sincerity.

The French Revolution had now been above a

twelvemonth in progress; at its commencement, as first emotions are generally honest, every one was in its favour; but, after some time, the probable consequences to monarchy and aristocracy began to be foreseen, and the partizans of both to retrench considerably in their admiration: at length, Mr. Burke's famous invective appeared; and this in due season produced Paine's reply, which he called "Rights of Man." This controversy, and the gigantic event which gave rise to it, changed in an instant the politics of Ireland. Two years before, the nation was in lethargy. The puny efforts of the Whig Club, miserable and defective as their system was, were the only appearance of any thing like exertion, and he was looked on as extravagant who thought of Parliamentary reform, against which, by the by, all parties equally set their faces. I have already mentioned that, in those days of apathy and depression, I made a blow at the supremacy of England, by my pamphlet on the expected rupture with Spain; and I have also fairly stated, that I found nobody who ventured to second my attempt or paid the least attention to the doctrine I endeavoured to disseminate. But the rapid succession of events, and, above all, the explosion which had taken place in France and blown into the elements a despotism rooted for fourteen centuries, had thoroughly aroused all Europe, and the eyes of every man, in every quarter, were turned anxiously on the French National Assembly. In England, Burke had the triumph completely to decide the public; fascinated by an eloquent publication which flattered so many of their prejudices, and animated by their unconquerable hatred of France, which no change of circumstances could alter, the whole English nation, it may be said, retracted from their first decision in favour of the glorious and successful efforts of the French people: they sickened at the prospect of the approaching liberty and happiness of that mighty nation: they calculated, as merchants, the probable effects which the energy of regenerated France might have on their commerce: they rejoiced when they saw the combination of despots formed to restore the ancient system, and perhaps to dismember the monarchy; and they waited with impatience for an occasion which, happily for mankind, they soon found, when they might, with some appearance of decency, engage in person in the infamous contest.

But matters were very different in Ireland,—an oppressed, insulted, and plundered nation. As we well knew, experimentally, what it was to be enslaved, we sympathised most sincerely with the French people, and watched their progress to freedom with the utmost anxiety; we had not, like England, a prejudice rooted in our very nature against France. As the revolution advanced, and as events expanded themselves, the public spirit of Ireland rose with rapid acceleration. The fears and animosities of the aristocracy rose in the same or a still higher proportion. In a little time the French Revolution became the test of every man's political creed, and the nation was fairly divided into two great parties, the Aristocrats and the Democrats, (epithets borrowed from France,) who have ever since been measuring each other's strength, and carrying on a kind of smothered war, which the course of events, it is highly probable, may soon call into energy and action.

It is needless, I believe, to say that I was a Democrat from the very commencement: and as all the retainers of Government (including the sages and judges of the law,) were, of course, on the other side, this gave the *coup de grace* to any expectations, if any such I had, of succeeding at the bar, for I soon became pretty notorious; but, in fact, I had for some time renounced all hope, and, I may say, all desire, of succeeding in a profession which I always disliked, and which the political prostitution of its members (though otherwise men of high honour and of great personal worth) had taught me sincerely to despise. I therefore seldom went near the four courts, nor did I adopt any one of the means, and, least of all, the study of the law, which are successfully employed by those young men whose object it is to rise in their profession.

As I came about this period rather more forward than I had hitherto done, it is necessary for the understanding my history, to take a rapid survey of the state of parties in Ireland, that is to say, of the members of the Established Religion, the Dissenters and the Catholics.

The first party, whom, for distinction's sake, I call the *Protestants*, though not above the tenth of the population, were in possession of the whole of the government, and of five-sixths of the landed property of the nation; they were, and had been for above a century, in quiet enjoyment of the church, the law, the revenue, the army, the navy, the magistracy, the corporations, in a word, of the whole patronage of Ireland. With properties whose title was founded in massacre and plunder, and being, as it were, but a colony of foreign usurpers in the land, they saw no security for their persons and estates but in a close connection with England, who profited by their fears, and, as the price of her protection, exacted the implicit surrender of the commerce and liberties of Ireland. Different events, particularly the revolution in America, had enabled and emboldened the other two parties, of whom I am about to speak, to hurry the Protestants into measures highly disagreeable to England and beneficial to their country; but in which, from accidental circumstances, the latter durst not refuse to concur. The spirit of the corps, however, remained unchanged, as has been manifested on every occasion since which chance has offered. This party, therefore, so powerful by their property and influence, were implicitly devoted to England, which they esteemed necessary for the security of their existence; they adopted, in consequence, the sentiments and the language of the British cabinet; they dreaded and abhorred the principles of the French Revolution, and were, in one word, an aristocracy, in the fullest and most odious extent of the term.

The Dissenters, who formed the second party, were at least twice as numerous as the first. Like them, they were a colony of foreigners in their origin, but, being mostly engaged in trade and manufactures, with few overgrown landed proprietors among them, they did not, like them, feel that a slavish dependance on England was essential to their very existence. Strong in their numbers and their courage, they felt that they were able to defend themselves, and soon ceased to consider themselves as any other than Irishmen. It was the Dissenters who composed the flower of the famous volunteer army in 1782, which extorted from the English Minister the restoration of what is affected to be called the Constitution of Ireland: it was they who first promoted and continued the demand of a Parliamentary Reform, in which, however, they were baffled by the superior address and chicanery of the aristocracy; and it was they, finally, who were the first to stand forward, in the most decided and unqualified manner, in support of the principles of the French Revolution.

The Catholics, who composed the third party, were about two-thirds of the nation, and formed, perhaps, a still greater proportion. They embraced the entire peasantry of three provinces; they constituted a considerable portion of the mercantile interest; but, from the tyranny of the penal laws enacted at different periods against them, they possessed but a very small proportion of the landed property, perhaps not a fiftieth part of the whole. It is not my intention here to give a detail of that execrable and infamous code, framed with the art and the malice of demons, to plunder and degrade and brutalize the Catholics. Suffice it to say, that there was no injustice, no disgrace, no disqualification moral, political or religious, civil or military, that was not heaped upon them : it is with difficulty that I restrain myself from entering into the abominable detail; but it is the less necessary, as it is to be found in so many publications of the day. This horrible system, pursued for above a century with unrelenting acrimony and perseverance, had wrought its full effect, and had, in fact, reduced the great body of the Catholic peasantry of Ireland to a situation, morally and physically speaking, below that of the beasts of the field. The spirit of their few remaining gentry was broken, and their minds degraded ; and it was only in the class of their merchants and traders, and a few members of the medical profession, who had smuggled an education in despite of the penal code, that any thing like political sensation existed. Such was pretty nearly the situation of the three great parties at the commencement of the French Revolution, and certainly a much more gloomy prospect could not well present itself to the eyes of any friend to liberty and his country. But, as the luminary of truth and freedom in France advanced rapidly to its meridian splendour, the public mind in Ireland was proportionably illuminated ;

and to the honour of the Dissenters of Belfast be it said, they were the first to reduce to practice their newly received principles, and to show, by being just, that they were deserving to be free.

The dominion of England in Ireland had been begun and continued in the disunion of the great sects which divided the latter country.* In effectuating this disunion, the Protestant party were the willing instruments; as they saw clearly that if ever the Dissenters and Catholics were to discover their true interests, and, forgetting their former ruinous dissensions, were to unite cordially and make common cause, the downfal of English supremacy, and, of course, of their own unjust monopoly, would be the necessary and immediate consequence. They therefore laboured continually, and for a long time successfully, to keep the other two sects asunder; and the English Government had even the address to persuade the Catholics that the non-execution of the penal laws, which were, in fact, too atrocious to be enforced in their full rigour, was owing to their clemency; that the Protestants and Dissenters, but especially the latter, were the enemies, and themselves, in effect, the protectors of the Catholic people. Under this arrangement, the machine of Government moved forward on carpet-ground; but the time was at length come, when this system of iniquity was to tumble in the dust, and the day of truth and reason to commence.

* At least since the reign of Elizabeth and James I.

So far back as the year 1783, the volunteers of Belfast had instructed their deputies to the convention held in Dublin for the purpose of framing a plan of parliamentary reform, to support the equal admission of the Catholics to the rights of freemen. In this instance of liberality, they were then almost alone; for it is their fate in political wisdom ever to be in advance of their country; it was sufficient, however, to alarm the Government, who immediately procured from Lord Kenmare, at that time esteemed the leader of the Catholics, a solemn disavowal, in the name of that body of any wish to be restored to their long-lost rights. Prostrate as the Catholics were at that period, this last insult was too much; they instantly assembled their General Committee, and disavowed Lord Kenmare and his disavowal, observing at the same time that they were not framed so differently from all other men as to be in love with their own degradation. The majority of the volunteer convention, however, resolved to consider the infamous declaration of Lord Kenmare as the voice of the Catholics of Ireland, and therefore, the emancipation of that body made no part of their plan of reform. The consequence natural to such folly and injustice immediately ensued: the Government, seeing the convention, by their own act, separate themselves from the great mass of the people, who could alone give them effective force, set them at defiance, and that formidable assembly which under better principles might have held the fate of Ireland in its hands was broken up with disgrace and ignominy, a memorable warning that those who know not to render their just rights to others will be found incapable of firmly adhering to their own.

The General Committee of the Catholics, of which I have spoken above, and which since the year 1792 has made a distinguished feature in the politics of Ireland, was a body composed of their bishops, their country gentlemen, and of a certain number of merchants and traders, all resident in Dublin, but named by the Catholics in the different corporate towns to represent them. The original object of this institution was to obtain the repeal of a partial and oppressive tax called quarterage, which was levied on Catholics only, and the Government, which found the committee at first a convenient instrument on some occasions, connived at its existence. So degraded was the Catholic mind at the period of the formation of their committee, about 1770, and long after, that they were happy in being allowed to go up to the Castle with an abominably slavish address to each successive Viceroy, of which, moreover, until the accession of the Duke of Portland, in 1782, so little notice was taken, that his Grace was the first who condescended to give them an answer; and, indeed, for above twenty years, the sole business of the General Committee was to prepare and deliver in those records of their depression! The effort which an honest indignation had called forth at the time of the volunteer convention in 1783, seemed to have exhausted their strength, and they sank back into their primitive nullity. Under this appearance of apathy, however, a new spirit was gradually arising in the body, owing principally to the exertions and the example of one man, John Keogh, to whose services his country, and more especially the Catholics, are singularly indebted. In fact, the downfal of feudal tyranny was acted in little on the theatre of the General Committee. The influence of their clergy and of their barons was gradually undermined; and the third estate, the commercial interest, rising in wealth and power, was preparing by degrees to throw off the yoke, in the imposing (or at least the perpetuating) of which the leaders of the body, I mean the prelates and aristocracy, to their disgrace be it spoken, were ready to concur. Already had those leaders, acting in obedience to the orders of the Government, which held them in fetters, suffered one or two signal defeats in the Committee, owing principally to the talents and address of John Keogh: the parties began to be defined, and a sturdy democracy of new men, with bolder views and stronger talents, soon superseded the timid counsels and slavish measures of the ancient aristocracy. Every thing seemed tending to a better order of things among the Catholics, and an occasion soon offered to call the energy of their new leaders into action.

The Dissenters of the north, and more especially of the town of Belfast, are, from the genius of their religion, and from the superior diffusion of political information among them, sincere and enlightened republicans. They had ever been foremost in the pursuit of Parliamentary Reform, and I have already mentioned the early wisdom and virtue of the town of Belfast in proposing the emancipation of the Catholics, so far back as the year 1783. The French Revolution had awakened all parties in the nation from the stupor in which they lay plunged from the time of the dispersion of the ever-memorable volunteer convention, and the citizens of Belfast were the first to raise their heads from the abyss, and to look the situation of their country steadily in the face. They saw at a glance their true object, and the only means to obtain it; conscious that the force of the existing Government was such as to require the united efforts of the whole Irish people to subvert it, and long convinced in their own minds, that to be free it was necessary to be just, they cast their eyes once more on the long-neglected Catholics, and profiting by past errors, for which however they had not to accuse themselves, they determined to begin on a new system, and to raise the structure of the liberty and independence of their country on the broad basis of equal rights to the whole people.

The Catholics, on their part, were rapidly advancing in political spirit and information. Every month, every day, as the Revolution in France went prosperously forward, added to their courage and their force, and the hour seemed at last arrived when, after a dreary oppression of above one hundred years, they were once more to appear on the political theatre of their country. They saw the brilliant prospect of success which events in France opened to their view, and they determined to avail themselves with promptitude of that opportunity which never returns to those who omit it. For this, the active members of the General Committee resolved to set on foot an immediate application to Parliament, praying for a repeal of the penal laws. The first difficulty they had to surmount arose in their own body; their peers, their gentry, (as they affected to call themselves,) and their prelates, either seduced or intimidated by Government, gave the measure all possible opposition; and at length, after a long contest, in which both parties strained every nerve and produced the whole of their strength, the question was decided, on a division in the committee, by a majority of at least six to one, in favour of the intended application. The triumph of the young democracy was complete; but, though the aristocracy were defeated, they were not yet entirely broken down. By the instigation of Government they had the meanness to secede from the General Committee, to disavow their acts, and even to publish in the papers, that they did not wish to embarrass the Government by advancing their claims of emancipation. It is difficult to conceive such a degree of political degradation; but what will not the tyranny of an execrable system produce in time? Sixty-eight gentlemen, individually of high spirit, were found, who publicly and in a body deserted their party and their own just claims, and even sanctioned this pitiful desertion by the authority of their signatures. Such an effect had the operation of the penal laws on the minds of the Catholics of Ireland, as proud a race as any in all Europe!

But I am in some degree anticipating matters, and, indeed, instead of a few memorandums relating to myself, I find I am embarking in a kind of *history of my own times*: let me return and condense as much as I can. The first attempts of the Catholic Committee failed totally. Endeavouring to accommodate all parties, they framed a petition so humble that it ventured to ask for nothing, and even this petition they could not find a single member of the Legislature to present; of so little consequence, in the year 1790, was the great mass of the Irish people! Not disheartened, however, by this defeat, they went on, and in the interval between that and the approaching session, were preparing measures for a second application. In order to add greater weight and consequence to their intended petition, they brought over to Ireland Richard Burke, only son of the celebrated Edmund, and appointed him their agent to conduct their application to Parliament. This young man came over with considerable advantages, and especially with the *eclat* of his father's name, who, the Catholics concluded, and very reasonably, would for his sake, if not for theirs, assist his son with his advice and directions. But their expectations in the event proved abortive. Richard Burke, with a considerable portion of talents from nature, and cultivated, as may be well supposed, with the utmost care by his father, who idolized him, was utterly deficient in judgment, in temper, and especially in the art of managing parties. In three or four months time during which he remained in Ireland, he contrived to embroil himself, and, in a certain degree, the committee, with all parties in Parliament, the Opposition as well as the Government, and, finally, desiring to drive his employers into measures of which they disapproved, and thinking himself strong enough to go on without the assistance of the men who introduced, and, as long as their duty would permit, supported him, (in which he miserably deceived himself,) he ended his short and turbulent career by breaking with the General Committee. That body, however, treated him respectfully to the last, and, on his departure, sent a deputation to thank him for his exertions, and presented him with the sum of two thousand guineas.

It was pretty much about this time that my connexion with the Catholic body commenced, in the manner which I am about to relate. I cannot pretend to strict accuracy as to dates, for I write entirely from memory; all my papers being in America.

Russell had, on his arrival to join his regiment at Belfast, found the people so much to his taste, and in return had rendered himself so agreeable to them, that he was speedily admitted into their confidence and became a member of several of their clubs. This was an unusual circumstance, as British officers, it may well be supposed, were no great favourites with the Republicans of Belfast. The Catholic question was, at this period, beginning to attract public notice; and the Belfast volunteers, on some public occasion, (I know not precisely what,) wished to come forward with a declaration in its favour. For this purpose Russell, who by this time was entirely in their confidence, wrote to me to draw up and transmit to him such a declaration as I thought proper, which I accordingly did. A meeting of the corps was held in consequence, but an opposition unexpectedly arising to a part of the declarations which alluded directly to the Catholic claims, that passage was, for the sake of unanimity, withdrawn for the present, and the declarations then passed unanimously. Russell wrote me an account of all this, and it immediately set me thinking more seriously than I had yet done upon the state of Ireland. I soon formed my theory, and on that theory have unvaryingly acted ever since.

To subvert the tyranny of our execrable Government, to break the connexion with England, (the never-failing source of all our political evils,) and to assert the independence of my country—these were my objects. To unite the whole people of Ireland; to abolish the memory of all past dissensions; and to substitute the common name of Irishman in place of the denominations of Protestant, Catholic, and Dissenter—these were my means. To effectuate such great objects, I reviewed the three principal sects. The Protestants I despaired of from the outset, for obvious reasons. Already in possession, by an unjust monopoly, of the whole power and patronage of the country, it was not to be supposed they would ever concur in measures, the certain tendency of which must be to lessen their influence as a party, how much soever the nation might gain. To the Catholics I thought it unnecessary to address myself, because that, as no change could make their political situation worse, I reckoned upon their support to a certainty; besides, they had already begun to manifest a strong sense of their wrongs and oppressions; and, finally, I well knew that, however it might be disguised or suppressed, there existed in the breast of every Irish Catholic an inextirpable abhorrence of the English name and power. There remained only the Dissenters, whom I knew to be patriotic and enlightened; however, the recent events at Belfast had shown me that all prejudice was not yet entirely removed from their minds. I sat down accordingly, and wrote a pamphlet addressed to the Dissenters, which I entitled " An Argument on behalf of the Catholics of Ireland," the object of which was to convince them that they and the Catholics had but one common interest and one common enemy; that the depression and slavery of Ireland was produced and perpetuated by the divisions existing between them, and that, consequently, to assert the independence of their country and their own individual liberties, it was necessary to forget all former feuds, to consolidate the entire strength of the whole nation, and to form for the future but one people. These principles I supported by the best arguments which suggested themselves to me, and particularly by demonstrating that the cause of the failure of all former efforts, and more especially of the Volunteer Convention in 1783, was the unjust neglect of the claims of their Catholic brethren. This pamphlet, which appeared in September, 1791, under the signature of "A Northern Whig," had a considerable degree of success. The Catholics (*with not one of whom I was at the time acquainted*) were pleased with the efforts of a volunteer in their cause, and distributed it in all quarters. The people of Belfast, of whom I had spoken with the respect and admiration I sincerely felt for them, and to whom I was also perfectly unknown, printed a very large edition, which they dispersed through the whole North of Ireland, and I have the great satisfaction to believe that many of the Dissenters were converted by my arguments. It is like vanity to speak of my own performances so much; and the fact is, I believe that I am somewhat vain on that topic; but as it was the immediate cause of my being known to the Catholic body, I may be perhaps excused for dwelling upon a circumstance which I must ever look on, for that reason, as one of the most fortunate of my life. As my pamphlet spread more and more, my acquaintance amongst the Catholics extended accordingly. My first friend in the body was John Keogh, and through him I became acquainted with all the leaders, as Richard McCormick, John Sweetman, Edward Byrne, Thomas Braughall, in short, the whole Sub-Committee, and most of the active members of the General Committee. It was a kind of fashion this winter, (1791) among the Catholics, to give splendid dinners to their political friends in and out of Parliament, and I was always a guest, of course. I was invited to a grand dinner given to Richard Burke, on his leaving Dublin, together with William Todd Jones, (who had distinguished himself by a most excellent pamphlet in favour of the Catholic cause,) as well as to several entertainments given by clubs and associations; in short, I began to grow into something like reputation, and my company was, in a manner, a requisite at all the entertainments of that winter.

But this was not all. The volunteers of Belfast, of the first or green company, were pleased, in consequence of my pamphlet, to elect me an honorary member of their corps, a favour which they were very delicate in bestowing, as I believe I was the only person, except the great Henry Flood, who was ever honoured with that mark of their approbation. I was also invited to spend a few days in Belfast, in order to assist in framing the first club of United Irishmen, and to cultivate a personal acquaintance with those men whom, though I highly esteemed, I knew as yet but by reputation. In consequence, about the beginning of October I went down with my friend Russell, who had by this time quitted the army, and was in Dublin, on his private affairs. The incidents of that journey, which was by far the most agreeable and interesting one I had ever made, I recorded in a kind of diary, a practice which I then commenced, and have ever since, from time to time, continued, as circumstances of sufficient importance occurred. To that diary I refer.* It is sufficient here to say, that my reception was of the most flattering kind, and that I found the men of the most distinguished public virtue in the nation the most estimable in all the domestic relations of life: I had the good fortune to render myself agreeable to them, and a friendship was then formed between us which I think it will not be easy to shake. It is a kind of injustice to name individuals, yet I cannot refuse myself the pleasure of observing how peculiarly fortunate I esteem myself in having formed connexions with Samuel Neilson, Robert Simms, William Simms, William Sinclair, Thomas Mc Cabe :—I may as well stop here; for, in enumerating my most particular friends, I find I am, in fact, making out a list of the men of Belfast most distinguished for their virtue, talent, and patriotism. To proceed. We formed our club, of which I wrote the declaration, and certainly the formation of that club commenced a new epoch in the politics of Ireland. At length, after a stay of about three weeks, which I look back upon as perhaps the pleasantest in my life, Russell and I returned to Dublin, with instructions to cultivate the leaders in the popular interest, (being Protestants,) and, if possible, to establish in the capital a club of United Irishmen. Neither Russell nor myself were known to one of those leaders; however, we soon contrived to get acquainted with James Napper

* See Appendix in Vol. II.

Tandy, who was the principal of them, and, through him, with several others; so that, in a little time, we succeeded, and a club was accordingly formed, of which the Honourable Simon Butler was the first chairman, and Tandy the first secretary. The club adopted the declaration of their brethren of Belfast, with whom they immediately opened a correspondence. It is but justice to an honest man who has been persecuted for his firm adherence to his principles, to observe here that Tandy, in coming forward on this occasion, well knew that he was putting to the most extreme hazard his popularity among the corporations of the city of Dublin, with whom he had enjoyed the most unbounded influence for nearly twenty years; and, in fact, in the event, his popularity *was* sacrificed. That did not prevent, however, his taking his part decidedly; he had the firmness to forego the gratification of his private feelings for the good of his country. The truth is, Tandy was a very sincere republican, and it did not require much argument to show him the impossibility of attaining a Republic by any means short of the united powers of the whole people; he therefore renounced the lesser object for the greater, and gave up the certain influence which he possessed (and had well earned) in the city, for the contingency of that influence which he might have (and well deserves to have) in the nation. For my own part, I think it right to mention that, at this time, the establishment of a Republic was not the immediate object of my speculations. My object was to secure the independence of my country under *any* form of government, to which I was led by a hatred of England, so deeply rooted in my nature, that it was rather an instinct than a principle. I left to others, better qualified for the inquiry, the investigation and merits of the different forms of government, and I contented myself with labouring on my own system, which was luckily in perfect coincidence as to its operation with that of those men who viewed the question on a broader and juster scale than I did at the time I mention. But to return. The club was scarcely formed before I lost all pretensions to any thing like influence in their measures,—a circumstance which at first mortified me not a little ; and perhaps had I retained more weight in their councils, I might have prevented, as on some occasions I laboured unsuccessfully to prevent, their running into indiscretions which gave their enemies but too great advantages over them. It is easy to be wise *after* the event. So it was, however, that I soon sank into obscurity in the club, which, nevertheless, I had satisfaction in seeing daily increase in numbers and consequence. The Catholics, particularly, flocked in by crowds, as well as some of the Protestant members of corporations most distinguished for their liberality and public spirit on former occasions ; and, indeed, I must do the society the justice to say, that I believe there never existed a political body which included amongst its members a greater portion of sincere uncorrupted patriotism, as well as a very respectable proportion of talents. Their publications, mostly written by Dr. Drennan, and many of them admirably well done, began to draw the public attention, especially as they were evidently the production of a society utterly disclaiming all party views or motives, and acting on a broad original scale, not sparing those who called themselves patriots more than those who were the habitual slaves of the Government; a system in which I heartily concurred, having long entertained a more serious contempt for what is called *opposition* than for the common prostitutes of the Treasury bench, who want at least the vice of hypocrisy. At length the Solicitor General, in speaking of the society, having made use of expressions in the House of Commons extremely offensive, an explanation was demanded of him by Simon Butler, chairman, and Tandy, secretary. Butler was satisfied—Tandy was not; and, after several messages, which it is not my affair to detail, the Solicitor General at length complained to the House of a breach of privilege, and Tandy was ordered, in the first instance, into custody. He was in consequence arrested by a messenger, from whom he found means to make his escape, and immediately a proclamation was issued, offering a reward for taking him. The society was now in a difficult situation, and I thought myself called upon to make an effort, at all hazards to myself, to prevent its falling by any improper timidity in the public opinion. We were in fact committed with the House of Commons on the question of privilege, and having fairly engaged in the contest, it was impossible to recede without a total forfeiture of character. Under these circumstances, I cast my eyes on Archibald Hamilten Rowan, a distinguished member of the society, whose many virtues, public and private, had set his name above the reach of even the malevolence of party; whose situation in life was of the most respectable rank, if rank be indeed respectable; and, above all, whose personal courage was not to be shaken,—a circumstance, in the actual situation of affairs, of the last importance. To Rowan, therefore, I applied; I showed him that the current of public opinion was rather setting against us in this business, and that it was necessary some of us should step forward and expose ourselves, at all risks, to show the House of Commons and the nation at large that we were not to be intimidated or put down so easily. I offered, if he would take the chair, that I would, with the society's permission, act as secretary, and that we would give our signatures to such publications as circumstances might render necessary. Rowan instantly agreed; and accordingly, on the next night of meeting, he was chosen chairman and I pro-secretary in the absence of Tandy; and the society having agreed to the resolutions proposed, (which were worded in a manner very offensive to the dignity of the House of Commons, and in fact amounted to a challenge of their authority,) we inserted them in all the newspapers, and printed 5,000 copies with our names affixed.

The least that Rowan and I expected in consequence of this step, which, under the circumstances, was, I must say, rather a bold one, was to be committed to Newgate for breach of privilege, and perhaps exposed to personal discussions with some of the members of the House of Commons; for he proposed, and I agreed, that, if any disrespectful language was applied to either of us in any debate which might arise on the business, we would attack the person, whoever he might be, immediately, and oblige him either to recant his words or give battle. All our determination, however, came to nothing. The House of Commons, either content with their victory over Tandy, who was obliged to conceal himself for some time, or not thinking Rowan and myself objects sufficiently important to attract their notice; or perhaps, which I rather believed, not wishing just then to embroil themselves with a man of Rowan's firmness and courage, (not to speak of his great and justly merited popularity,) took no notice whatsoever of our resolutions, and, in this manner, he and I had the good fortune, and, I may say, the merit, to rescue the society from a situation of considerable difficulty without any actual suffering, though certainly with some personal hazard on our part: We had likewise the satisfaction to see the society, instead of losing ground, rise rapidly in public opinion by its firmness on the occasion. Shortly after, on the last day of the sessions, Tandy appeared in public, and was taken into custody, the whole society attending him in a body to the House of Commons. He was ordered by the Speaker to be committed to Newgate, whither he was conveyed, the society attending him as before; and the Parliament being prorogued in half an hour after, he was liberated immediately, and escorted in triumph to his own house. On this occasion Rowan and I attended of course, and were in the gallery of the House of Commons. As we were not sure but we might be attacked ourselves, we took pains to place ourselves in a conspicuous situation, and to wear our Whig-club uniforms, which were rather gaudy, in order to signify to all whom it might concern, that there we were. A good many of the members, we observed, remarked us, but no further notice was taken: our names were never mentioned; the whole business passed over quietly, and I resigned my pro-secretaryship, being the only office I ever held in the society, into the hands of Tandy, who resumed his functions. This was in Spring, 1792: I should observe, that the day after the publication above-mentioned, when I attended near the House of Commons in expectation of being called before them to answer for what I had done, and had requested my friend, Sir Lawrence Parsons, to give me notice, in order that I might present myself, the house took fire by accident, and was burned to the ground.

The Society of United Irishmen beginning to attract public notice considerably, in consequence of the events which I have mentioned, and it being pretty generally known that I was principally instrumental in its formation, I was one day surprised by a visit from the barrister who had about two years before spoken to me on the part of the Whig leaders, a business of which I had long since discharged my memory. He told me he was sorry to see the new line I was adopting in politics, the more so as I might rely upon it that the principles I now held would never be generally adopted, and consequently I was devoting myself without advancing any beneficial purpose; he also testified to me surprise at my conduct, and insinuated pretty directly, though with great civility, that I had not kept faith with the Whigs, with whom he professed to understand I had connected myself, and whom, in consequence, I ought to have consulted before I took so decided a line of conduct as I had lately done. I did not like the latter part of his discourse at all; however, I answered with great civility on my part, that, as to the principles he mentioned, I had not adopted them without examination; that, as to the pamphlet I had written in the Catholic cause, I had not advanced a syllable which I did not conscientiously believe, and, consequently, I was neither inclined to repent nor retract; as to my supposed connexion with the Whigs, I reminded him that I had not sought them; on the contrary, they had sought me; if they had, on reflection, not thought me worth cultivating, that was no fault of mine. I observed, also, that Mr. George Ponsonby, whom I looked upon as principal in the business, had never spoken to me above a dozen times in my life, and then merely on ordinary topics; that I was too proud to be treated in that manner; and if I was supposed capable of rendering service to the party, it would only be by confiding in, and communicating with me, that I could be really serviceable, and on that footing only would I consent to be treated; that probably Mr. Ponsonby would think this rather a lofty declaration, but it was my determination, the more as I knew he was himself rather a proud man. Finally, I observed, my visitor had my permission to report all this, and that I looked on myself as under no tie of obligation whatsoever; that I had written a pamphlet, unsolicited, in favour of the party; that I had consequently been employed in a business, professionally, which produced me eighty guineas; that I looked on myself as sufficiently rewarded, but I also considered the money as fully earned; that I had at present taken my party; that my principles were known, and I was not at all disposed to retract them: what I had done I had done, and was determined to abide by it. My friend then said he was sorry to see me so obstinate in what he must consider an indiscreet line of conduct, and protesting that his principal object was to serve me (in which I believed him), he took his leave, and this put an end completely to the idea of a connexion with the Whigs. I spoke rather haughtily in this affair, because I was somewhat provoked at the insinuation of duplicity, and, besides, I wished to have a blow at Mr. George Ponsonby, who seemed desirous to retain me as a kind of pamphleteer in his service, at the same time that he industriously avoided any thing like communication with me, a situation to which I was neither so weak nor so mean as to suffer myself to be reduced; and as I well knew he was one of the proudest men in Ireland, I took care to speak on a footing of the most independent equality. After this discussion, I for the second time dismissed all idea of Ponsonby and the Whigs, but had good reason, a long time after, to believe that he had not so readily forgotten the business as I, and indeed he was very near having his full revenge of me, as I shall mention in its place.

I have already observed that the first attempts of the Catholic Committee, after the secession of their aristocracy, were totally unsuccessful. In 1790, they could not even find a member of Parliament who would condescend to present their petition. In 1791, Richard Burke, their then agent, had prepared, on their behalf, a very well-written philippic, but certainly no *petition*, which, after considerable difficulties, resulting in a great degree from his want of temper and discretion, after being offered to, and accepted by, different members, was at length finally refused, a circumstance which, by disgusting him extremely with all parties, I believe determined him to quit Ireland. After his departure, another petition was prepared and presented by * * *, but no unfortunate paper was ever so maltreated. The committee in general, and its more active and ostensible members in particular, were vilified and abused in the grossest manner; they were called a rabble of obscure porter-drinking mechanics, without property, pretensions, or influence, who met in holes and corners, and fancied themselves the representatives of the Catholic body, which disavowed and despised them; the independence and respectability of the sixty-eight renegadoes who had set their hands so infamously to their act of apostasy were extolled to the skies, while the lowest and most clumsy personalities were heaped upon the leaders of the committee, particularly Edward Byrne and John Keogh, who had the honour to be selected from their brethren, and exposed as butts for the small wit of the prostitutes of the Government. Finally, the petition of the Catholics, three millions of people, was, by special motion of David Latouche, taken off the table of the House of Commons, where it had been suffered to lie for three days, and rejected. Never was an address to a legislative body more unpitifully used. The people of Belfast, rapidly advancing in the career of wisdom and liberality, had presented a petition in behalf of the Catholics much more pointed than that which the Catholics presented for themselves, for their petition was extremely guarded, asking only the right of elective franchise, and equal admission to grand juries, whereas that of Belfast prayed for their entire admission to *all* the rights of citizens. This petition was also, on motion of the same member, taken off the table and rejected, and the two papers sent forth together to wander as they might.

There seems, from this time, a special providence to have watched over the affairs of Ireland,

and to have turned to her profit and advantage the deepest-laid and most artful schemes of her enemies. Every measure adopted, and skilfully adopted, to thwart the expectations of the Catholics, and to crush the rising spirit of union between them and the Dissenters, has, without exception, only tended to confirm and fortify both, and the fact I am about to mention, for one, is a striking proof of the truth of this assertion. The principal charge in the general outcry raised in the House of Commons against the General Committee was, that they were a self-appointed body, not nominated by the Catholics of the nation, and, consequently, not authorised to speak on their behalf. This argument, which in fact was the truth, was triumphantly dwelt upon by the enemies of the Catholics; but in the end, it would have been perhaps more fortunate for their wishes if they had not laid such a stress upon this circumstance, and drawn the line of separation so strongly between the General Committee and the body at large. For the Catholics throughout Ireland, who had hitherto been indolent spectators of the business, seeing their brethren of Dublin, and especially the General Committee, insulted and abused for their exertions in pursuit of that liberty which if attained must be a common blessing to all, came forward as one man from every quarter of the nation, with addresses and resolutions, adopting the measures of the General Committee as their own, declaring that body the only organ competent to speak for the Catholics of Ireland, and condemning, in terms of the most marked disapprobation and contempt, the conduct of the sixty-eight apostates who were so triumphantly held up by the hirelings of Government as the *respectable* part of the Catholic community. The question was now fairly decided. The aristocracy shrank back in disgrace and obscurity, leaving the field open to the democracy, which body wanted neither talents nor spirit to profit by the advantages of their present situation.

The Catholics of Dublin were, at this period, to the Catholics of Ireland, what Paris, at the commencement of the French Revolution, was to the Departments. Their sentiment was that of the nation, and whatever political measure they adopted was sure to be obeyed. Still, however, there was wanting a personal communication between the General Committee and their constituents in the country; and, as the Catholic question had now grown to considerable magnitude, so much indeed as to absorb all other political discussion, it became the first care of the leaders of the Committee to frame a plan of organization for that purpose. It is to the sagacity of Myles Keon, of Keonbrook, county Leitrim, that his country is indebted for the system on which the General Committee was to be framed anew, in a manner that should render it impossible to bring it again in doubt whether that body was or was not the organ of the Catholic will. His plan was to associate to the Committee, as then constituted, two members from each county and great city, actual residents of the place which they represented, who were, however, only to be summoned upon extraordinary occasions, leaving the common routine of business to the original members, who, as I have already related, were all residents of Dublin. The Committee, as thus constituted, would consist of half town, and half country members; and the elections for the latter he proposed should be held by means of primary and electoral assemblies, held, the first in each parish, the second in each county and great town. He likewise proposed, that the town members should be held to correspond regularly with their country associates, these with their immediate electors, and these again with the primary assemblies. A more simple, and at the same time, more comprehensive organization could not be devised. By this means the General Committee became the centre of a circle embracing the whole nation, and pushing its rays instantaneously to the remotest parts of the circumference. The plan was laid, in writing, before the General Committee by Myles Keon, and, after mature discussion, the first part, relating to the association and election of the country members, was adopted with some slight variation; the latter part, relating to the constant communication with the mass of the people, was thought, under the circumstances, to be too hardy, and was, accordingly, dropped, *sub silentio*.

About this time it was that the leaders of the Committee cast their eyes upon me to fill the station left vacant by Richard Burke. It was, accordingly, proposed by my friend John Keogh to appoint me their agent, with the title of assistant secretary, and a salary of 200*l.* sterling a year, during my continuance in the service of the committee. This proposal was adopted unanimously. John Keogh and John Sweetman were ordered to wait on me, with the proposal in writing, to which I acceded immediately by a respectful answer, and I was that very day introduced in form to the sub-committee, and entered upon the functions of my new office.

I was now placed in a very honourable, but a very arduous situation. The Committee having taken so decided a step as to propose a general election of members to represent the Catholic body throughout Ireland, was well aware that they would be exposed to attacks of all possible kinds, and they were not disappointed; they were prepared, however, to repel them, and the literary part of the warfare fell, of course, to my share. In reviewing the conduct of my predecessor, Richard Burke, I saw that the rock on which he split was an overweening opinion of his own talents and judgment, and a desire, which he had not art enough to conceal, of guiding, at his pleasure, the measures of the Committee. I therefore determined to model my conduct with the greatest caution in that respect; I seldom or never offered my opinion, unless it was called for, in the sub-committee, but contented myself with giving my sentiments without reserve in private, to the two men I most esteemed, and who had, in their respective capacities, the greatest influence on that body—I mean John Keogh, and

Richard Mc Cormick, Secretary to the General Committee. My discretion in this respect was not unobserved, and I very soon acquired, and I may say, without vanity, deserved, the entire confidence and good opinion of the Catholics. The fact is, I was devoted most sincerely to their cause, and being now retained in their service, I would have sacrificed every thing to ensure their success, and they knew it. I am satisfied they looked upon me as a faithful and zealous advocate, neither to be intimidated nor corrupted, and in that respect they rendered me but justice. My circumstances were, at the time of my appointment, extremely embarrassed, and of course the salary annexed to my office was a considerable object with me. But though I had now an increasing family totally unprovided for, I can safely say that I would not have deserted my duty to the Catholics for the whole patronage of the Government consolidated into one office, if offered me as the reward. In these sentiments I was encouraged and confirmed by the incomparable spirit of my wife, to whose patient suffering under adversity, (for we had often been reduced, and were now well accustomed to difficulties,) I know not how to render justice. Women in general, I am sorry to say it, are mercenary; and especially if they have children, are ready to make all sacrifices to *their* establishment. But my dearest love had bolder and juster views. On every occasion of my life I consulted her; we had no secrets one from the other, and I unvaryingly found her think and act with energy and courage combined with the greatest prudence and discretion. If ever I succeed in life, or arrive at any thing like station or eminence, I shall consider it as owing to her counsels and example. But to return. Another rule which I adopted for my conduct was, in all the papers I had occasion to write, to remember I was not speaking for myself but for the Catholic body, and consequently to be never wedded to my own compositions; but to receive the objections of every one with respect, and to change without reluctance whatever the Committee thought fit to alter, even in cases where perhaps my own judgment was otherwise. And trifling as this circumstance may seem, I am sure it recommended me considerably to the Committee, who had been, on former occasions, more than once embarrassed by the self-love of Richard Burke, and indeed even of some of their own body, men of considerable talents, who had written some excellent papers on their behalf, but who did not stand criticism as I did, without wincing. The fact is, I was so entirely devoted to their cause, that the idea of literary reputation as to myself never occurred to me; not that I am at all insensible on that score, but that the feeling was totally absorbed in superior considerations; and I think I may safely appeal to the sub-committee whether ever, on any occasion, they found me for a moment set up my vanity or self-love against their interests, or even their pleasure. I am sure that by my discretion on the points I have mentioned, which indeed was no more than my duty, I secured the esteem of the Committee, and, consequently, an influence in their counsels, which I should justly have forfeited had I seemed too eager to assume it; and it is to the credit of both parties that, from the first moment of our connexion to the last, neither my zeal and anxiety to serve them, nor the kindness and favour with which they received my efforts, were ever, for a single moment, suspended.

Almost the first business I had to transact was to conduct a correspondence with Richard Burke, who was very desirous to return to Ireland once more, and to resume his former station, which the Committee were determined he should not do. It was a matter of some difficulty to refuse without offending him, and I must say he pressed us rather forcibly; however, we parried him with as much address as we could, and after two or three long letters, to which the answers were very concise and civil, he found the business was desperate, and gave it up accordingly.

This (1792) was a memorable year in Ireland. The publication of the plan for organizing anew the General Committee gave instant alarm to all the supporters of the British Government, and every effort was made to prevent the election of the country members; for it was sufficiently evident that, if the representatives of three millions of oppressed people were once suffered to meet, it would not afterwards be safe, or indeed possible, to refuse their just demands. Accordingly, at the ensuing assizes, the grand juries, universally, throughout Ireland, published the most furious, I may say frantic, resolutions against the plan and its authors, whom they charged with little short of high treason. Government, likewise, was too successful in gaining over the Catholic Clergy, particularly the Bishops, who gave the measure at first very serious opposition. The Committee, however, was not daunted; and, satisfied of the justice of their cause, and of their own courage, laboured, and with success, to inspire the same spirit in the breasts of their brethren throughout the nation. For this purpose, their first step was an admirable one. By their order, I drew up a state of the case, with the plan for the organization of the Committee annexed, which was laid before Simon Butler and Beresford Burton, two lawyers of great eminence, and, what was of consequence here, King's counsel, to know whether the Committee had in any respect contravened the law of the land, or whether, by carrying the proposed plan into execution, the parties concerned would subject themselves to pain or penalty. The answers of both the lawyers were completely in our favour, and we instantly printed them in the papers, and dispersed them in handbills, letters, and all possible shapes. This blow was decisive as to the legality of the measure. For the Bishops, whose opposition gave us great trouble, four or five different missions were undertaken by different members of the sub-committee into the provinces, at their own expense, in order to hold conferences with them, in which, with much difficulty, they succeeded so far as to secure the co-operation of some, and the neutrality of the rest of the Prelates. On these missions the most active members were John Keogh and Thomas Braughall, neither of whom spared purse nor person where the interests of the Catholic body were concerned. I accompanied Mr. Braughall in his visit to Connaught, where he went to meet the gentry of that province at the great fair of Ballinasloe. As it was late in the evening when we left town, (the postilion who drove us having given warning, I am satisfied, to some footpads,) the carriage was stopped by four or five fellows at the gate of the Phœnix Park. We had two cases of pistols in the carriage, and agreed not to be robbed. Braughall, who was at this time about sixty-five years of age, and lame from a fall off his horse some years before, was as cool and intrepid as man could be. He took the command, and by his orders I let down all the glasses, and called out to the fellows to come on, if they were so inclined, for that we were ready; Braughall desiring me at the same time not to fire till I could touch the scoundrels. This rather embarrassed them, and they did not venture to approach the carriage, but held a council of war at the horses' heads. I then presented one of my pistols at the postilion, swearing horribly that I would put him instantly to death if he did not drive over them, and I made him feel the muzzle of the pistol against the back of his head; the fellows on this took to their heels and ran off, and we proceeded on our journey without further interruption. When we arrived at the inn, Braughall, whose goodness of heart is equal to his courage, and no man is braver, began by abusing the postilion for his treachery, and ended by giving him half a crown! I wanted to break the rascal's bones, but he would not suffer me, and this was the end of the adventure.

All parties were now fully employed preparing for the ensuing session of Parliament. The Government, through the organ of the corporations and grand juries, opened a heavy fire upon us of manifestos and resolutions. At first we were like young soldiers, a little stunned with the noise, but after a few rounds we began to look about us, and seeing nobody drop with all this furious cannonade, we took courage and determined to return the fire. In consequence, wherever there was a meeting of the Protestant ascendancy, which was the title assumed by that party, (and a very impudent one it was,) we took care it should be followed by a meeting of the Catholics, who spoke as loud and louder than their adversaries; and, as we had the right clearly on our side, we found no great difficulty in silencing the enemy on this quarter. The Catholics likewise took care, at the same time, that they branded their enemies, to mark their gratitude to their friends, who were daily increasing, and especially to the people of Belfast, between whom and themselves the union was now completely established. Among the various attacks made on us this summer, the most remarkable for their virulence were those of the Grand Jury of Louth, headed by the Speaker of the House of Commons; of Limerick, at which the Lord Chancellor assisted; and of the Corporation of the city of Dublin; which last published a most furious manifesto, threatening us, in so many words, with resistance by force. In consequence, a meeting was held of the Catholics of Dublin at large, which was attended by several thousands, where the manifesto of the corporation was read and most ably commented upon by John Keogh, Dr. Ryan, Dr. Mc Neven, and several others, and a counter-manifesto being proposed, which was written by my friend Emmet, and incomparably well done, it was carried unanimously, and published in all the papers, together with the speeches above-mentioned; and both the speeches and the manifesto had such an infinite superiority over those of the corporation, which were also published and diligently circulated by the Government, that it put an end, effectually, to this warfare of resolutions.

The people of Belfast were not idle on their part; they spared neither pains nor expense to propagate the new doctrine of the union of Irishmen through the whole north of Ireland, and they had the satisfaction to see their proselytes rapidly extending in all directions. In order more effectually to spread their principles, twelve of the most active and intelligent among them subscribed 250*l.* each, in order to set on foot a paper whose object should be to give a fair statement of all that passed in France, whither every one turned their eyes; to inculcate the necessity of union amongst Irishmen of all religious persuasions; to support the emancipation of the Catholics; and finally, as the necessary, though not avowed, consequence of all this, to erect Ireland into a republic, independent of England. This paper, which they called very appositely the Northern Star, was conducted by my friend Samuel Neilson, who was unanimously chosen editor, and it could not have been delivered into abler hands. It is, in truth, a most incomparable paper, and it rose, instantly on its appearance, into a most rapid and extensive sale. The Catholics every where through Ireland (I mean the leading Catholics) were, of course, subscribers, and the Northern Star contributed effectually towards accomplishing the union of the two great sects, by the simple process of making their mutual sentiments better known to each other.

It was determined by the people of Belfast to commemorate this year the anniversary of the taking of the Bastille, with great ceremony. For this purpose they planned a review of the volunteers of the town and neighbourhood, to be followed by a grand procession, with emblematical devices, &c. They also determined to avail themselves of this opportunity to bring forward the Catholic question in force, and, in consequence, resolved to publish two addresses, one to the people of France, and one to the people of Ireland. They gave instructions to Dr. Drennan to prepare the former, and the latter fell to my lot. Drennan executed his task admirably; and I made my address, for my part, as good as I knew how. We were invited to assist at the ceremony, and a great number of the leading members of the Catholic Committee determined to take this opportunity of showing their zeal for the success of the cause of liberty in France, as well as their respect and gratitude to their friends in Belfast. In consequence, a grand assembly took place on the 14th July. After the review, the volunteers and inhabitants, to the number of about 6,000, assembled in the Linen-Hall, and voted the address to the French people unanimously. The address to the people of Ireland followed, and as it was directly and unequivocally in favour of the Catholic claims, we expected some opposition, but were soon relieved from our anxiety, for the address passed, I may say, unanimously: a few ventured to oppose it indirectly, but their arguments were exposed and overset by the friends to Catholic emancipation, amongst the foremost of whom we had the satisfaction to see several dissenting clergymen of great popularity in that country, as Sinclair Kilburne, William Dixon, and T. Birch. It was William Sinclair who moved the two addresses. The hospitality shown by the people of Belfast to the Catholics on this occasion, and the personal acquaintance which the parties formed, riveted the bonds of their recent union, and produced in the sequel the most beneficial and powerful effects.

## CONNECTING SKETCH,

### BY THE EDITOR.

In the preceding abstract, written at Paris, from memory and amidst the most anxious cares, my father, it will be seen, brought down the narrative of his life to the middle of July, 1792. From thence to his arrival in France elapsed a space of upwards of three years. I feel it my duty to account and apologize for the scantiness of my materials relative to this period, perhaps the most interesting of his career. It was during this time that, young and unknown, acting against all the power and influence of a party secure in the long enjoyment of unopposed usurpation and insolent authority, he roused the energies of his oppressed countrymen, and rallied the mass of the people, so long divided by conflicting interests and religious animosities, to assert their national independence.

From the moment he engaged in this cause, he made it a rule to consign in a Diary, destined for the sole perusal of his family and most intimate friends, the passing events of the times, his comments upon them, and his own thoughts and actions. Of this spirited and lively journal, we yet possess, and now publish, the part which begins at his arrival in France, and extends to the date of the last expedition in which he perished. But, on his departure from America, he left in my mother's hands that which contained the diary of his efforts in Ireland whilst forming the Society of the United Irishmen, and acting as Agent and Secretary to the Catholic sub-committee. The experience of our former journey had proved what little respect was then paid by the British cruizers to the neutral American flag, and how unsafe it would have been to have carried such papers along with him.

When, at the close of the year 1796, my mother sailed from America to join him, the same reasons still existed. As he had left with Dr. Reynolds, of Philadelphia, an old friend and associate in his political career, an unlimited power of attorney to protect his family and manage their affairs in his absence, she trusted to his charge all our little property in America, amounting to some hundreds of pounds sterling, a select library of six hundred volumes, and, above all, my father's papers, essays, and manuscripts, including those journals, and enclosed in a strong corded and sealed trunk, of which she kept the key. I am pained to add, that this sacred trust, this pledge of confidence and of friendship, he violated by an unpardonable negligence. Neither during my father's life, nor after his death, could our repeated demands, nor our letters and messages by the most respectable and confidential friends who went to America, procure any answer. At length, in the year 1807, when the state of my health compelled us to undertake a sea voyage and we came to Philadelphia, we called the unfortunate man to an account: but he could give none, and, reduced by repeated and severe illness, was then tottering on the verge of life. What could we do? Serious as the sacrifice was in our circumstances, we offered him a full release for the remainder of the property, if he could only put us in the way of recovering the papers. But it was all in vain, for he had them not; he begged me to search his house, and I found the trunk broken open and empty. With a great deal of difficulty I recovered some fragments dispersed in different hands, and now published. But his journals of the most important and interesting years, of 1793, 1794, and 1795, were irrecoverably gone. The manuscripts of the numerous pamphlets and essays which my father composed at that time—a great number of which were anonymous, and often ascribed to other hands—as well as the materials of a philosophical and political history of Ireland which he was then compiling, and had already begun to write, were also lost. Dr. Reynolds died within a few weeks, and we were obliged to give up all hopes of discovering them.

By this loss, inappreciable to our feelings, we are deprived of the means of tracing accurately my father's career during those three eventful years, in which he was constantly employed in supporting the spirit of union and independence in his country, and performing, as agent to the Catholic Committees, those services which, by their parting vote of thanks, they declared "no gratitude could overrate, and no remuneration overpay." As it is not my purpose to write a history of Ireland, nor a political dissertation on the state of that country under its former, and never-to-be-forgotten nor forgiven Government, I will merely indicate, from my mother's recollections and from the scanty materials which we have recovered, a few of those prominent events in which he was then engaged, and which may elucidate some passages in his subsequent memoirs.

Of the journals which formed the most interesting part in this collection, we have recovered those of October, 1791, with some trifling fragments of an earlier date, those of July, August, September, October, and November, 1792, and part of January and February, 1793. My father states, in his own memoir, that he began to keep them regularly in 1791, when he engaged seriously in the politics of the day. From thence, they extended in a regular series to the middle of 1795, when he sailed for America; but all the remainder, though he frequently refers to them in his other writings, are irrecoverably lost. This loss may, it is true, be partly supplied by an abstract of the operations of the General Committee and delegation which carried the petition of the Catholics to England, and of their subsequent negotiations with the Irish Government, from the beginning of December, 1792, to the end of April, 1793. This elegant and lucid report, which we will insert in this portion of his life, as it properly forms a continuation of it, will show how qualified he was to write that history of Ireland which he had begun, and of which it was probably destined to form a part.

Along with these papers others have been recovered, in a very mutilated state, written on flying scraps of paper, and relating to various periods of his life. These were the materials from whence his journals were afterwards written, when sitting, surrounded by his wife and children, as I yet remember him, in the evening leisure of his home.

We have already seen, in the preceding narrative, that in 1791 he wrote that pamphlet, in favour of the Catholic cause, signed " A Northern Whig," the success of which was so prodigious, and on which he was appointed secretary and agent to the sub-committee, in the place of Richard Burke. The following year, 1792, was the most busy period in his political career. In the course of a few months, constantly engaged in the same great pursuit, he performed three journeys to Belfast, to effect the union between the Catholics and Dissenters, (in which he succeeded at length completely,) besides several other journeys in Connaught and elsewhere, to rally the Catholics themselves in the common cause, and calm the agitated passions of the Dissenters. The details of these journeys, written in a most playful and lively style, are contained in the journals which we have saved, as well as his negotiations with the Whig leaders, Grattan, Lord Moira, and the Marquis of Abercorn, on behalf of the Catholics. During the same period he founded the first clubs of the United Irishmen, whose organization and object were then very different from those which the tyranny of the Government afterwards drove them to, when they had spread all over the country. The primitive object of these societies was merely to form a union of all religious denominations, whose members, abjuring every former feud, should join their efforts to reform the abuses of the government and constitution of the country, and restore the rights of free and equal citizenship to Irishmen of every sect and religion. Their oath of secrecy and regular organization was introduced at a later period, and by other leaders, when my father had ceased to have any influence over them, and scarcely held any correspondence with their councils.

Towards the close of that year, 1792, his arduous efforts to unite the mass of the nation in the sacred cause of union and independence presented more favourable symptoms of success than at any former period. The Catholics and Dissenters were united, and a new and complete system of representation was, as we have seen, organized among the former, which enabled them to concentrate in one voice the grievances and opinions of 3,000,000 of men. This great result was obtained by the unremitting efforts of the sub-committee of Dublin, as well as of my father.

In the beginning of December, 1792, that General Committee of the Catholics of Ireland, which first represented the whole strength of their body, opened their meetings; and the single circumstance of their sitting with all the forms of a legislative assembly in the capital, produced a kind of awe and stupefaction in the Government. Never did such a convention begin its proceedings under auspices more favourable. Their friends were roused, their enemies stunned; and the British Government, extremely embarrassed at home, showed no desire to interfere. From a letter of Richard Burke, (mentioned in my father's journals of 23d and 24th July, 1792, (See Appendix,) they concluded that England was determined on remaining neutral in the controversy. To yield without a struggle, and recommend themselves as well as they could to the ruling party, as that gentleman advised, was a counsel too cowardly to be followed. They felt secure in their own strength, which their adversaries, and even their friends, had much undervalued; in the spirit and union of the people; and in the support of the Dissenters; and determined on bringing matters to a close by addressing the Monarch directly against their own Government. Had they persevered in the same spirit with which they began, they would undoubtedly have succeeded.

The immediate purpose of the meeting which followed was to draw a statement of their grievances, a vindication of the Catholics, and a petition to the King, and to address them directly to his Majesty, without sending them through the channel of the Irish administration. These papers, the first which fairly represented the whole extent of their grievances and claimed the total repeal of those penal laws by which nine-tenths of the population were deprived of the rights of citizenship, and almost of humanity, in their own country, were all drawn up by my father, the only Protestant in the assembly, and he accompanied the delegation which presented them to the Sovereign.

On this occasion I must observe that, notwithstanding the affected alarm of the Irish Government at a mere playful and theoretical letter of his, which, as already stated, fell afterwards into their hands, at this time he only sought to obtain, without the struggles of a revolution, the gradual emancipation of his country by legal and constitutional means; by uniting the Dissenters and Catholics, who formed the mass of the people, to overwhelm the ruling and oppressive minority of the Protestant ascendancy, and deprive it of its usurped privileges. And well would it have been for England if her administration had had the sense and determination to support the cause of justice, instead of that of oppression. The millions which have been expended, and the oceans of blood which have been shed in Ireland, would have been spared; she would have secured the gratitude and attachment of its warm-hearted population, and acquired a faithful and useful ally to fight by her side in her subsequent contests, instead of a chained enemy, requiring the constant employment of half her forces to keep him at her feet.

In the following narrative, the only circumstance which my father has passed over in silence was his own share in these great events; his part in these councils, and in planning and framing these acts; as well as the two special votes of thanks which he received from the Committee when they closed their sittings—the first in December, and the second in April. The beginning of this interesting abstract is lost, but it must have comprized the organization of the convention, and the account of its first meeting.

ACCOUNT OF THE PROCEEDINGS OF THE GENERAL COMMITTEE OF THE CATHOLICS OF IRELAND; OF THE DELEGATION WHICH PRESENTED THEIR PETITION TO THE KING; AND OF THE PASSAGE OF THE FIRST BILL FOR THEIR RELIEF.

THE Catholics were thus once more, after a dreary interval of 104 years of slavery, fully and fairly represented by members of their own persuasion. The last Catholic assembly which Ireland had seen was the Parliament summoned by James II. in 1688, a body of men whose wisdom, spirit, and patriotism reflect no discredit on their country or their sect. The great object of this Parliament was national supremacy. By an act of navigation they wisely guarded the commerce, and, by a declaration of rights, boldly asserted the independence of their native land, both scandalously betrayed to the monopoly and the pride of England by their immediate successors, the Protestant Parliament of William. The patriots of the present day found their best claim to public regard on maintaining principles first advanced by an assembly to whose merits no historian has yet ventured to do justice, but whose memory, when passion and prejudice are no more, will be perpetuated in the hearts of their grateful countrymen.

The proceedings of the General Committee fully justified the foresight, and far surpassed the hopes, of those who had devised the measure. On the first moment of their meeting, when they looked round and reviewed their numbers and their strength, they at once discarded the unworthy habits of deference and submission which their unhappy situation had so long compelled them to assume. They felt and acted with the decision of men who deserved to be free, and with the dignity becoming the representatives of 3,000,000 of people. The spirit of liberty ran like electric fire through every link of their chains, and before they were an hour convened, the question of their emancipation was, in fact, decided.

The first act of the assembly was, unanimously, to call to the chair Mr. Edward Byrne, a mark of distinction equally honourable to him and to themselves. In their cause he had exposed himself to every species of calumny and abuse; his name had been held up as a target against which the arrows of prejudice, falsehood, and corruption, had been unceasingly discharged, and, after a persecution of many months, he had come forth unhurt. The General Committee, by thus placing him at their head, as their first President, at once discharged a debt of gratitude they had incurred, and marked their utter contempt for the impotent malice of those who had vilified and abused him, only for his eminent services in the public cause.

The attempts which had been made to introduce members who under the old constitution had an indubitable right to attend, rendered it necessary for the General Committee to close the question. They therefore resolved, that the meeting as then constituted, with the Peers and Prelates, formed the only organ competent to speak the sense of the Catholic body,—a measure which wisdom, and indeed necessity, impelled them to adopt. A faint attempt was made to oppose it, on the ground that the circular letter, under which the meeting was convened, had stated that the rights of no person, then a member of the Committee, were intended to be abridged; and it was proposed, by a nice distinction, to say, that the meeting was "*competent*," and not "*only competent*," to speak the sense of the people at large. But it was answered to this by Captain Sweetman, of Wexford, that the sub-committee could not, by their act, tie up the hands of the great body of the Catholics, then present by their representatives, who were alone empowered to determine this question. And that admitting a confusion of personal and representative rights was but to lay a foundation for future dissension, since it might so happen that, on a division, all those of one description might secede, and thereby enable the enemies of the Catholics to take shelter behind a specious pretence, of which, as they had formerly seized it with avidity, they would be glad again to avail themselves.

These arguments appeared conclusive; the opposition was withdrawn, and the motion passed unanimously. Thus, by a material change in the constitution of the General Committee, all future claims grounded on personal rights were extinguished; the right of *representation* was established, and the strength of the whole Catholic people consolidated into one great and indivisible mass. The wisdom of the measure was justified by the event.

The General Committee next resolved, that a petition be prepared to his Majesty, stating the grievances of the Catholics of Ireland, and praying relief, and the members of the sub-committee were ordered to bring in the same forthwith, which being done, and the petition read in the usual forms, it was again read, paragraph by paragraph, each passing unanimously, until the last. A spirited and intelligent member, who represented a great northern county,[*] then rose and said, "That he must object to this paragraph, on the ground of its being limited in its demand. His instructions from his constituents were to require nothing short of total emancipation; and it was not consistent with the dignity of this meeting, and much less of the great body whom it represented, to sanction, by any thing which could be construed into acquiescence on their part, one fragment of that unjust and abominable system, the penal code. It lay with the paternal wisdom of the Sovereign to ascertain what he thought

---

[*] Luke Teeling, Esq. of Lisburn, county Antrim.

fit to be granted, but it was the duty of this meeting to put him fully and unequivocally in possession of the wants and wishes of his people." He therefore moved, "that in place of the paragraph then read, one should be inserted, praying that the Catholics might be restored to the equal enjoyment of the blessings of the constitution."

It is not easy to describe the effect which this speech had on the assembly. It was received with the most extravagant applause. A member of great respectability, and who had ever been remarked for a cautious and prudent system in his public conduct,* rose to declare his entire and hearty concurrence in the spirit of the motion. "Let us not," said he, "deceive our Sovereign and our constituents, nor approach the throne with a suppression of the truth. Now is our time to speak. The whole Catholic people are not to be called forth to acquiesce in the demand of partial relief." The question would now have been carried by acclamation, but for the interposition of a member to whose opinion, from his past services and the active part he had ever taken, the Committee were disposed to pay every respect,—Mr. J. Keogh. He said, "that he entirely agreed with the spirit of the motion, and was satisfied that they had but to ask and they should receive. But the meeting had already despatched a great deal of business, the hour was now late, and the question of the very last importance.—Have you," said the

* D. T. O'Brien, Esq. of Cork.

speaker, " considered the magnitude of your demand and the power of your enemies? have you considered the disgrace and the consequences of a refusal, and are you prepared to support your claim?" The whole assembly rose, as one man, and raising their right hands, answered, " WE ARE." It was a sublime spectacle. " Then," continued he, " I honour and rejoice in a spirit which must render your success infallible ; but let it not be said that you took a resolution of this infinite magnitude in a fit of enthusiasm. Let us agree to retire. We meet again to-morrow. We will consider this question in the mean time, and whatever be the determination of the morning, it will not be accused of want of temperance or consideration." This argument prevailed, and the meeting adjourned.

But the business of the day was, perhaps, not less effectually promoted by the convivial parties which followed than by the serious debates which occupied the sitting of the Committee. Those members resident in Dublin, whom it had been the policy of the enemies to Catholic emancipation grossly to malign and misrepresent in the remote parts of the kingdom, had taken care to offer the rites of hospitality to the delegates from the country ; and, in unreserved communication, both parties compared their common grievances and mutually entered into each other's sentiments. All distrust was banished at once, and a comparison of ideas satisfied them that their interests were one and the same, and that the only enemy to be dreaded was disunion among themselves. The delegate from Antrim, who sat beside the delegate from Kerry, at the board of their brother in the capital, needed but little argument to convince him, that as the old maxim, "divide and conquer," had been the uniform rule of conduct with their common enemies, so, mutual confidence and union among themselves were the infallible presage and most certain means of securing their approaching emancipation. The attrition of parties, thus collected from every district of the kingdom, demolished in one evening the barriers of prejudice which art and industry and the monopolising spirit of corruption had, by falsehood and soothing, by misrepresentation and menaces, been labouring for years, and but too successfully, to establish between them.

In this spirit the assembly met on the next day. The business was opened by the same member, (Mr. Teeling) who had introduced the amendment. He stated that it was the duty of the Catholics not to wrong themselves by asking less than complete emancipation. That it was also the idea of the friends of the Catholics in the province from whence he came, and this coincidence of sentiments would establish that union from which the Catholic cause had already derived such essential benefit, and which had been found so formidable to their enemies. Something had been insinuated about danger; he saw none: violence was neither the interest nor the wish of the meeting. "But," continued he, "we have been asked, what we shall do in case of a refusal? I will not, when I look round me, suppose a refusal. But, if such an event should take place, our duty is obvious. We are to tell our constituents; and they, not we, are to determine. We will take the sense of the whole people, and see what *they* will have done." Similar sentiments were avowed by every member who followed him; and, on the question being put, the amendment, praying for complete restitution of the rights of the Catholics, was carried by the unanimous acclamation of the whole assembly.

It was not to be supposed that perfect secrecy could be preserved in so numerous a meeting, or that the industry of the enemies to Catholic freedom would not be exerted in so important a crisis and on so material a question as that which was now determined with such unanimity. On the morning of the day it was whispered that, if the prayer for complete emancipation was persisted in, a large number of the most respectable country delegates would instantly quit the meeting, and publish their dissent. Whether such a measure was ever seriously intended or not, is not accurately known: certainly, had it been carried into execution, a secession of so formidable a nature would have extremely embarrassed, if not totally destroyed, a system which had cost so much time and labour to bring to its present state. Be that as it may, such was the force of virtuous example, so powerful the effect of public spirit in an assembly uncontaminated with places or pensions, and freely chosen by the people, that not a murmur of dissent was heard; and a day which opened with circumstances of considerable doubt and anxiety, terminated in the unanimous adoption of the great principle which, whilst it asserted, secured the emancipation of the Catholics.

The prayer of the petition having been thus agreed upon, it was proposed by Mr. Fitzgerald, that the signatures of the delegates should not be affixed, until the mode of transmission should be first determined. The object of this motion was obviously to embarrass, and, if possible, to prevent a measure which, from the spirit of the meeting, it was more than suspected would be tried. Apprehensions were entertained that the usual form in presenting petitions would be broken through, and that, by a direct application to the throne, a very pointed mark of disapprobation would be attached to the Government of this country. If to prevent administration from being exposed to such an insult was the object of the motion, it failed completely. The Committee decreed, that the signing the petition should precede all debate as to the mode of transmission: and not only so, but it was unanimously resolved, (on the motion of Mr. Edward Sweetman, of Wexford) that every delegate should instantly pledge himself to support, with his hand and signature, the sense of the majority; an engagement which was immediately and solemnly taken by the whole assembly.

The petition having been thus agreed upon, and

signed, the important question arose as to the mode of presenting it to his Majesty. The usual method had been to deliver all former addresses to the Lord Lieutenant, who transmitted them to the King; and certainly, to break through a custom invariably continued from the first establishment of the General Committee was marking, in the most decided manner, that the Catholics had lost all confidence in the administration of the country. But, strong as this measure was, it was now to be tried. The petition having been read for the last time, a spirited young member, whose property gave him much, and his talents and virtues still more, influence in the assembly, and who represented a county, perhaps the first in Ireland for Catholic property and independence,* rose, and moved, without preface, that the petition should be sent to the foot of the throne by a deputation to be chosen from the General Committee. He was seconded by a delegate from a county adjacent to his own.†

A blow of this nature, striking so directly at the character, and almost at the existence of the administration, could scarcely be suffered to pass without some effort on their part to prevent it. As the attack had been foreseen, some kind of a negotiation had been attempted with individuals, who were given to understand that, if the petition was sent through the usual channel, administration would instantly dis-

* Mr. Christopher Dillon Bellew, of Galway.
† Mr. J. J. Macdonnell, of Mayo.

patch it by express, and back it with the strongest recommendations. The negotiation was not yet concluded when the dreaded motion was made, and with some difficulty the assembly agreed to wait half an hour for the result of one more interview. There can hardly be imagined a revolution more curious and unexpected than that which was occurring in the General Committee. The very men who, a few months before, could not obtain an answer at the Castle, sat with their watches in their hands, minuting that Government which had repelled them with disdain. At length the result of the interview was made known, and it appeared that the parties had either mistaken each other, or their powers, or the intentions of the administration, for it was stated by Mr. Keogh, the member who reported it, that what had been supposed to be offered was merely a conversation between a very respectable individual and himself, but he had nothing to communicate from any authority. This, which the majority of the assembly considered, whether justly or not, as an instance of duplicity in administration, and as trifling with their own time and dignity, determined them to stigmatize, as far as in them lay, a Government which they now looked upon as having added insult to injury. " Will you," cried Keogh, " trust your petition with such men?" The assembly answered with a unanimous, repeated, and indignant negative!

Yet still, a few individuals were found who started at the idea of fixing so gross an insult on administration. It was suggested, rather than argued, that it was not perhaps respectful, even to majesty itself, to pass over with such marked contempt his representative in Ireland, and that the usual mode was the most constitutional, or, at least, the most conciliatory. But the spirit of the meeting was now above stooping to conciliate the favour of those whom they neither respected nor feared. The member who moved the question (Mr. C. Bellew) again rose to support it. He said he did not ground his motion merely on the insults which the Catholics, through their delegates, had so often received, but on this, that he had no confidence in men who kept no faith with Catholics, and the attempt of the present day had satisfied his mind. Faith had been broken, even with those gentlemen (Lord Kenmare and the sixty-eight) who, in support of administration, had seceded from their own body. The engagement entered into with them had been mutilated and curtailed. "It has been said," continued he, "my plan is disrespectful to administration. I answer, *it is intended to be so*. It is time for us to speak out like men. We will not, like African slaves, *petition* our task-masters. Our Sovereign will never consider it disrespectful, that we lay before his throne the dutiful and humble petition of 3,000,000 of loyal and suffering subjects. For my part, I know I speak the sentiments of my county. I wish my constituents may know my conduct; and the measure which I have now proposed, I am ready to justify in any way." These were strong expressions; they were followed by others no less energetic. "We have not come thus far," said Mr. M'Dermott, a delegate from Sligo, " to stop short in our career. Gentlemen tell us of the wounded pride of the administration. I believe it will be wounded, but I care not; I consider only the pride of the Catholics of Ireland." The last attempt was now made, to postpone the further consideration of the question until the next day, but this was immediately and powerfully resisted. "We will stay all night, if necessary," cried a spirited young member (Mr. P. Russell, of Louth,) "but this question must be decided before we part, If it go abroad that you waver, you are undone." " Let us mark," cried Mr. J. Edw. Devereux, of Wexford, " our abhorrence of the measures of our enemies, for they are the enemies of Ireland. The present administration has not the confidence of the people." The whole assembly confirmed his words by a general exclamation, while the orator proceeded: " Our allegiance and attachment are to King, Lords, and Commons, not to a bad ministry, who have calumniated and reviled us throughout the Kingdom." His assertions were ratified by repeated and universal plaudits.

The question on the original motion was at length unanimously decided in the affirmative. By passing over the administration of their country, in a studied and deliberate manner, and on solemn debate, the General Committee published to all the world, that his Majesty's ministers in Ireland had so far lost the confidence of no less than 3,000,000 of his subjects, that they were not even to be entrusted with the delivery of their petition. A stigma more severe it has not been the fortune of many administrations to receive.

On the 7th of December, the General Committee proceeded to choose, by ballot, five of their body, who should present their petition to his Majesty in person; and the gentlemen appointed were Edward Byrne, John Keogh, Christopher Dillon Bellew, James Edward Devereux, and Sir Thomas French. The only instruction they received was to adhere strictly to the spirit of the petition, and to admit nothing derogatory to the union which is the strength of Ireland:—and this instruction, for greater solemnity, was delivered to them, engrossed on vellum, signed by the Chairman, and countersigned by the Secretary of the meeting.

The petition being thus disposed of, the next measure which occupied the attention of the General Committee was to prepare a vindication of the Catholic body from the many foul imputations which had lately been thrown out against their principles and conduct. For many months, patiently listening to the calumnies and falsehoods which affected terror and real corruption had unremittingly vented, and attending only to the great measure, the universal election of their delegates, they had not suffered themselves to been trapped into the snare of political controversy. They had consequently made no defence against the torrent of abuse which poured upon them from all quarters. They were not seduced even by the glory of a contest with great names or high authorities, but proceeded in their march right onward, slowly and steadily, alike unmoved at the turbulent attacks of the numerous county meetings, the well-feigned alarms of the selected grand juries, and dictated and loyal fears of the obedient corporations. But now, success had afforded them leisure, and the present opportunity was seized to give one general replication to all the invectives thrown out against them they, therefore, framed and published their vindication, which was intended as a commentary on their petition, a defence of their own conduct, and a refutation of the malicious and unfounded charges of their adversaries.

On the principle of this vindication, the assembly was unanimous; but, as to one or two particular passages, a doubt arose in the minds of certain of the delegates. Among the number of the enemies to their emancipation were to be found personages of the most exalted political situation, some of whom had presided, and others assisted, at meetings, whence publications had issued of the most violent hostility to the Catholic cause. In replying to these publications, it was hardly possible to avoid statements and expressions which must be directly offensive to the exalted characters concerned; for, as the attacks were not merely political, but, from their extreme acrimony, partook of somewhat of a personal feeling, so the nature of the defence, and, indeed, the nature of man, suggested, and in a manner enforced, a language which, in a controversy of a milder kind, could not have arisen. It was not to be wondered at, if men felt some degree of caution at committing themselves in this species of warfare with such grave and high authorities. The question, therefore, on those parts of the vindication which remotely alluded to, or directly named, the most potent of their adversaries (Lord Chancellor Fitzgibbon), was very fully debated and maturely considered.

The conduct of the personages under deliberation could not be defended on any principle, in an assembly of Catholics. Those, therefore, who doubted on the propriety of thus repelling force by force, among whom were Messrs. Fitzgerald, Daly, Lynch, &c., contented themselves with the common-place topics of the necessary respect to high station, and the danger of speaking evil of dignities. But these were arguments to which the great majority of the assembly was now very little disposed to pay any respect. Feeling their own strength and unanimity, and galled by the remembrance of the wanton abuse which had been so profusely lavished upon them, they determined not to let pass an opportunity which fortune and their own wise and spirited conduct had put into their hands, but to mark their adversaries in their turn. Almost every man was eager to express his contempt and abhorrence of those whom the assembly now considered as fallen tyrants, and the feeble attempt to rescue them from a public stigma was drowned in one universal outcry of disapprobation. "What?" it was asked, "are we to spare one man, who smells of the blood of our peasantry?[*] or another who made it his public and profligate boast that he would prostrate the chapels of the Catholics?[†] We know that man, the road to his favour is through his fears. Let us become formidable to him, and we shall be respected. He is the calumniator of the people, and therefore he has our hatred and our contempt. Loyalty itself becomes stupidity and vice, where there is no protection; and are we to tender gratuitous submission to men who have held, and would hold us in fetters, in mockery, and in scorn? What have we to fear, but our own disunion? Let us boldly acknowledge our friends, and mark our enemies. Let us respect ourselves, and the world will respect us; and, above all, let us not disgrace our cause, or the great body which we represent, by indecision, temporising, or equivocation." The assembly then unanimously decreed that the passages which had been objected to should remain unaltered.

The great and important business for which the General Committee had been summoned was now, in effect, terminated, at least as far as their labours could advance it. What remained of their time was occupied in discharging the debt of gratitude to their friends, and forming an arrangement for their future assembling. They voted their unanimous thanks to the citizens of Belfast, "to whom," said

---

[*] Mr. Foster.
[†] Lord Fitzgibbon, afterwards Earl Clare.

a delegate, " we owe that we meet here in safety; they stand sentinels at our doors; they support you, Mr. President, in that chair;" a sentiment which was received with acclamation by the whole meeting. They voted their thanks to those illustrious members who had supported the cause of the Catholics in Parliament. They thanked those patriotic characters, who had devoted their time and talents to forwarding the emancipation of their brethren. They thanked their officers; they thanked their sub-committee. They empowered that body to act for them in the intervals between their rising and their next meeting; but they made a material alteration in its constitution, by associating to the twelve members who then formed it, the whole of the country delegates, each of whom was henceforward to be, *ipso facto*, a member thereof. They then resolved, unanimously, that they would re-assemble when duly summoned by the sub-committee, who were invested with powers for that purpose. "We will attend," cried a member from a remote county, (Mr. O'Gorman, of Mayo,) " if we are summoned to meet across the Atlantic!"

One occurrence deserves to be particularly noted. It had been the policy of the enemies of the Catholic cause, for a long time, to foment and continue divisions between the clergy and laity, and, in some instances, their acts had so far succeeded as, perhaps, nearly to produce a difference between the pastor and the flock. It has already been mentioned that it was not without difficulty some of the prelates had been induced to concur with the General Committee in the plan for the electing of delegates, a circumstance not to be wondered at when we consider the peculiar delicacy and responsibility of their situation, and the uncommon diligence and art which were used to deter them from any interference. But, whatever might at first have been their doubts and diffidence, when they saw the great body of the laity come forward and unanimously demand their rights, they manfully cast away all reserve, and declared their determination to rise or fall with their flocks—a wise and patriotic resolution, which was signified to the General Committee by two venerable prelates, Dr. Troy, Archbishop of Dublin, and Dr. Moylan, Bishop of Cork, who assisted at the meeting, and signed the petition in the name, and on behalf, of the great body of the Catholic clergy of Ireland. They were received by the assembly with the utmost deference and respect, due not less to their sacred functions and private virtues, than to the great and useful accession of strength which they brought to the common cause.

The members of the General Committee having returned to their counties, the delivery of their petition to the King became the immediate and urgent business of the gentlemen delegated to that honourable duty. It so happened that there was no packet-boat ready in the harbour, and the wind was contrary. They therefore determined to go by a route longer, it is true, but less subject to accidental delays. To go by Scotland, it was necessary to pass through the north of Ireland, and, especially, through Belfast. On their arrival in that town they were met by a number of the most active and intelligent inhabitants, who had distinguished themselves in the abolition of prejudice, and the conciliation of the public mind in Ulster to the claims of the Catholics. On their departure, their horses were taken off, and they were drawn along with loud acclamations by the people, among whom were numbers of an appearance and rank very different from what are usually seen on such occasions. To the honour of the populace of Belfast, it should be mentioned, that they refused a liberal donation which was offered by the Catholic delegates; and, having escorted them beyond the precincts of the town, and cordially wished them success in their embassy, they dismissed them with three cheers.

Trifling as this circumstance may appear, it was the subject of much observation. By some it was considered as throwing additional difficulties on a measure already supposed to be sufficiently unpalatable to the British Minister, by avowing a connection with men notoriously obnoxious to him. By others it was applauded, on the ground of strengthening that union of the great sects, the beneficial effects of which had already begun to operate in the elevation of the Catholic mind—an advantage which was thought to carry an intrinsic weight and power far beyond the uncertain favour of any minister. Whatever effect it might have on the negotiation in England, it certainly tended to raise and confirm the hopes of the Catholics at home. " Let our delegates," said they, " if they are refused, return by the same route." To those who looked beyond the surface it was an interesting spectacle, and pregnant with material consequences, to see the Dissenter of the north drawing with his own hands the Catholic of the south in triumph through what may be denominated the capital of Presbyterianism. However repugnant it might be to the wishes of the British Minister, it was a wholesome suggestion to his prudence, and when he scanned the whole business in his mind, was probably not dismissed from his contemplation.

On the arrival of the delegates in London, their first business was to apprize the Secretary for the Home Department, (the Hon. H. Dundas) that they were deputed to present to the King the humble petition of the Catholics of Ireland, and they requested to know at what time they should attend him with a copy for his Majesty's perusal. The minister having appointed a day, the delegates met him, and, in a long conversation, very fully detailed the situation and wishes of the Catholic body. It is not to be supposed that the minister, on his part, was equally communicative, but he heard them with particular attention, and dismissed them with respectful politeness. His object was to procure the petition to be delivered through his hands; that of the delegates, to deliver it to the King himself, in person. Some dexterity was exhibited on both sides in negotiating this point, but the minister was, at length, obliged to concede, and the firmness of the delegates prevailed.

It is but justice to the merit of an illustrious character, to state here the obligation which the Catholics of Ireland owe to their countryman, the Earl of Moira, at that time Lord Rawdon.* He had immediately on the arrival of the delegates in London, waited on them, and offered them the hospitality of his mansion and the command of his household; he entertained them repeatedly in a style of splendid magnificence; and if the dignity of their mission could have received lustre from the support of an individual, they would have found it in the zeal and friendship of the Earl of Moira. But his services were not confined to acts of hospitality and politeness. He assisted in their councils, and, in a manner, committed his public character with their cause; for, on the emergency, when the minister was dallying with the earnestness of the delegates to procure admission to their Sovereign, and probably presumed that they would not readily find another channel of access, Lord Moira came forward and told them that, if it became necessary, *he* would, as a peer, demand an audience of his Majesty, and be himself their introducer; adding, at the same time, with the frankness and candour of his profession and character, that, flattering as such a distinction would be to himself, it was his wish that the minister should rather have the honour,

* The late Marquess of Hastings.

inasmuch as he thought it would better serve their cause. "As an Irishman and a military man," continued he, "it might be esteemed to wear, perhaps, too peremptory an appearance, were I to introduce you, and when the minister finds that you are, at all events, secure of admission, he will, probably, be less reluctant to have the credit of it himself. If, however, he should persist in his refusal, you may then command me." The event justified his prediction; the minister relaxed; and Wednesday, the 2d of January, was fixed as the day of their introduction. On that day the delegates were introduced at St. James's in the usual forms by Mr. Dundas, and, agreeably to their instructions, delivered into the King's own hands the petition of his Catholic subjects of Ireland. Their appearance was splendid, and they met with what is called in the language of courts a most gracious reception; that is, his Majesty was pleased to say a few words to each of the delegates in his turn. In such colloquies, the matter is generally of little interest, the manner is all; and with the manner of the Sovereign the delegates had every reason to be content.

Thus had the Catholics, at length, through innumerable difficulties, fought their way to the foot of the throne; the King had, in the most solemn manner, received their petition, and his ministers were in full possession of their situation, their wants, and their wishes. Their delegates had now executed their mission, and began to prepare for their return. After allowing a decent interval of a few days, they attended on the minister, for the last time, to learn, if they could, his determination, and to take what may be called their audience of leave. In this conversation, as in every former one, the claims of the Catholics were powerfully enforced and impressed on the mind of the minister in language stronger than is often used to men in his high station, and which would most probably have shocked the delicacy of a gentleman-usher. He was given to understand, in terms scarcely equivocal, that the peace of Ireland, or, in other words, the submission of the Catholics, depended on the measures which Government might adopt on their behalf. Yet, the cool and guarded temper of the minister was not to be disturbed, and, though he heard them with attention, and, apparently, at times, with emotion, he was not to be driven from the diplomatic caution behind which he had carefully intrenched himself. After much of that general language which is vernacular in official stations, the delegates were told, that his Majesty was sensible of their loyalty and attachment to the principles of the constitution; that, in consequence, they should be recommended in the speech from the throne at the opening of the impending session, and that Ministers in England desired approbation and support from them only in proportion to the measure of relief afforded. If the elasticity of this answer, which would dilate or compress to any magnitude, did not appear entirely satisfactory to the plain and uncourtly understandings of the delegates, they were told, and probably with some truth, that the minister had gone farther than custom in similar circumstances would warrant; and that, preserving the decorum due to the independent government and legislature in Ireland, more could not, with propriety, be said on the one hand, or required on the other. With this answer they were forced to be content, and satisfied themselves in the reflection that nothing on their part had been left undone to procure one more definite.

It now became necessary to consider of the report which should be made to their constituents in Ireland. The expressions of the minister, according to all received rules of construction, were to be taken most strongly against himself; the King was sensible of their loyalty; they were to be liberally recommended, and their gratitude was to be commensurable with their relief. Combining these expressions with the general behaviour of the minister, and the effect produced on their minds in the various conferences, and making allowance for the delicacy of his station, which did not permit him to be more explicit, they resolved that the answer of the minister was satisfactory, (and satisfaction to Catholic minds, then inferred the idea of *complete relief*,) a construction which they founded not on this or on that expression, but adopted as a general impression resulting from the whole tenor of Mr. Dundas's conduct from the commencement to the termination of their negotiation.

In pursuance of this principle, as the session had already opened, two of their body were instantly despatched to state to the sub-committee all that had been done, and what the deputation conceived to be the sentiments of the Ministry in England. The other members followed more leisurely; and, in the course of a few days, the deputation was collected, with the exception of one gentleman, Mr. Devereux, of Wexford, who remained in London as a kind of *Chargé d'Affaires.*

The opening of the session of 1793 was, perhaps, as critical a period as had occurred for a century in Ireland. In consequence of the regulation beforementioned, every country gentleman, delegated for either county or city, was now a member of the subcommittee, and the anxiety which they felt for the event of a question in which their dearest interests and warmest hopes were so deeply involved, had detained a number of the most active, spirited, and intelligent of the Catholic gentry in town during the whole period of the absence of their deputation. On its return, the sub-committee was, in consequence, very diligently attended, and the process of the measures intended for the relief of the Catholics fully investigated, and, on several material points, debated in crowded meetings and with considerable heat.

At the adjournment of the General Committee in December, and for some time after, administration in Ireland was in a state of deplorable depression and dismay. Already stunned with the rude shock received from the Catholics, the Minister, at the opening of the session, was a perfect model of conciliatory concession. To the astonishment of the nation, the principle of Parliamentary Reform was asserted unanimously by the House of Commons, and admitted without a struggle, almost without a sigh, by administration. The people seemed to have but to demand and to obtain their long withheld rights, and sanguine men began to indulge the hope that the constitution of their country would, at length, be restored to its theoretical simplicity and justice, and all its impurities be purged away. But this vision, so bright in the perspective, was soon dispelled, and the nation, in the course of a few short weeks, awakened from its fancied triumph over inveterate corruption to a very solid and substantial system of coercion. To follow in detail many of the measures which materially contributed to this sudden and unexpected change would now be, at best, useless, perhaps prejudicial; yet truth requires that some of them should be developed: the investigation of past errors, if it cannot recall lost opportunity, may, at least, prevent their repetition in similar circumstances, should such ever occur again.

The solid strength of the people was their union. In December, the Catholics had thundered out their demands,—the imperious, because unanimous, requisition of 3,000,000 of men; they were supported by all the spirit and intelligence of the Dissenters. Dumourier was in Brabant, Holland was prostrate before him; even London, to the impetuous ardour of the French, did not appear at an immeasurable distance; the stocks were trembling; war seemed inevitable; the minister was embarrassed; and under those circumstances, it was idle to think that he would risk the domestic peace of Ireland to maintain a system of monopoly utterly useless to his views. The Catholics well knew this; they well knew their own strength and the weakness of their enemies; and therefore it was that the sub-committee derided the empty bluster of the Grand Juries, and did not fear, in the moment that they stigmatized the administration, to approach their Sovereign with a demand of unlimited emancipation. Happy had the same decided spirit continued to actuate their councils! But it would be fruitless to deny what it is impossible to conceal. From whatever cause, the system was changed, the simple universality of demand was subjected to discussion, and, from the moment of the first interview with the Minister of Ireland, the popular mind became retrograde, the confidence of administration and their strength returned, and the same session which afforded a mutilated though important relief to the Catholics carries on its records a militia bill, a gunpowder act, and an act for the suppression of tumultuous assemblies. These bills are now the law of the land. In times like the present, it is not safe to descant on their merits; they will be appreciated by the fair and impartial judgment of posterity. But, though a critical investigation of their excellencies, however curious or interesting, be, for the present, denied to him who feels himself indignantly bound by their extensive operation, it is not yet, perhaps, criminal to relate, historically, in a work like the present, the progress of measures so closely connected with the Catholic question, or to conjecture the probable views of those who planned, those who supported, and those who connived at those famous statutes.

The General Committee had framed their demand for total emancipation; their instructions to the deputation had been to adhere to the spirit of the petition. These instructions had been faithfully observed, perhaps exceeded, in every interview with the British minister. Even in the unimportant circumstance of the day of their introduction, they had refused to consult his convenience or his caprice, and they parted from him with a reiteration of the principle which, in every conversation, they had maintained, that nothing short of total emancipation would be esteemed satisfactory by the Catholics of Ireland. But when they had returned, having executed the object of their mission, certain it is, that this unaccommodating spirit relaxed, and something of a more conciliatory nature, and a system of less extensive demand, appeared to pervade the councils of the Catholics. In the first interview with the Irish minister, the two Houses of Parliament were at once given up, and the question began to be, not how much must be conceded, but how much might be withheld. So striking a change did not escape the vigilance of administration : they instantly recovered from the panic which had led them into such indiscreet, and, as it now appeared, unnecessary concessions at the opening of Parliament; they dexterously seduced the Catholics into the strong ground of negotiation, so well known to themselves, so little to their adversaries; they procrastinated and they distinguished, they started doubts, they pleaded difficulties; the measure of relief was gradually curtailed; and, during the tedious and anxious progress of discussion,—whilst the Catholic mind, their hopes and fears, were unremittingly intent on the process of their bill, which was obviously and designedly suspended, the acts already commemorated were driven through both Houses with the utmost impetuosity, and, with the most cordial and unanimous concurrence of all parties, received the royal assent.

This negotiation, however, did not proceed without serious opposition amongst the Catholics themselves. Many warm debates occurred in the sub-committee, and several of the members strenuously resisted the idea of compromising the general demand. It is not necessary, nor could it now be useful, to detail these various combats, in which the same ground was fought over again and again with equal obstinacy and the same success. It may suffice to give the substance of one debate, as a specimen.

During the progress of the bill, the minister having sent for the gentlemen appointed to communicate with him, informed them that he could not pretend to answer for the success of the bill, unless he was enabled, from authority, to reply to a question proposed to him by a noble Lord in debate, " Whether the Catholics would be satisfied with the measure of relief intended?" By "satisfied," he meant that the public mind should not be irritated in the manner it had been for some time back; he did not mean to say, that future applications might not be made; but if they, the Catholics, would not for the present be satisfied, it were better to make a stand here than to concede, and therefore to give them strength, by which they might be able farther to embarrass administration—perhaps next session. This was pretty strong language from the minister, (Secretary Hobart,) and very unlike what he had held at the opening of the session; but the aspect of the political hemisphere had been materially altered in that short space. The very night before this interview, the House of Commons had voted an army of 20,000, and a militia of 16,000 men, a measure in which the opposition party had outrun the hopes and almost the wishes of administration. Every measure for strengthening the hands of Government was adopted by one party with even more eagerness than it was proposed by the other; the nation was submitted implicitly to the good pleasure of the minister, and the leader of opposition was contented, in *terms*, to implore the gratuitous clemency of the man to whom he could have dictated the law; a mode of proceeding that seems to have been more sentimental than wise, as the subsequent measures of the administration abundantly verified. Government was invested with dictatorial powers;—to what purpose were exerted, posterity may safely, and will impartially, determine. But to return.

The deputation having reported the speech of the Secretary, a very warm debate ensued in the sub-committee, which, it may be necessary to repeat, then comprised a great portion of the spirit and ability of the General Committee. The question was, " Whether they would accede to the wish of the minister, and, by admitting their satisfaction at the present bill, sanction a measure short of complete emancipation ?"

Those who argued in the affirmative, stated, That the people out of doors would disown them if they were, after bringing the question thus far prosperously, now to refuse purchasing a bill conveying such solid benefits at so cheap a price. That the minister did not say the Catholics were to acquiesce for ever under the measures intended, but only that the public mind should not be irritated ; that every accession of strength enabled them the better to secure the remainder; that what was now offered might be accepted, and, under the terms of the stipulation, application might, in two or three years, be made for what was withheld ; that no man could deny that the present bill afforded substantial relief; that the members who might suffer by what was refused were very few, in comparison with those who would be satisfied with what was granted ; that, taking the bench as an example, few Catholic lawyers could be, even in point of standing, fit for that station in many years, long before which time, it was presumed, all distinctions would be done away ; that as to seats in Parliament, if all distinctions between the sects were at that moment abolished, no Catholic gentleman was prepared, by freeholders or otherwise, for an immediate contest; so that, in case of a general election immediately, the Protestant gentry must come in without opposition; that a few years would alter this, and enable the Catholics to make their arrangements so as to engage in the contest on equal terms; that what was given by the bill, and particularly the right of elective franchise, was an infallible means of obtaining all that remained behind:— it was again and again pressed, and relied on, that the people would not be with them who would reject the terms; and finally it was asked, were they prepared, under these circumstances, for the consequences of a refusal,—that is, were they ready to take " the tented field ?"

To these arguments, which were certainly of great cogency, it was replied, That what had been once determined by the general will of the Catholics of Ireland, assembled, could not be reversed by persons merely appointed to carry that will into execution; that the sub-committee had not even the power of discussing the minister's proposition; that, if the Catholics were still to be kept from an equal share of the benefits of the constitution, it was not for them to sanction the exclusion by concurring themselves in the principle; that it would ill become them now, when they had obtained the royal approbation of their claims, when they had the support of the entire north, and so many respectable meetings of their Protestant brethren, joined to their own united and compact strength, to ask less than they had unanimously done in December last, when so many fortunate circumstances had not yet concurred in their favour; that the proposal under debate had originated with men who had ever been enemies to the Catholics, and was now brought forward, evidently, with a view to distract and divide them; that the people would support the sub-committee, which might be inferred from the universal approbation which the resolution of the General Committee to go for complete emancipation had given to all ranks and descriptions of Catholics; that they were unable to cope with their enemies in the intricate arts of negotiation; but that, if the minister persisted in desiring that expression of satisfaction which the sub-committee neither could nor ought to give, he should be told that the General Committee would be summoned, the mention of which would probably deter him from pressing it further; that, as to taking the " tented field," such language was not to be held out to an unarmed people, pursuing their just rights, and using, and desiring to use, no other weapons than a sulky, unaccommodating, complaining, constitutional loyalty. Finally, it was again pressed and insisted on, that the General Committee having already decided in favour of the whole measure, no body nor individuals among the Catholics had power to sanction any thing short of absolute and complete relief.

The result of these arguments, which brought conviction to neither side, was a compromise. The deputation again saw the minister, and, with a nice distinction, they refused, in the name of the body, to express the wished-for satisfaction; they refused to express it officially as members of the sub-committee, but, as individuals of the Catholic body, they admitted that the bill did contain *substantial relief*, and even this admission was guarded with a stipulation that it should not be quoted in debate. But the minister had ascertained all that he wished to know, by the proposal; he saw that the Catholics would acquiesce in a measure short of complete relief, and he inferred that they would not risk the safety of their bill by opposition to any measures, however repugnant to their own feelings, or subversive of the general interest; and the whole process of the session justified his sagacity. The expression of satisfaction was therefore no longer required, and the bill proceeded in the usual forms.

But, while it was in progress through the House of Commons, a very serious blow was struck at the hopes of the Catholics and the honour of the sub-committee in the House of Lords. A noble peer, high in legal station (Lord Fitzgibbon), and to whom not Envy herself can deny the praise of consistency on the subject of Catholic emancipation, had early in the session declared his opposition in terms of the bitterest invective. Very shortly after, advantage was taken of the riotous and tumultuous outrages committed by the rabble in certain counties, and a committee of secrecy was appointed by the Lords, to inquire into the causes of the disorders and disturbances which prevailed in several parts of the kingdom. In due time this committee published a report, whose object was two-fold ;—to attach a suspicion on the most active members of the sub-committee of having fomented those disturbances, and to convey a charge little short of high treason on certain corps of volunteers, particularly in Belfast, preparatory to disarming or otherwise suppressing that formidable body. In the first of these schemes, the authors of the measure completely failed ; in the last, they were but too successful.

On the merits of that report I am, with deep reluctance, compelled to refrain. The examples which I have seen of victims to the unforgiving revenge of offended privilege force me to bury in silence the ardent spirit of resentment which I feel. What single man will again be found to encounter the strong hand of power for a country that would suffer him to rot in a dungeon ? When I reflect on that publication, a thousand ideas crowd at once into my mind and struggle for a vent. Perhaps a time may come ——.

The sub-committee could not overlook an attack of so very serious a nature, containing charges which, if established, would subject them to penalties of the severest kind. Their Secretary, Richard M'Cormick, Esq., a man universally respected in public and in private life, was more peculiarly marked out, and though it might be thought that such charges, if at all founded, should be instantly followed by criminal prosecution, and that, where no such prosecution did ensue, it was probable that no foundation existed for the imputation;—yet the sub-committee, knowing, in the pending state of the Catholic bill, how severely a stigma like that conveyed in the report might affect their dearest hopes; and conjecturing that such was the object of the framers of that paper; determined to give it an immediate answer, disclaiming, in the most solemn manner, every article of the charges alleged against them, and tendering themselves, their publications, and their accounts, to the most severe and public scrutiny that the malice of their enemies could devise. Their secretary likewise published a separate defence, in which he very fully explained those circumstances which, were they not contained in a report of a committee of the House of Lords, might be said to be grossly and wilfully misstated. Yet the defence of the sub-committee and the vindication of the Secretary were languid, compared with former publications. The body and the individual were confined to a defensive war, and obliged to parry, without returning the blow; a situation more severe to an honourable mind cannot well be imagined. The felon in the dock has his irons knocked off, that his mind may be free for his defence. The sub-committee were arraigned at the bar of their country with their hands manacled, their feet shackled, and the halter of undefined privileges dangling on their necks.

Fortunately, however, the measure of Catholic relief had now taken such deep root, that it was not to be subverted even by this storm. The bill, after a long and tedious discussion of several weeks, at length passed the House of Commons, and was transmitted to the Lords. Through that house it also passed without alteration, receiving, however, in its transit, one more severe philippic from the exalted character who had, with undeviating consistency, condemned the measures intended for Catholic relief in this and the preceding session; and, finally, on the 9th day of April, 1793, it received, with the usual solemnities, the royal assent.

It would, in a work like the present, be impossible to do justice to the talents displayed in support of the Catholic claims by all their advocates in Parliament. It would be invidious, perhaps, to make a selection, yet the self-love of none amongst them will be wounded by the acknowledgment of the superior talents manifested by Mr. Grattan. He was the early, the steady, and the indefatigable friend of Catholic emancipation. The splendour of his talents reflected a light upon the cause in the darkest moments of its depression. To that great object he bent the undivided powers of his mind, and did not scruple to hazard his popularity by a manly declaration in its favour, at a time when the tide of popular clamour ran most strongly against it, and when his own constituents were foremost in the cry. He saw that clamour subside at his feet; the voice of truth and reason prevailed over the storm, and the same man had the rare and unexampled good fortune to be foremost in restoring a people to the constitution, as he had been in restoring a constitution to the people.

By one comprehensive clause of this bill, all penalties, forfeitures, disabilities, and incapacities, are removed.—The property of the Catholic is completely discharged from the restraints and limitations of the penal laws, and his liberty in a great measure restored, by the restoration of the right of elective franchise, so long withheld, so ardently pursued. The right of self-defence is established by the restoration of the privilege to carry arms, subject to a restraint which does not seem unreasonable, as excluding none but the very lowest orders. The unjust and unreasonable distinctions affecting Catholics as to service on grand and petty juries are done away; the army, navy, and all offices and places of trust are opened to them, subject to exceptions afterwards mentioned. Catholics may be masters or fellows of any college hereafter to be founded, subject to two conditions, namely, that such college be a member of the University, and that it be not founded exclusively for the education of Catholics. They may be members of any lay body-corporate, except Trinity College, notwithstanding any law, statute, or by-law, of such corporation to the contrary. They may obtain degrees in the University of Dublin.—These, and some lesser immunities and privileges, constitute the grant of the bill, the value of which will be best ascertained by reference to the petition, whence it will appear, that every complaint *recited* has been attended to; every grievance *specified* has been removed. Yet the prayer of the petition was for *general* relief. The bill is not coextensive with the prayer. The measure of redress must, however, be estimated by the extent of the previous suffering and degradation of the Catholics set forth by themselves, and, in this point of view, the bill will undoubtedly justify those who admitted that it afforded *solid and substantial relief*.

But though many and most important privileges were now secured to the Catholics, it will appear that much was withheld, and withheld in the manner most offensive to their feelings, because the bill, admitting the lower orders of the Catholic people to all the advantages of the constitution which they are competent to enjoy, excludes the whole body of their gentry from those functions which they are naturally entitled to fill. A strange inconsistency! During the whole progress of the Catholic question, a favourite and plausible topic with their enemies was the ignorance and bigotry of the multitude, which rendered them incompetent to exercise the functions of freemen. That ignorance and bigotry are now admitted into the bosom of the constitution, whilst all the learning and liberality, the rank and fortune, the pride and pre-eminence, of the Catholics, are degraded from their station, and stigmatized by act of Parliament. Of the bead-roll of disqualifications, many indeed are unnecessary, doing that by act of Parliament which his Majesty is already competent to do by his royal discretion. The exclusion is the more invidious, from the utter improbability of any Irish Catholic being called to fill the stations of Lord Lieutenant, Lord Deputy, or

Lord High Chancellor, which are formally excepted in the bill, merely, as it should seem, to affix on the body a mark of distrust and inferiority. But these are exceptions offensive only to their pride;—there are others directly trenching on their interests.

By their exclusion from the two Houses of Parliament, the whole body of the Catholic gentry of Ireland, a high-spirited race of men, are insulted and disgraced, thrown down from the level of their fortune and talents, and branded with a mark of subjugation, the last relic of interested bigotry. This is the radical defect of the bill. If the Catholics deserved what has been granted, they deserved what has been withheld; if they did not deserve what has been withheld, what has been granted should have been refused. There is an inconsistency not to be explained on any principle of reason or justice, in admitting the alleged ignorance, bigotry and numbers of the Catholics into the pale of the constitution, and excluding all the birth, rank, property and talents. By granting the franchise, and withholding seats in Parliament, the Catholic gentry are at once compelled and enabled to act with effect as a distinct body, and a separate interest. They receive a benefit with one hand and a blow with the other, and their rising gratitude is checked by their just resentment; a resentment which in the same moment they obtain the means and the provocation to justify. If it was not intended to emancipate them also, they should have been debarred of all share of political power. Will they not say that they have received just so much liberty as will enable them to serve the interests of others? to be useful freeholders and convenient voters, artificers of the greatness and power in which they must not share, subaltern instruments in the elevation of those whom their honest pride tells them are in no respect better than themselves? A mortifying state of degradation to men of ardent spirit and generous feelings! As the law now stands, a Catholic gentleman of the first rank and fortune is, in a political point of view, inferior to the meanest of his tenants; combining their situation and their feelings, *they* are fully emancipated,—*he* drags along an unseemly and galling link of his ancient chain.

An attempt was made to do justice to the Catholics, to preserve the consistency of Parliament, and to carry into execution his Majesty's paternal wish for the complete union of all his subjects in support of the established constitution. On the day of the committal of the bill in the House of Commons, the Hon. George Knox, member for Dungannon, moved that the committee be empowered to receive a clause to make it lawful for Catholics to sit and vote in Parliament. The justice and magnanimity of the principle were supported by the spirit and ability of the mover, who, in a strain of eloquence unanswered, because unanswerable, enforced the wisdom of the measure and the claims of the Catholics by arguments drawn not merely from local or temporary topics, but from the principles of good government and the feelings and nature of man.

"What," said he, " is the object of this bill? To admit the Catholics to some degree of civil liberty. On what principle then, with what object, have you singled out that portion which you are about to concede?" (Vide Hibernian Journal, March 18th, 1793.) It will not much impeach the abilities of the opposers of the motion to say, that to these arguments they were unable to reply. It does not, however, always happen that the weight of argument concurs with the weight of members. Notwithstanding the powerful exertions of the friends to Catholic emancipation, and the talents they are known to possess, and which were never displayed in greater lustre, the motion was lost by a very large majority, seventy-one members voting in the affirmative, and no less than one hundred and sixty-five in the negative. Yet even this defeat compared with the last session of Parliament, was a victory. But few men could then be found to vote for receiving a petition which, in effect, asked for nothing; whilst now seventy-one members, constituting a great portion of the character, the property, and, above all, the talents of the House, voted for the complete admission of the Catholics to the privileges of the constitution.

The denial of the right to sit and vote in Parliament is now, undoubtedly, the chief grievance of the Catholics of Ireland. Another function from which they are excluded is, however, of material import. They may not be high sheriffs nor sub-sheriffs; an exception which diminishes extremely the value of the concessions whereby they are admitted to serve on grand juries. When it is considered that the office is never conferred but on gentlemen of property and figure, it is not easy to see any good reason for the exclusion of a man, in all other respects unexceptionable, merely because he is a Catholic. Every argument which can be used for their admission to Parliament, applies with much greater force to their filling the office of sheriff; and the danger, if danger can be apprehended, ought surely to vanish in the reflection that the appointment to that office appertains to the crown, whose discretion and whose advisers may, in this prerogative, be safely trusted. Excluding Catholics by law, therefore, is at best an unnecessary precaution, and every such precaution, as springing from a principle of distrust and suspicion, is for so much an insult, and an insult solely on the men of family, property, and education.

From another function, and of considerable importance likewise, Catholics are yet excluded in fact, though not in express terms. By the bill, " they may be members of any lay body-corporate, any rule or by-law to the contrary, notwithstanding." But this is, in effect, a nugatory license. There are but three ways of obtaining freedom of corporations; by birth, by service, or by special grace. From the first Catholics are excluded, for their fathers, for generations back, have been slaves. From the second they are excluded, because it has been hitherto a part of the oath of a freeman, that he would take as an apprentice no bondman's son, a clause which effectually shuts out the Catholics. The third door may be opened by the liberality of Protestant corporators; but in this instance, our laws have outrun our manners. In the metropolis, the vigilant bigotry of the corporation of the city has been successfully exerted to effect, and, as far as in them lay, to perpetuate the exclusion of Catholics, and this unworthy spirit has been manifested in the refusal of their freedom to some who have passed through the ordeal of their respective guilds, among whom are men of character and respectability equal to any, not merely in the corporation, but in the community. The unbounded influence which administration is known to possess in that body renders such conduct, in this instance, the more paradoxical, and it certainly wears a great appearance of insincerity, to grant the Catholics a valuable privilege, and, in the very same moment, to render them incapable to avail themselves of its benefits.

It is not my wish to aggravate discontent, by dwelling on those parts of the bill which have disappointed the Catholic hope. Some of them are above, and some of them below, the general contemplation. Those parts which I have selected are, in form, offensive to the feelings, and in substance, subversive of the interests, of the Catholic body. But the radical and fundamental defect of the bill is, that it still tends to perpetuate distinctions, and, by consequence, disunion amongst the people. While a single fibre of the old penal code, that cancer in the bosom of the country, is permitted to exist, the mischief is but suspended, not removed; the principle of contamination remains behind and propagates itself. Palliatives may, for awhile, keep the disease at bay, but a sound and firm constitution can only be restored by its total extirpation.

# FARTHER CONNECTING SKETCH,

### BY THE EDITOR.

On reviewing the transactions detailed in this important fragment, the causes of the sudden and unfortunate change which shortly followed will remain no longer a mystery. During the whole course of the year 1792, the progress of the Catholic interest had been rapid and decisive; at its close, the Government of Ireland seemed paralysed, and the General Committee, supported by the whole power of the Dissenters, by all the liberal Protestants in the country, and the Whig party in Parliament, conquered the Monarch's approbation of their claims and the assent of the British Ministry. The weakness of some of their own leaders, and the skill, promptitude, and decision, of their adversaries, soon altered this favourable prospect.

In a better cause, the able and energetical measures of the Irish Government and Protestant ascendancy party would deserve the highest admiration. Threatened in the vital principle of their unjust monopoly of power, and unsupported by the

British Ministry, they were stunned for a moment at the unexpected vigour of a party which they had too long despised; but, recovering shortly from the panic, they felt the pulse of those leaders, who seemed astonished at their own success. It is remarkable, and belongs perhaps to an innate principle of human nature, that the Catholic leaders displayed much more spirit in pleading their cause amongst strangers, and before the Monarch himself, than when they had to settle the terms of that relief already granted with those subordinate ministers of his, before whose insolence and oppression they had bent so long in submission. They then seemed to recognize that frown to which they had been accustomed, and the Irish administration, perceiving its advantages, instantly assumed a higher tone. Offering the repeal of such of the penal statutes as were too odious, and had fallen into disuse, and granting the elective franchise, which, in the organization of society and property in Ireland, could confer no effectual power on the Catholics, they retained the monopoly of all the real elements of power, and artfully delaying the passage of the bill, thus mutilated, made them understand that it should depend on their passive and quiet demeanour. In the meantime, having secured, for the moment, the silence of the expecting Catholics, they bent all their efforts against the reformers and the republicans of the north, who had so powerfully assisted them. They profited by the alarm excited by the horrors of the French Revolution; they roused the fears of all men of property and timidity; they secured, by sacrificing the interests of their country, the co-operation of the mercantile and manufacturing classes in England, and overawed and intimidated even the British Ministry. The very cloak of patriotism served their designs: they exclaimed against the interference of that Ministry as an encroachment on the national independence of the Imperial Crown of Ireland, and were readily supported by those who possessed the monopoly of that independence. At home, they possessed all the powers of the Government, the army and treasury, the judiciary, magistracy, clergy, landed property, and corporations; they rallied all their efforts, and, on pretence of some trifling troubles in the north between the Defenders and Peep-of-day Boys, called out all the forces of the nation, augmented the army, raised the militia and yeomanry, and disarmed the people. The gentry, magistracy, and clergy of the established church, every where seconded these efforts. Unscrupulous as to their means; bloody, unsparing, and uncompromising with their enemies,—they established at the same time and under the same pretext, with the consent of the Whig as well as the Tory interest, that secret committee, whose operations soon equalled, in cruelty and illegal violence, those of the Star-chamber in England, the Inquisition in Spain, the bloody tribunals of the Duke of Alva, and the *Comité de Salut public*, in France. In short, under pretence of resisting a revolutionary spirit in Ireland, they assumed themselves a revolutionary vigour beyond the law. When secure of all those means, they passed at length that mutilated bill, cramped by so many restrictions, and granted with such manifold reluctance, that it was received by the mass of the Catholic body with as little gratitude as it deserved.

Those measures of the Irish administration, though able and vigorous, and calculated to rescue them from their impending danger, were however founded on narrow and short-sighted views. They succeeded; but it was evident that they would finally render that Government so odious and unpopular that it would be unable to stand. The British Ministry acted on principles of more long-sighted policy. Their sagacity cannot be doubted. Aiming already, in all probability, at the future incorporation of that country, the more unpopular its Government rendered itself, the better was it for their ends in the long run :—in fact, the most violent declamations of the United Irishmen, which led them by thousands to the dungeon, the transport-hulk, the picket, and the halter, never pictured its crimes in more glowing colours than they were afterwards displayed in by Lord Castlereagh himself, (long the remorseless agent of its cruelties, and then the venal instrument of its dissolution,) in his speeches on the Union. The British Ministry foresaw that both parties, exhausted by the approaching and inevitable struggle, and weakened by their mutual hatred and disunion, would be obliged to yield up the independence of their country as the price of peace and protection.

If so, their calculation, however cruel and selfish, was justified by the event.

In Ireland the confusion and disorder into which these determined operations threw the councils of all the well-wishers to reform, union, and independence, was, for awhile, very great. The indignant Dissenters exclaimed that they were deserted and betrayed by those whom they had assisted; the great body of the Catholics were equally dissatisfied with such an imperfect termination to their high-raised hopes, and with the want of spirit in their leaders. It must be observed, however, that in the beginning of these affairs there was a radical difference between those two parties. The Dissenters, from the early character of their sect, were mostly republicans from principle;—the great mass of the Catholics only became so through oppression and persecution. Had the latter not been goaded by tyranny in every hour and in every act of their lives, had they been freely admitted to an equal share in the benefits of the constitution,—they would have become, by the very spirit of their religion, the most peaceable, obedient, orderly, and well-affectioned subjects of the empire. Their proud and old gentry, and their clergy, inclined even to feudal and chivalrous, and somewhat to Tory principles, rather than to those of democracy :—but common sufferings now united them in a common hatred of the Government and desire for its subversion.

The next session of the General Committee, which

opened a few days after this act of partial relief, was stormy in the extreme. The cause of freedom and of union was advocated in some of the most brilliant speeches recorded in the annals of Irish eloquence; the attacks of the patriotic members on the Government, and on their own leaders, were formidable and vigorous. The defence of these leaders was, however, plausible. Charged with a very difficult negotiation, they had in fact obtained, as they asserted, a very real and substantial, although a partial relief. But the crisis for freeing their country was passed; the favourable opportunity was lost, perhaps never to return. The Government felt its strength, and began, from that moment, to act on the infernal system of goading the people to desperation and open insurrection, in order to colour and justify the violence of their measures. The assembly parted, at length, with the usual vote of thanks to their real and pretended friends, but without coming to any important decision on the great object of their meeting.

This change of circumstances was most disheartening to those eager and disinterested spirits who had devoted themselves to the cause of the Catholics; because, in the first place, it was just, and in the second, their enfranchisement was a necessary preliminary to the emancipation of Ireland, to the reform of her government, and to the establishment of a free and equal system of national representation. The bitter feelings which filled my father's breast at this first failure of hopes which had been so nearly gratified, and the further views which he then began to meditate, may be traced more freely in his journals of January and February, 1793, (see Appendix,) where he gave way to them without control, than in the preceding abstract, which was evidently written with caution, and destined for publication. They will also appear in the following loose fragment of his thoughts, which I have found amongst his papers, dated March 27th, 1793.

"Sudden change of Deputation, on our return from England—Last conversation previous to leaving London—Bellew's visit, and mine, to the Castle—All set aside by the first visit of the whole Deputation—Negotiation, giving up both Houses of Parliament—People then unanimous and spirited, but soon disheartened by this unaccountable conduct of their former leaders—Great advantages of the Castle over us in negotiation—My own opposition to compromise—Compelled to give it up at last—Consequence of this dereliction, a loss of all public spirit—Low state of Government at the opening of the Session, as appeared from their admitting the principle of reform—Their recovery, from the indecision of Catholics—Consequent carrying, under cover of the Catholic bill, the gunpowder and militia acts, augmentation of army, proclamations, &c.—Motives of Catholic leaders: not corruption—Some negotiation carried on by one of them in London, unknown to the others—The others, probably, unwilling to risk their estates.

"Suppression of Belfast volunteers—Feelings of

the North thereupon—Probable consequences of any mishap befalling the English in the war—*Ten thousand French would accomplish a separation.*

" Secret Committee—First object to vilify the Catholic Committee; failing that, to fix a charge of separation on the people here, and thereby induce the English Minister to support a *union.*—Possible, by *proper* means, to carry said union; also possible to fail, and then the countries infallibly separated.

" War unpopular here—trade very bad—credit rather better than in England.

" Government apparently strong and people subdued; probably both appearances fallacious—Accessions to people, permanent; to Government, but temporary—Gunpowder act no prevention, if the people are determined to have arms—Militia will not dragoon the people; bad policy to exasperate them, and then make militia of them; that is, give them arms and discipline." [To the eternal dishonour of the Irish militia, my father was mistaken in this particular; he did not calculate sufficiently on the effect of the *esprit de corps* in embodied troops.]

" Secret Committee examine, even about me; have my letter to Russell; proof of their weakness, when they descend so low."

Such were the ideas fermenting in his mind. But the increasing insolence and cruelty of the administration soon roused the spirit of the people, and rallied their angry and divided parties. Openly trampling on law and decency, its oppressive measures fired the hearts of the multitude with indignation, and spread the fraternity of the United Irishmen more rapidly than could have been done by all the efforts of the patriotic leaders. Their views were no longer bounded to Catholic emancipation and reform of Parliament; they aimed at separation, liberty, and even revenge. Their societies took a fiercer character, and then, for the first time, began those secret oaths and associations by which their members bound themselves; whilst the Orange lodges, with forms at least as illegal as those of the United Irishmen, and purposes as diabolical as those of the others were pure and liberal, were encouraged by the Government all over the country. To unite all sects and parties for the independence of Ireland, was the professed object of the first; to support the exclusive privileges of the members of the Anglican church, and keep the rest of the nation in slavery for ever, of the second—and in opposing the principles of the two societies, I have selected those only which were openly avowed by either body.

The two parties being thus arrayed in opposition to each other, it soon became evident that the contest could only be finally decided by force, and that if England continued to support the ruling party with all her power and influence, the other had no resource but to break the connexion between the two countries, and establish a national and independent government. This idea had often mingled with the dreams of my father's youth; but he now, for the first time, began to consider it seriously. As foreign aid was indispensable for this purpose, since their enemies had all the power of administration and that of England to back them, the Irish leaders, and he among the rest, naturally cast their eyes and hopes, although no positive overtures were made till some time afterwards, towards the rising fortunes of the French Republic. She was then struggling, with unparalleled spirit and success, against the arms of all Europe, and animated by the most violent resentment against England. In the beginning of their revolution, the French had looked up to that country with hope and confidence; they had expected the praises and countenance of the freest and most liberal people in Europe, for breaking their own chains; and on the first celebration of their independence, had blended in one wreath the flags of England and America with their own tri-colour. But England, supporting the coalition of the European kings, began then to oppose the springing liberties of the remainder of mankind, as if she wished to monopolize the benefits of freedom as well as those of trade and manufactures.

My father's part during this period was most trying and difficult. With the Whig party he was utterly disgusted. In his opinion, whatever professions they had formerly made were violated by their joining the Government in those extraordinary and illegal measures. They showed themselves as much afraid of a real and radical reform in the social organization and government of the country as the Tories themselves; and yet so unnatural was the state of Ireland, that such a change was indispensable before it could be settled in a state of any stability. As for the revolutionary spirit, of which they now affected such fears, it might have been totally suppressed by an early conciliation of the Catholics and a just allowance of their claims. With the Catholics and United Irishmen he had to combat alternate fits of despondency and enthusiasm, and to reconcile continual discords. At one time, when it was endeavoured to form a corps of volunteers from all the religious sects, they expressed their alarm and distrust at the small number of Protestants who presented themselves. "And are you not the nation?" replied he. "Do without them;—will you not *keep*, unless you are *corned* with Protestants?"

At other times, on the contrary, their enthusiasm, roused by the energetical efforts and dazzling exploits of the French Republicans, and their indignation kindled by the oppression of the Government, burst out into imprudent and extravagant excesses. My father endeavoured to restrain these; but the only consequence of his efforts was, that he lost all influence in the United Irish clubs, his own creation, but which had now assumed a new spirit and organization. As in all periods of popular ferment, the loudest and boldest talkers took the lead, and the papers teemed daily with the most imprudent and inflammatory publications. These ebullitions of impotent resentment, by which they only favoured the views of the administration, he always condemned. Numbers of them agreed to call each other by the title of citizen, and he frequently received letters through the post-office, written in imitation of the popular style of the French Jacobins, and addressed to Citizen Theobald Wolfe Tone. His good sense pointed out to him the danger and folly of such idle demonstrations. " Make yourselves free," would he say, " and call yourselves what you please. But you are no more citizens for shutting yourselves up in a room, and calling yourselves by that name, than you would be all Peers and Noblemen, by calling each other, My Lord." Such was his general dissatisfaction at the state of affairs, that he retired in a great degree from the political arena, and spent most of his time at a small country seat, which he inherited by the death of his uncle, Capt. Jonathan Tone. On every occasion, however, of danger and difficulty, he was prominent, and ready to assume the post of peril and honour.

But it is not my purpose to write a history of Ireland. During the year which followed the passing of the Act of April, 1793, the storm did not yet burst, but it was lowering and thickening every hour with terrific and portentous gloom. Blood had not yet flowed, and the reign of torture had not yet commenced; but a noxious crowd of informers, from the fæces of society, began to appear like the vermin and insects from the mud of Egypt, under the fostering patronage of the Castle; state prosecutions were multiplied beyond example; juries were packed and iniquitous judgments rendered; the soldiery were quartered on the disaffected districts, and indulged in every licence; the affections of the people were alienated for ever, and their irritation increased to madness. It is not my intention to enter into the details of these odious transactions. Amongst the most marking events which indicated the increasing violence of all parties, and the approaching crisis of the storm, were the arrest, trial, and imprisonment of my father's friends, Archibald Hamilton Rowan, Simon Butler, and Oliver Bond. The declarations and speeches for which they were arrested, and those made on their trials, are in every history of the times and in every recollection. It is needless here to dwell upon or recapitulate them.

At length, in the month of April, 1794, William Jackson was arrested on a charge of high treason. This gentleman was sent by the French Government to sound the people of Ireland as to their willingness to join the French, and had received his instructions from one Madgett, an old Irishman long settled in France in the office of the Department for Foreign Affairs, and whose name is repeatedly mentioned in my father's journals. The sincerity of Jackson was fully demonstrated by his heroic death, but his imprudence and indiscretion rendered him totally unfit for such a mission. On his passage through England, he opened himself to an English Attorney, Cockayne, an old acquaintance of his, who instantly sold his information to the British Government, and was ordered by the police to follow him as an official spy. The leaders of the patriotic party and Catholics in Ireland, desirous as they were to open a communication with France, were unwilling to compromise themselves with a stranger, by answering directly to his overtures. My father undertook to run the risk, and even engaged himself to bear their answer to that country, and deliver to its Government a statement of the wants and situation of Ireland. But, after some communications with Jackson, he was deeply disgusted by the rash and unlimited confidence which that unfortunate man seemed to repose in Cockayne. He made it a point never to open himself in his presence, and insisted on it with Jackson :—" This business," said he, " is one thing for us Irishmen; but an Englishman who engages in it *must* be a traitor one way or the other." At length, on a glaring instance of Jackson's indiscretion, he withdrew his offers, (taking care that it should be in the presence of Cockayne, who could testify nothing further against him,) and declined engaging any longer in the business. Jackson was shortly after arrested.

This was an awful period of my father's life. Although Cockayne could only give positive evidence against Jackson, the latter might undoubtedly have saved his life by giving information. The most violent suspicions were directed against my father, as being at least privy to these plots, if not engaged in them. Every night he expected to be arrested for examination before the Secret Committee. Several of the patriotic and Catholic leaders, most from attachment to him, some for fear of being compromised by his arrest, urged him to abscond, and many of those highly respectable and beloved friends, whom, notwithstanding the difference of their political opinions, his amiable character and social qualities had secured to him amongst the aristocracy and higher classes, joined in the same request, and pressed upon him the means necessary for that purpose. He constantly refused them. The great body of the Catholics behaved, on this occasion, with firmness and dignity, and showed a proper sense of gratitude for his former services. Several of the Whig leaders, (amongst whom I am sorry to include the honourable name of Grattan,) whose party he had mortally offended by refusing to engage in their service as a pamphleteer, advised them to abandon him to his fate, urging, How could their Parliamentary friends support them whilst they retained in their service a man so obnoxious and so deeply compromised?" They rejected all such overtures. I must however observe, that though my father had put himself forward in their cause on this occasion, most of their leaders were as deeply engaged as himself, and could neither in honour, in justice, nor in prudence, act otherwise—a circumstance of which Grattan was probably not aware.

During all this time he refused, much against the advice of his friends, to conceal himself; but remained, generally, at his home in the country, compiling his history of Ireland, and making occasional visits to Dublin, where he continued to act as secretary to the Catholic sub-committee. At length, by the most pressing instances with the Government, his aristocratical friends succeeded in concluding an agreement, by which, on his engaging simply to leave Ireland as soon as he could settle his private affairs, no steps were to be taken against him. I cannot think that the most furious partisans of that Government could blame those generous and disinterested efforts, (for these friends were opposed to him in politics,) or that their names can suffer in the slightest degree by the publication of these facts. One of them, the Hon. Marcus Beresford, (the amiable and accomplished,) is now no more; the other, the honourable and high-minded George Knox, will, I am sure, see with pleasure this homage to his virtues by his own god-son and the only surviving child of his departed friend.

As this compromise engaged him (and these true friends would never have proposed any other) to nothing contrary to his principles, and left his future course free, he accepted it; giving in to them a fair and exact statement of how far and how deep he had been personally engaged in this business; and adding, that he was ready to bear the consequences of whatever he had done, but would, on no account, charge, compromise, or appear against any one else.

Of this transaction he drew, before his departure from Ireland, the following full and manly narrative, which we insert entire, adding the statement above mentioned. The only fact which, in both these papers, he passes over in silence, from obvious and generous reasons, is, that any others were privy to these communications with Jackson. He assumes them as the sole act of his own will.

STATEMENT OF MR. TONE'S COMPROMISE WITH THE IRISH GOVERNMENT.

Having seen in a newspaper report of the trial of the Rev. Wm. Jackson, the testimony of Mr. Keane, in which he mentions that he understands I have compromised with Government, I think it a duty incumbent upon me, feeling as I do that the expression carries a very invidious import, to state what the nature of that compromise is. At the time of Mr. Jackson's arrest, Mr. Rowan's escape, and Dr. Reynolds' emigration, my situation was a very critical one. I felt the necessity of taking immediate and decided measures to extricate myself. I therefore went to a gentleman high in confidence with the then administration, and told him at once fairly, every step I had taken. I told him, also, that I knew how far I was in danger; that my life was safe, unless it were unfairly practised against, which I did not at all apprehend; but that it was certainly in the power of the Government, if they pleased, to ruin me as effectually as they possibly could do by my death; that on two points I had made up my mind;—the first was, that I would not fly; the other, that I would never open my lips, as a witness, either against Mr. Rowan, (to whom I felt myself bound by the strongest ties of esteem and regard, or against Mr. Jackson, who, in whatever conversations he had held in my presence, must have supposed he was speaking to a man who would not betray him : that I had no claim whatsoever on the Government, nor should I murmur at any course they might please to adopt. What I had done, I had done, and, if necessary, I must pay the penalty ; but, as my ruin might not be an object to them, I was ready, if I were allowed and could at all accomplish it, to go to America. In the mean time, here I was, ready to submit to my fate whatever that might be, but inflexibly determined on the two points which I have mentioned above, and from which I would sacrifice my life a thousand times, rather than recede. The gentleman to whom I addressed myself, after a short time assured me, that I should neither be attacked as a principal nor summoned as a witness ; an assurance he repeated to me afterwards on another occasion, and which has been very faithfully kept. This assurance was given me unclogged by any stipulation or condition whatsoever ; and I have ever since, to the best of my judgment, observed a strict neutrality. Whether this, which is the whole of the communication between Government and me, be a *compromise* or not, I hope, at least, it is no dishonourable one. I have betrayed no friend ; I have revealed no secret ; I have abused no confidence. For what I had done, I was ready to suffer ; I would if necessary submit, I hope, to death, but I would not to what I consider disgrace. As to that part of my conduct which was introductory to this unfortunate business, I leave it, without anxiety, to the censure of all inclined to condemn it.

## STATEMENT OF MR. TONE'S COMMUNICATIONS WITH JACKSON.

Some days previous to the Drogheda assizes, I was informed by A——, that there was a gentleman in town, who was very recently arrived from France, and who, he suspected, was in the confidence of the *Comité de Salut Public*. I was very desirous to see him, in order to hear some account of the state of France which might be depended on. A—— accordingly wrote a note, which he gave me to deliver, stating that he could not have the pleasure of seeing the gentleman next day, being Sunday, but would be glad he would call any other time; and, I believe, added, that the bearer was his particular friend. *I did not then, nor since, ask A—— how he became acquainted with the gentleman, nor do I yet know who introduced him.* I went with this note, and saw the gentleman and another person\* at the hotel where they lodged. I stayed about half an hour, and the conversation was either on mere general politics or the want of accommodation for travellers in Ireland; the superiority of England in that respect, &c. On my rising to depart, the gentleman asked me to dine with him on Wednesday subsequent, which I accordingly agreed to do. On

\* Cockayne.—*Editor.*

the Monday after, as I recollect, I paid a visit to A—, which I was in the habit of doing daily, for some time back; and while I was there, the gentleman above-mentioned and his friend came in together; and after some time he and A— entered into close conversation, and his friend and I retired to a distant part of the room, where we talked of the mode of travelling in Ireland, and amused ourselves looking over Taylor's map, for about half an hour. *Neither of us heard, nor could hear, the conversation between A— and the gentleman.* A—, at length, beckoned me over, and I went. He then said, they had been talking of the state of the country; that I knew what that state was as well as any body; and that it was that gentleman's opinion, that if it were made fully known to people in France, they would, to a certainty, afford every assistance to enable the Irish to assert their independence. I said, that it would be a most severe and grievous remedy for our abuses, but that I saw no other; for, that liberty was shackled in Ireland in such a variety of ways, that the people had no way left to expose their sentiments but by open resistance. That, in the alternative between this and unconditional submission, many would differ; but that I was one of those who, seeing all the danger and horror of a contest, still thought the independence of the country an object worth risking all to obtain; satisfied as I was that, until that were secured, Ireland would never attain to her natural state of power, opulence, and glory. In these sentiments A.— concurred, and the gentleman, as I recollect, again said, "*If this were known in France, assistance might certainly be obtained.*" The conversation, at that time, went no farther. I had a latent suspicion he might possibly be an emissary of the British Minister, and therefore, to mortify him, if that were the case, I spoke with the greatest asperity of the English nation, and of their unjust influence on the Government of Ireland. His friend sat at a distance during this conversation, and I am sure could have heard no part of it, neither *did I inquire, nor do I know*, what conversation A— and the gentleman had previous to their beckoning me over; and the reason I did not inquire was that, not knowing how the affair might terminate, and especially not knowing but this person might be an English spy, I determined I would know as little of other people's secrets as I could, consistent with my taking any part in the business.

The next day, I think, I saw A— again. He showed me a paper, admirably drawn up, in my judgment, which he said he had got from the gentleman above mentioned. The paper went to show the political state of England, and the deduction was, that an invasion there would only tend to unite all parties against the French. I said the state of Ireland was totally different, and that it would be easy, in the same compass, to explain that on paper. He bade me try, and I agreed to do so. I do not recollect that we had any further conversation at that time. I went home, and that evening made a sketch of the state of Ireland, as it appeared to me, and the inference of my paper was, that circumstances in Ireland were favourable to a French invasion. I made no copy.

On Wednesday morning, the day I had fixed to dine with the gentleman and his friend, I found myself called upon to go down to Drogheda immediately, to arrange matters preparatory to the trial of MM. Bird and Hamill, &c. I therefore wrote, and sent an apology, stating the fact. I then went, as usual, to call on Mr. A—, and showed him the paper. Shortly after, the gentleman and his friend came in. After a short general conversation of regret at the disappointment, &c. A—, the gentleman, and I, retired to a window at one end of the room, and his friend took up a book and retired to the other end. The conversation between us was carried on in a very low voice, so that he could not possibly hear us. I then said, I had seen the English paper, and had attempted a similar sketch as to Ireland, which I read. When I had done, the gentleman asked me, "Would I intrust the paper to him?" I gave it without hesitation, but, immediately after, saw I had been guilty of a gross indiscretion, (to call it no worse,) in delivering such a paper to a person whom I hardly knew, and without my knowing to what purposes he might apply it. I therefore, in about five minutes, demanded it back again; he returned it immediately, having neither opened nor read it, nor any part of it. I then gave it to A—; and I believe the precise words I used, (but certainly the purport of them,) were, "that if he had a mind, he might make a copy, in which case I desired him to burn the one I gave him." The conversation then turned, as before, on the state of Ireland, the necessity of seeking aid from France, and her readiness and ability to afford it, if a proper person could be found who would go over, and lay the situation of things here before the *Comité de Salut Public*. But I do not recollect that either A—, the gentleman, or I, came to the definite point of myself being that proper person. I went away, leaving the paper, as I said, in the hands of A—, and set off directly for Drogheda.

On Saturday morning, I received a letter from A—, (a circumstance which I had forgotten, until my sitting down to write, and referring to dates for greater accuracy, revived it in my memory,) expressing an earnest desire to see me immediately on indispensable business. In consequence, I set off instantly, posted up to town, and called directly on A—. He told me that the gentleman was in a great hurry to be off, and wanted to see me of all things. I could not, however, learn that any new matter had occurred, and therefore was a little vexed at being hurried up to town for nothing. I said, nevertheless, I could call on the gentleman the next morning (Sunday) at nine, which I was, however, determined not to do, and in consequence, instead of calling on him, set off for Drogheda at six o'clock. On Thursday I returned to town, and received a rebuke from A— for breaking my engagement. He then told me, to my unspeakable astonishment and vexation, that he had given two or three copies of the paper I had left with him to the gentleman, with several alterations, but that he had burned my copy, as I had desired him. Seeing the thing done and past recall, I determined to find no fault, but to withdraw myself as soon as I could from a business wherein I saw such grievous indiscretion. I am not sure whether it was on that or the next morning that the gentleman and his *friend* came in. But after some time the conversation was taken up on the usual topics, and, for the first time to my knowledge, the gentleman's friend made one. Before that, he seemed to me to avoid it. I then took an opportunity, on the difficulty of finding a proper person to go to France being stated, and it being mentioned, (*I cannot precisely recollect by whom of the party*) that no one was, in all respects, so fit as myself, to recapitulate pretty nearly what I had said in all the preceding conversations on the general state of the country; and I then added, that, with regard to my going to France, I was a man of no fortune; that my sole dependence was on a profession; that I had a wife and three children, whom I dearly loved, solely depending on me for support; that I could not go and leave them totally unprovided for, and trusting to the mercy of Providence for existence; and that, consequently, with regard to me, the going to France was a thing totally impossible. They all agreed that what I said was reasonable, but there *was no offer of money or pecuniary assistance of any kind held out to induce me to change my determination*; a circumstance which I mention merely because I understand it is believed that some such was made.

The gentleman before-mentioned was about to point out certain circumstances which would facilitate such an expedition, if a person could be found; but I stopped him, adding that, as I could make no use of the information, I did not desire to become the depositary of secrets useless to me, and which might be dangerous to him. I think it was at this conversation (the last I was at previous to the gentleman's being arrested,) that some one, I cannot at all ascertain whom, mentioned a letter being put into the post-office, containing the papers before-mentioned, and directed to a person at some neutral port, but I am utterly ignorant how, or when, or to whom, the letter was addressed, or what were its contents, other than as I have now stated; and the reason of my not knowing is, that I studiously avoided burthening my mind with secrets which I might afterwards be forced to betray, or submit to very severe inconveniences. What happened after the gentleman's being arrested I know not other than by common report, having only seen him for about two minutes in A—'s apartment on the night of his committal, when all the conversation I recollect was, that I declared, and so did A—, that if we were brought before the privy council, we would each of us state the truth as nearly as we could consistently with our personal safety; for, that

all attempts at fabrication would only add infamy to peril, and that we must now take our chance.

I have thus stated, as well as my memory enables me, all the material facts which came to my knowledge, or in which I took any share. I find I was present at three conversations, instead of two, as I at first thought, but that makes no difference of consequence. I cannot answer for the precise accuracy of dates, but I believe they are exact.

I have framed the foregoing narrative, relying implicitly on the honour of the gentlemen to whom I willingly confide it, that no use whatsoever shall be made of it against any one of the parties concerned, in any judicial transaction; I give it for political purposes solely.

With regard to myself, the part I have taken appears on the face of the narrative. Whatever may be the consequence, I shall make no attempt to withdraw myself or to avoid the fate, whatever that be, which awaits me. I have but one thing to add, that there is no circumstance which can befall me, not even excepting an ignominious death, that I will not rather undergo, than appear as an evidence in a court of justice, to give testimony against *any one* of the parties concerned.

Dublin, *May 3d*, 1794.

THEOBALD WOLFE TONE.

When my father delivered this paper, the prevalent opinion, which he then shared, was that Jackson was a secret emissary employed by the British Go-

vernment. It required the unfortunate man's voluntary death to clear his character of such a foul imputation. What renders this transaction the more odious is that, before his arrival in Ireland, the life of Jackson was completely in the power of the British Government. His evil genius was already pinned upon him; his mission from France, his every thought, his every view, were known. He was allowed to proceed, not in order to *detect* an existing conspiracy in Ireland, but to *form* one, and thus increase the number of victims. A more atrocious instance of perfidious and gratuitous cruelty is scarcely to be found in the history of any country but Ireland.

Soon afterwards, the efforts of his friends, and the generous interference of Arthur Wolfe, afterwards Lord Kilwarden, and then Attorney General, effected the compromise abovementioned. I am aware many persons may think that my father did not show sufficient gratitude to the Irish Government, in whose power he certainly was to a very dangerous degree. To this I can only reply that he considered his duty to his country paramount to any personal feeling or consideration; that *their* tyranny grew more and more atrocious every day, and that, even in that extreme peril, he constantly refused to tie his hands by any engagement for the future. He would, however, have accepted the offer which they made at first to send him to the East Indies, out of the reach of European politics; perhaps they feared him even there, when they altered their minds. But confiding

in the prostrate state of Ireland, they finally allowed him to withdraw his head, like the crane in Esop's fables, from the jaws of the wolf, and depart free and disengaged for his voluntary exile.

The state of his affairs did not, however, allow him to proceed on his journey for several months. During all that time, Jackson's trial was still pending, and he was frequently threatened by the more violent members of the Government that he should be compelled to appear, and be examined as a witness—a menace which he constantly spurned at. A whole year, from the arrest of Jackson in April 1794, to his trial and death in April 1795, was spent in this anxious suspense.

Towards the beginning of the year 1795, a glimpse of hope and sunshine shone for an instant on the Irish horizon, by the momentary triumph of the Whigs, and the appointment of Earl Fitzwilliam to the Vice-Royalty. On this occasion, overtures were again made to my father by that party, at first to set up a newspaper, and afterwards to write in support of their administration. The Catholic leaders, who felt the utility of which he might be to them, in such a situation, entered with eagerness into the idea, and pressed the administration, whose favour they enjoyed, on the subject. He always felt repugnant to it, and his ideas on the occasion are couched in the following short memorandum:—

" FEB. 7, 1795,—MM. Byrne, Hamill, and

Keogh, waited on Mr. Grattan to recommend me to the new administration as a person who had done and suffered much in the Catholic cause. Previous to their going, I thought it right to apprize Mr. Hamill, (the other two being already, and Mr. Keogh particularly, thoroughly acquainted with the circumstances of such objections as I thought might arise, on Grattan's part, against me) first, that I was a United Irishman, and probably the author of papers offensive to the late Government. But on the other hand, I assured him, as the fact most truly was, that in that club I never had any influence; so far from it, I was always looked on as a suspicious character, or, at best a Catholic partizan endeavouring to make the club an instrument of their emancipation, at the sacrifice of all its other objects; that, since May, 1793, I had never attended its meetings, nor taken any part in its concerns, which conduct I had adopted in consequence of an address, carried totally against my judgment, and calling on the Catholics, immediately on the passing of their bill, to come forward and demand a reform,—a measure which I looked upon as mischievous and insidious; that I had never written but one paper, on the committal of Butler and Bond by the Secret Committee, which paper would be found, I did think, a very moderate one, and that I was, of course, not the author of the papers offensive to the *present* administration. The next probable objection which I thought might arise, was about the national guards. In answer to which, I stated that, during the whole of that business, as well as of the publication, 'Citizen-soldiers, to arms!' I was in London, attending the Catholic delegates, and, of course, could not be concerned, for which I appealed to Mr. Keogh. The third objection was more serious, which was, the part I had in Jackson and Rowan's business, which is fully detailed in other parts of my memorandums. That, with regard to that, all I could say was, my conduct had been undoubtedly very indiscreet in the business, but such as it was, I had stated it fully to the late administration, who after consideration maturely had, were not of opinion that it was such as to call for punishment; that I had positive assurances to that effect, and even a letter written by Secretary Hamilton, by order of Lord Westmoreland, guaranteeing me from all attack; that, therefore, I did hope I should find myself, if not bettered, at least not injured by the late change in the Government. The rest of the topics of defence on this head I left to Keogh, with whom I had, at great length, mooted the whole affair a few days back.

"Hamill said, 'All this is very fair; but was he to understand that they were at liberty to state to Mr. Grattan my inclination to support the present Government?' I said, 'By no means; if that were to be so, it would become a matter of bargain and sale, without any compliment paid to the great body whom he was to represent; that I wished it should have no relation to the future, but should rest on the merits of past services rendered to the Catholics. At the same time, I added, he might state a disposition on my part towards the new administration, grounded on some of their measures, which had already developed themselves, such as Catholic Emancipation and the nominations to the Primacy and Provostship. This, however, I guarded, by saying there were others, to the support of which I would not be purchased by their whole patronage: such as this infamous war, or any thing reflecting on the north of Ireland, or on Parliamentary Reform; that, sooner than lend any countenance to such measures, I would, if necessary, put 50*l*. in my pocket, and transport myself to the farthest corner of the earth. Subject, however, to this exception, there were many topics, particularly all Catholic measures, in which I could promise them my most cordial support, but that I feared (and I am sure the fact is so) that the measures I should object to, would be, perhaps, the only ones which they would thank me for defending.

"Having had this eclaircissement, the deputation went off, and I write these memorandums, waiting the event of their application, I thank God, with the most perfect serenity. I have never indulged any idle or extravagant expectations, and, therefore, it is not in the power of man to disappoint me. My belief is, the application will fail, and if so, I am no worse than I was.

"I should have added above, in its place, that I told Mr. Hamill I did not *wish* to form any connexion with the present administration, because I thought I foresaw they would not long retain nor deserve the confidence of the people; and I again repeated I wished to stand solely on the recommendation of the Catholic body, and not on any services rendered, or to be rendered, by myself."

My father finally refused this offer, declaring that he felt the highest respect for Lord Fitzwilliam's character; that he entertained no doubt his measures would always deserve support; that he would support them, as an individual, as long as he approved of them; but that he could enter into no engagement. In fact, his political principles had taken, from a very early period, a loftier flight than those of the Whigs. He thought their views narrow, their ends selfish, and their measures tending rather to the aggrandizement of their party than to the permanent and general good of the country. The Whigs were highly irritated at this refusal; and Mr. Ponsonby, who expected to be appointed Attorney General, hinted that, " perhaps Mr. Tone would not find the next Attorney General so accommodating as the last." On Lord Fitzwilliam's recall, in March, 1795, my father received a new proof of the affection and confidence of the Catholics, by their appointing him, in this precarious situation, to accompany the deputation which they sent to solicit from the Monarch the continuance of his Lordship in the administration, and to draw up the petition for this purpose and the address to his Lordship. In the month of April following, soon after his return, the trial of Jackson took place. It nobly redeemed his previous errors.

With the Vice-Royalty of Lord Camden began the triumvirate of those three noble Earls, Camden, Carhampton, and Clare; who, by a series of increasing persecutions, succeeded at length in driving the people to madness and open and general insurrection. But towards the beginning of that administration, my father put in execution his agreement with the Government to leave Ireland. He received votes of thanks from the Catholics of Dublin, on resigning his appointment as their Secretary and Agent; and the honours which were paid to him there and in Belfast, his last secret instructions to follow up the negotiation begun with Jackson, and the events which occurred between his departure from Ireland and his arrival in France, are contained in the following continuation of his Memoirs, which he wrote before embarking in the Bantry Bay expedition, and which is dated from Rennes, September 28, 1796.

## AUTOBIOGRAPHY RESUMED.

As my time is growing shorter, I pass over a very busy interval of my life, (all the important events of which are detailed in different diaries among my papers,*) and hasten to the period when, in consequence of the conviction of William Jackson for high treason, I was obliged to quit my country and go into exile in America. A short time before my departure, my friend Russell being in town, he and I walked out together to Rathfarnham, to see Emmet, who has a charming villa there. He showed us a little study, of an elliptical form, which he was building at the bottom of the lawn, and which he said he would consecrate to our meetings, if ever we lived to see our country emancipated. I begged of him, if he intended Russell should be of the party, in addition to the books and maps it would naturally contain, to fit up a small cellaret, which should enclose a few dozens of his best old claret. He showed me that he had not omitted that circum-

* The fate of which has been already detailed.

stance, which he acknowledged to be essential, and we both rallied Russell with considerable success. I mention this trifling anecdote because I love the men, and because it seems now, at least, possible that we may yet meet again in Emmet's study. As we walked together into town, I opened my plan to them both. I told them that I considered my compromise with Government to extend no farther than the banks of the Delaware, and that the moment I landed, I was free to follow any plan which might suggest itself to me for the emancipation of my country; that, undoubtedly, I had been guilty of a great offence against the existing Government; that, in consequence, I was going into exile, which I considered as a full expiation for the offence, and therefore felt myself at liberty, having made that sacrifice, to begin again on a fresh score. They both agreed with me in those principles, and I then proceeded to tell them that my intention was, immediately on my arrival in Philadelphia, to wait on the French Minister; to detail to him, fully, the situation of affairs in Ireland,—to endeavour to obtain a recommendation to the French Government, and, if I succeeded so far, to leave my family in America, set off instantly for Paris, and apply, in the name of my country, for the assistance of France, to enable us to assert our independence. It is unnecessary, I believe, to say, that this plan met with the warmest approbation and support from both Russell and Emmet. We shook hands, and having repeated our professions of unalterable regard and esteem for each other, we parted; and this was the last interview which I was so happy as to have with those two invaluable friends together. I remember it was in a little triangular field that this conversation took place; and Emmet remarked to us that it was in one exactly like it in Switzerland where William Tell and his associates planned the downfall of the tyranny of Austria. The next day Russell returned to Belfast.

As I was determined not to appear to leave Ireland clandestinely, whatever might be the hazard, I took care, on the day of Jackson's trial, to walk up and down in the most public streets in Dublin, and to go, contrary to my usual custom, into several of the most frequented coffee-houses, and to my bookseller's, which was still more frequented. In this place I was seen by Lord Mountjoy, who gave himself the pains to call on the Attorney General* the next day, and inform him that I was to be found, for that he had seen me in Archer's the day before. The Attorney General gave him, however, no thanks for his pains, and so the affair ended; my obligation, nevertheless, to his Lordship is not the less, for his good intentions. Having made this sacrifice to appearances, I set with all diligence to prepare for my departure; I sold off all my little property of every kind, reserving only my books, of which I had a very good selection of about six hundred volumes, and determined to take leave of nobody. I also resolved not

* Wolfe, afterwards Lord Kilwarden.

to call on any of my friends, not even Knox or Emmet; for, as I knew the part I had taken in Jackson's affair had raised a violent outcry against me with a very numerous and powerful party, I resolved not to implicate any of those I regarded in the difficulties of my situation. Satisfied as I was of the rectitude of my own conduct and of the purity of my motives, I believe I should have had fortitude to bear the desertion of my best friends; but, to their honour be it spoken, I was not put to so severe a trial. I did not lose the countenance and support of any one man whom I esteemed; and I believe that I secured the continuance of their regard by the firmness I had shown all along through this most arduous and painful trial; and, especially, by my repeated declarations, that I was ready to sacrifice my life, if necessary, but that I would never degrade myself by giving testimony against a man who had spoken to me in the confidence that I would not betray him. I have said that after Jackson's death I visited nobody; but all my friends made it, I believe, a point to call on me; so that for the short time I remained in Dublin after, we were never an hour alone. My friends M'Cormick and Keogh, who had both interested themselves extremely, all along, on my behalf, and had been principally instrumental in passing the vote for granting me the sum of 300*l.* in addition to the arrears due to me by the Catholics, were, of course, amongst the foremost. It was hardly necessary to men of their foresight, and who knew me perfectly, to mention my plans; however, for greater cer-

all attempts at fabrication would only add infamy to peril, and that we must now take our chance.

I have thus stated, as well as my memory enables me, all the material facts which came to my knowledge, or in which I took any share. I find I was present at three conversations, instead of two, as I at first thought, but that makes no difference of consequence. I cannot answer for the precise accuracy of dates, but I believe they are exact.

I have framed the foregoing narrative, relying implicitly on the honour of the gentlemen to whom I willingly confide it, that no use whatsoever shall be made of it against any one of the parties concerned, in any judicial transaction; I give it for political purposes solely.

With regard to myself, the part I have taken appears on the face of the narrative. Whatever may be the consequence, I shall make no attempt to withdraw myself or to avoid the fate, whatever that be, which awaits me. I have but one thing to add, that there is no circumstance which can befall me, not even excepting an ignominious death, that I will not rather undergo, than appear as an evidence in a court of justice, to give testimony against *any one* of the parties concerned.

*Dublin, May 3d,* 1794.

THEOBALD WOLFE TONE.

When my father delivered this paper, the prevalent opinion, which he then shared, was that Jackson was a secret emissary employed by the British Go-

vernment. It required the unfortunate man's voluntary death to clear his character of such a foul imputation. What renders this transaction the more odious is that, before his arrival in Ireland, the life of Jackson was completely in the power of the British Government. His evil genius was already pinned upon him; his mission from France, his every thought, his every view, were known. He was allowed to proceed, not in order to *detect* an existing conspiracy in Ireland, but to *form* one, and thus increase the number of victims. A more atrocious instance of perfidious and gratuitous cruelty is scarcely to be found in the history of any country but Ireland.

Soon afterwards, the efforts of his friends, and the generous interference of Arthur Wolfe, afterwards Lord Kilwarden, and then Attorney General, effected the compromise abovementioned. I am aware many persons may think that my father did not show sufficient gratitude to the Irish Government, in whose power he certainly was to a very dangerous degree. To this I can only reply that he considered his duty to his country paramount to any personal feeling or consideration; that *their* tyranny grew more and more atrocious every day, and that, even in that extreme peril, he constantly refused to tie his hands by any engagement for the future. He would, however, have accepted the offer which they made at first to send him to the East Indies, out of the reach of European politics; perhaps they feared him even there, when they altered their minds. But confiding

all attempts at fabrication would only add infamy to peril, and that we must now take our chance.

I have thus stated, as well as my memory enables me, all the material facts which came to my knowledge, or in which I took any share. I find I was present at three conversations, instead of two, as I at first thought, but that makes no difference of consequence. I cannot answer for the precise accuracy of dates, but I believe they are exact.

I have framed the foregoing narrative, relying implicitly on the honour of the gentlemen to whom I willingly confide it, that no use whatsoever shall be made of it against any one of the parties concerned, in any judicial transaction; I give it for political purposes solely.

With regard to myself, the part I have taken appears on the face of the narrative. Whatever may be the consequence, I shall make no attempt to withdraw myself or to avoid the fate, whatever that be, which awaits me. I have but one thing to add, that there is no circumstance which can befall me, not even excepting an ignominious death, that I will not rather undergo, than appear as an evidence in a court of justice, to give testimony against *any one* of the parties concerned.

*Dublin, May 3d,* 1794.

THEOBALD WOLFE TONE.

When my father delivered this paper, the prevalent opinion, which he then shared, was that Jackson was a secret emissary employed by the British Go-

vernment. It required the unfortunate man's voluntary death to clear his character of such a foul imputation. What renders this transaction the more odious is that, before his arrival in Ireland, the life of Jackson was completely in the power of the British Government. His evil genius was already pinned upon him; his mission from France, his every thought, his every view, were known. He was allowed to proceed, not in order to *detect* an existing conspiracy in Ireland, but to *form* one, and thus increase the number of victims. A more atrocious instance of perfidious and gratuitous cruelty is scarcely to be found in the history of any country but Ireland.

Soon afterwards, the efforts of his friends, and the generous interference of Arthur Wolfe, afterwards Lord Kilwarden, and then Attorney General, effected the compromise abovementioned. I am aware many persons may think that my father did not show sufficient gratitude to the Irish Government, in whose power he certainly was to a very dangerous degree. To this I can only reply that he considered his duty to his country paramount to any personal feeling or consideration; that *their* tyranny grew more and more atrocious every day, and that, even in that extreme peril, he constantly refused to tie his hands by any engagement for the future. He would, however, have accepted the offer which they made at first to send him to the East Indies, out of the reach of European politics; perhaps they feared him even there, when they altered their minds. But confiding

period of our voyage. As it was, in spite of every thing we were tolerably healthy; we lost but one passenger, a woman; we had some sick aboard, and the friendship of James Macdonnell, of Belfast, having supplied me with a small medicine-chest and written directions, I took on myself the office of physician. I prescribed and administered accordingly; and had the satisfaction to land all my patients safe and sound. As we distributed liberally the surplus of our sea stores, of which we had great abundance, and especially as we gave, from time to time, wine and porter to the sick and aged, we soon became very popular aboard, and I am sure there was no sacrifice to our ease or convenience, in the power of our poor fellow-passengers to make, that we might not have commanded. Thirty days of our voyage had now passed over without any event, save the ordinary ones of seeing now a shoal of porpoises, now a shark, now a set of dolphins, (the peacocks of the sea), playing about, and once or twice a whale. We had, indeed, been brought to, when about a week at sea, by the William Pitt, Indiaman, which was returning to Europe with about twenty other ships, under convoy of four or five men-of-war; but on examining our papers, they suffered us to proceed. At length, about the 20th of July, some time after we had cleared the banks of Newfoundland, we were stopped by three British frigates, the Thetis, Captain Lord Cochrane, the Hussar, Captain Rose, and the Esperance, Captain Wood, who boarded us, and after treating us with the greatest insolence, both officers and sailors, they pressed every one of our hands, save one, and near fifty of my unfortunate fellow-passengers, who were most of them flying to America to avoid the tyranny of a bad Government at home, and thus unexpectedly fell under the severest tyranny (one of them at least,) which exists. As I was in a jacket and trowsers, one of the lieutenants ordered me into the boat, as a fit man to serve the king, and it was only the screams of my wife and sister which induced him to desist. It would have been a pretty termination to my adventures if I had been pressed and sent on board a man-of-war. The insolence of these tyrants, as well to myself as to my poor fellow-passengers, in whose fate a fellowship in misfortune had interested me, I have not since forgotten, and I never will. At length, after detaining us two days, during which they rummaged us at least twenty times, they suffered us to proceed.

On the 30th July, we made Cape Henlopen; the 31st we ran up the Delaware, and the 1st of August landed safe at Wilmington, not one of my party, providentially, having been for an hour indisposed on the passage, nor even sea-sick. Those only who have had their wives, their children, and all in short that is dear to them floating for seven or eight weeks at the mercy of the winds and waves, can conceive the transport I felt at seeing my beloved and our darling babies ashore once again in health and safety. We put up at the principal tavern, kept by an Irishman, one Captain O'Byrne O'Flynn, (I think,) for all the taverns in America are kept by majors and captains, either of militia or continentals, and in a few days we had entirely recruited our strength and spirits, and totally forgotten the fatigues of the voyage.

During our stay in Wilmington, we formed an acquaintance which was of some service and a great deal of pleasure to us, with a General Humpton, an old continental officer. He was an Englishman, born in Yorkshire, and had been a Major in the 25th regiment, but on the breaking out of the American war, he resigned his commission, and offered his services to Congress, who immediately gave him a regiment, from which he rose by degrees to his present rank. He was a beautiful, hale, stout old man, of near seventy, perfectly the soldier and the gentleman, and he took a great liking to us, as we did to him. On our removal to Philadelphia, he found us a lodging with one of his acquaintance, and rendered all the little services and attentions that our situation as strangers required, which indeed he continued without remission during the whole of my stay in America, and I doubt not equally since my departure. I have a sincere and grateful sense of the kindness of this worthy veteran.

Immediately on my arrival in Philadelphia, which was about the 7th or 8th of August, I found out my old friend and brother exile, Dr. Reynolds, who seemed, to my great satisfaction, very comfortably settled. From him I learned that Hamilton Rowan had arrived about six weeks before me from France, and that same evening we all three met. It was a singular rencontre, and our several escapes from an ignominious death seemed little short of a miracle. We communicated our respective adventures since our last interview, which took place in the gaol of Newgate, in Dublin, fourteen months before. In Reynolds's adventures there was nothing very extraordinary. Rowan had been seized and thrown into prison immediately on his landing near Brest, from whence he was rescued by the interference of a young man named Sullivan, an Irishman in the service of the Republic, and sent on to Paris, to the Committee of Public Safety, by Prieur de la Marne, the Deputy on Mission. On his arrival, he was seized with a most dangerous fever, from which he narrowly escaped with his life; when he recovered, as well as during his illness, he was maintained by the French Government; he gave in some memorials on the state of Ireland, and began, from the reception he met with, to conceive hopes of success; but immediately after came on the famous 9th Thermidor, the downfall of Robespierre, and the dissolution of the Committee of Public Safety. The total change which this produced in the politics of France, and the attention of every man being occupied by his own immediate personal safety, was the cause of Rowan and his plans being forgotten in the confusion. After remaining, therefore, several months, and seeing no likelihood of bringing matters to any favourable issue, he yielded to the solicitude of his family and friends, and embarked at Havre for New York, where he arrived about the middle of June, 1795, after a tedious passage of eleven weeks.

It is unnecessary to detail again my adventures, which I related to them at full length, as well as every thing relating to the state of politics in Ireland, about which, it may be well supposed, their curiosity and anxiety were extreme. I then proceeded to tell them my designs, and that I intended waiting the next day on the French Minister with such credentials as I had brought with me, which were the two votes of thanks of the Catholics, engrossed on vellum, and signed by the Chairman and Secretaries; and my certificate of admission into the Belfast volunteers; and I added, that I would refer to them both for my credibility, in case the Minister had any doubts. Rowan offered to come with me, and introduce me to the Minister, Citizen Adet, whom he had known in Paris: but I observed to him, that as there were English agents without number in Philadelphia, he was most probably watched, and, consequently, his being seen to go with me to Adet, might materially prejudice his interests in Ireland. I therefore declined his offer, but requested of him a letter of introduction, which he gave me accordingly, and the next day I waited on the Minister, who received me very politely. He spoke English but imperfectly, and I French a great deal worse; however, we made a shift to understand one another; he read my certificates and Rowan's letter, and begged me to throw on paper, in the form of a memorial, all I had to communicate on the subject of Ireland. This I accordingly did in the course of two or three days, though with great difficulty, on account of the burning heat of the climate, so different from what I had been used to, the thermometer varying between ninety and ninety-seven. At length, however, I finished my memorial, such as it was, and brought it to Adet, offering at the same time, if he thought it would forward the business, to embark in the first vessel which sailed for France; but the Minister, for some reason, seemed not much to desire this, and eluded my offer by reminding me of the great risk I ran, as the British stopped and carried into their ports indiscriminately all American vessels bound for France: he assured me, however, that I might rely on my memorial being transmitted to the French Government, backed with his strongest recommendations; and he also promised to write particularly to procure the enlargement of my brother Matthew, who was then in prison at Guise; all which I have since found he faithfully performed.

I had now discharged my conscience, as to my duty to my country; and it was with the sincerest and deepest sorrow of mind that I saw this, my last effort, likely to be of so little effect. It was barely possible, but I did not much expect it, that the French Government might take notice of my memorial; and if they did not, there was an end to all my hopes. I now began to endeavour to bend my mind to my situation, but to no purpose. I moved my family, first to Westchester, and then to Downingstown, both in the state of Pennsylvania, about thirty miles from Philadelphia; and I began to look about for a small plantation, such as might suit the shattered state of my finances, on which the enormous expense of living in Philadelphia (three times as dear as at Paris, or even London,) was beginning to make a sensible inroad. While they remained there, in the neighbourhood of our friend General Humpton, whose kindness and attention continued unabated, I made divers excursions, on foot and in the stage-waggons, in quest of a farm. The situation of Princeton, in New Jersey, struck me for a variety of reasons, and I determined, if possible, to settle in that neighbourhood. I accordingly agreed with a Dutch farmer for a plantation of one hundred acres, with a small wooden house, (which would have suited me well enough,) for which I was to pay 750*l.* of that currency; but the fellow was too covetous, and after all was, as I thought, finished, he retracted and wanted to screw more out of me, on which I broke off the treaty in a rage, and he began to repent, but I was obstinate. At length I agreed with a Captain Leonard for a plantation of 180 acres, beautifully situated within two miles of Princeton, and half of it under timber. I was to pay 1,180*l.* currency, and I believe it was worth the money; in consequence I moved my family to Princeton, where I hired a small house for the winter, which I furnished frugally and decently;

I fitted up my study, and began to think my lot was cast to be an American farmer.

In this frame of mind I continued for some time, waiting for the lawyer who was employed to draw the deeds, and expecting next Spring to remove to my purchase and to begin farming at last, when one day I was roused from my lethargy by the receipt of letters from Keogh, Russell, and the two Simms's, wherein, after professions of the warmest and sincerest regard, they proceeded to acquaint me that the state of the public mind in Ireland was advancing to republicanism faster than even I could believe; and they pressed me, in the strongest manner, to fulfil the engagement I had made with them at my departure, and to move heaven and earth to force my way to the French Government, in order to supplicate assistance. William Simms, at the end of a most friendly and affectionate letter, desired me to draw upon him for 200*l.* sterling, and that my bill should be punctually paid; an offer, at the liberality of which, well as I knew the man, I confess I was surprised. I immediately handed the letters to my wife and sister, and desired their opinion, which I foresaw would be that I should immediately, if possible, set out for France. My wife, especially, whose courage and zeal for my honour and interests were not in the least abated by all her past sufferings, supplicated me to let no consideration of her or our children stand for a moment in the way of my engagements to our friends and my duty to my country; adding, that she would answer for our family during my absence, and that the same Providence which had so often, as it were miraculously, preserved us, would, she was confident, not desert us now. My sister joined her in those intreaties, and it may well be supposed I required no great supplication to induce me to make one more attempt in a cause to which I had been so long devoted. I set off, accordingly, the next morning, (it being this time about the end of November) for Philadelphia, and went, immediately on my arrival, to Adet, to whom I showed the letters I had just received, referring him to Rowan, who was then in town, for the character of the writers. I had the satisfaction, contrary to my expectations, to find Adet as willing to forward and assist my design now, as he seemed, to me at least, lukewarm when I saw him before, in August. He told me, immediately, that he would give me letters to the French Government, recommending me in the strongest manner, and also money to bear my expenses, if necessary. I thanked him most sincerely for the letters, but declined accepting any pecuniary assistance. Having thus far surmounted my difficulties, I wrote for my brother Arthur, who was at Princeton, to come to me immediately, and fitted him out with all expedition for sea. Having entrusted him with my determination of sailing for France in the first vessel, I ordered him to communicate this immediately on his arrival in Ireland, to Neilson, Simms, and Russell, in Belfast, and to Keogh and M'Cormick only, in Dublin. To every one else, including especially my father and mother, I desired him to say that I had purchased and was settled upon my farm near Princeton. Having fully instructed him, I put him on board the Susanna, Captain Baird, bound for Belfast, and on the 10th of December, 1795, he sailed from Philadelphia, and, I presume, arrived safe, but as yet I have had no opportunity of hearing of him. Having despatched him, I settled all my affairs as speedily as possible. I drew on Simms for 200*l.* agreeably to his letter, 150*l.* sterling of which I devoted to my voyage; my friend Reynolds procured me louis-d'ors at the bank for 100*l.* sterling of silver. I converted the remainder of my little property into bank stock, and having signed a general power of attorney to my wife, I waited finally on Adet, who gave me a letter in cypher, directed to the *Comité de Salut Public,* the only credential which I intended to carry with me to France. I spent one day in Philadelphia with Reynolds, Rowan, and my old friend and fellow-sufferer James Napper Tandy, who, after a long concealment and many adventures, was recently arrived from Hamburgh; and at length, on the 13th December at night I arrived at Princeton, whither Rowan accompanied me, bringing with me a few presents for my wife, sister, and our dear little babies. That night we supped together in high spirits, and Rowan retiring immediately after, my wife, sister, and I, sat together till very late, engaged in that kind of animated and enthusiastic conversation to which our characters, and the nature of the enterprise I was embarked in, may be supposed to give rise. The courage and firmness of the women supported me, and them too, beyond my expectations; we had neither tears nor lamentations, but, on the contrary, the most ardent hope and the most steady resolution. At length, at four the next morning I embraced them both for the last time, and we parted with a steadiness which astonished me. On the 16th December I arrived in New York, and took my passage on board the ship Jersey, Captain George Baron. I remained in New York for ten days, during which time I wrote continually to my family, and a day or two before my departure, received a letter from my wife, informing me that she was with child, a circumstance which she had concealed so far, I am sure, lest it might have had some influence on my determination. On the 1st January, 1796, I sailed from Sandy Hook, with nine fellow-passengers, all French, bound for Havre de Grace. Our voyage lasted exactly one month, during the most part of which we had heavy blowing weather; five times we had such gales of wind as obliged us to lie under a close-reefed mizen stay-sail; however, our ship was stout. We had plenty of provisions, wine, brandy, and especially (what I thought more of, remembering my last voyage) excellent water, so that I had no reason to complaint of my passage. We did not meet a single vessel of force, either French or English; but passed three or four Americans, bound mostly, like ourselves, to France. On the

27th we were in soundings, at eighty-five fathoms; on the 28th we made the Lizard, and at length, on the 1st of February, landed in safety at Havre de Grace, having met with not the smallest accident during our voyage. My adventures from this date are fully detailed in the ensuing Diary, which I have kept regularly since my arrival in France.

# DIARY.

### February, 1796.

2. I landed at Havre de Grace yesterday, after a rough winter passage from New York of thirty-one days. The town ugly and dirty, with several good houses in alleys, where it is impossible to see them. Lodged at the Hotel de Paix, formerly the Hotel of the Intendant, but reduced to its present state by the Revolution. " My landlord is civil, but dear as the devil." Slept in a superb crimson damask bed; great luxury, after being a month without having my clothes off.

3. Rose early; difficult to get breakfast; got it at last; excellent coffee, and very coarse brown bread, but, as it happens, I like brown bread. Walked out to see the lions; none to see. Mass celebrating in the church; many people present, especially women; went into divers coffee-houses; plenty of coffee, but no papers. *No bread* in two of the coffee-houses, but pastry; singular enough! Dinner: and here, as matter of curiosity, follows our bill of fare, which proves clearly that France is in a starving situation:—An excellent soup; a dish of fish, fresh from the harbour; a fore-quarter of delicate small mutton, like the Welsh; a superb turkey, and a couple of ducks roasted; pastry, cheese, and

fruit after dinner, with wine *ad libitum,* but still the *pain bis;* provoked with the Frenchmen grumbling at the bread; made a saying: *Vive le pain bis et la liberté!* I forgot the vegetables, which were excellent; very glad to see such unequivocal proofs of famine. Went to the Comedie in the evening: a neat theatre, and a very tolerable company; twenty performers in the orchestra: house full; several officers, very fine looking fellows: the audience just as gay as if there was no such thing as war and brown bread in the world. Supper just like our dinner, with wine, &c. N. B. *Finances.* The louis worth 5000 livres, or about 200 times its value, in assignats; the six-franc piece in proportion. My bill *per diem,* for such entertainment as abovementioned, is six francs, (five shillings), and my crimson damask bed 20 sols, or ten pence; coffee in the morning 12 sols, or sixpence; so that I am starving in the manner I have described, for the enormous sum of 6*s.* 4*d.* a day: sad! sad! Paid for my seat at the theatre, in the box next to that of the Municipalité, 80 livres in assignats, or about fourpence sterling. Be it remembered, I lodge at the principal hotel in Havre, and I doubt not but I might retrench, perhaps, one-half, by changing my situation; but hang saving!

4. A swindler in the hotel; wishes to take me in; wants to travel with me to Paris; says he is an American, and calls me Captain; is sure he has seen me *somewhere.* Tell him perhaps it was *in Spain.* " A close man, but warm;" it won't do. He tries his wily arts on an old Frenchman, and, to my great

surprise, tricks him out of about one guinea. The Frenchman finds it out, and is in a rage; going to beat the *aventurier*, who is forced to refund. This is our first adventure. My friend was no American, which I very soon found out; for " there is no halting before cripples," as poor Richard says.

5. A new arrangement with my landlord; I now pays 5*s.* a day for every thing, including my crimson damask bed; walk out; every third man a soldier, or with something of the military costume about him. In the evening the Comedie; *Blaise et Babet*, and the *Rigueurs du Cloître*, a revolutionary piece; applauses and honourable mention. I can account for the favourable reception of the latter piece, but the former is as great a favourite, though the fable is as simple as possible. Two lovers fall out about a nosegay and a ribbon, and, after squabbling through two acts, are reconciled at last, and marry. The sentiments and the music are pretty and pastoral; but what puzzles me is, to reconcile the impression which the piece, such as I have described it, seemed to make on the audience, with the sanguinary and ferocious character attributed to the French.

6. It is very singular, but I have had several occasions already to observe that there is more difficulty in passing silver than paper. I have seen money refused where assignats have been taken currently. This is a phenomenon I cannot understand, especially when the depreciation is considered. The republican silver is received with great suspicion. People have got it into their heads that it is adulte-

rated; but, even so, surely it is worth, intrinsically, more than a bit of paper. So it is, however, that assignats are more current. The Comedie again. The Marseillaise Hymn sung every night, and the verse, " *Tremblez, Tyrans!*" always received with applause. The behaviour of the young men extremely decorous and proper; very unlike the riotous and drunken exhibitions I have been witness to in other countries. The women ugly, and some most grotesque head-dresses. Supper, as usual, excellent; the servants at the hotel remarkably civil, attentive, and humble, which I mention, because I have been so often tormented with blockheads arguing against liberty and equality as subversive of all subordination. I have nowhere met with more respectful attendance than here, nor better entertainment; and all for five shillings a-day.

7. (*Sunday.*) I was curious to observe how this day would be kept in France. I believe nobody worked; the shops were half open, half shut; as I have seen them on holidays in other countries; everybody walking the streets. A vessel from Boston was wrecked last night within twenty yards of the Basin, and an unfortunate Frenchwoman lost, with two little children. She had fled to America early in the Revolution, and was now returning to her husband on the restoration of tranquillity. God Almighty help him! She might have been saved alone, but preferred to perish with her infants: it is too horrible to think of. Oh, my babies! my babies! if your little bodies were sunk in the Ocean, what

should I do? But you are safe, thank God! Well! no more of that. Comedie again: house quite full, being Sunday; Mad. Rousselois principal singer; just such another in person, age, manner, and voice, as the late Mrs. Kennedy, but a much better actress.

8. An arrangement for Paris at last. An American has a hired coach, a very good one, and we (*viz.* D'Ancourt, my fellow-traveller, and I,) are to pay one louis a-piece for our seats, and bear two thirds of the travelling expenses, post-horses, &c. This is very comfortable; cheaper and much better than any public carriage. We are to set off early on Wednesday. I have now waited eight days on my companion, who, by-the-by, does not improve on acquaintance; he is as proud as Lucifer, and as mean as avarice can make him. I foresee that we shall not live long together at Paris, but at first he will be absolutely necessary to me. "Damn it, and sink it, and rot it for me," that I cannot speak French. *Rues* they call them here. "Oh! that I had given that time to the tongues that I have spent in fencing and bear-baiting! Well, "'Tis but in vain," &c. With God's blessing, my little boys *shall* speak French. Comedie in the evening as usual.

9. My lover, the swindler, has been too cunning for us; he has engaged the fourth place in the coach, so we shall have the *pleasure* of his company on to Paris. He certainly has some design on our pockets, but I hope he will find himself defeated. Wrote to my family and to Dr. Reynolds of Philadelphia; and gave the letters to Capt. Baron. Tired

of Havre, which is dreadfully monotonous; and D'Aucourt's peevishness, proceeding partly from ill health, makes him not the pleasantest company in the world. Got our passports; engaged post-horses, &c. I do not bear the separation from my family well, yet I certainly do not wish them at present in France. If I can make out my brother Matthew, I shall be better off. Poor P. P.! I shall never meet with such another agreeable companion in a post-chaise. Well, hang sorrow! But I am dreadfully low-spirited: "*Croaker* is a rhyme for *joker.*"— Poor Dick! Comedie as usual; sad trash this evening; a boy of fifteen in love and married! introduced to his spouse by his nurse; confined to his room by his papa, and let out in order to be married; much fitter to peg a top or play marbles; yet the audience did not seem to feel any incongruity, though, to heighten the absurdity, his lover was Madame Rousselois, a fat woman of forty. It was excessively ridiculous to see her and the "*Amoureux de quinze ans*" together, and to hear her singing " *Lindor a su me plaire.*" She was easily pleased.— The dresses at the theatre of Havre are handsomer and better appointed than I have seen any where except at London; which is wonderful, considering it is but a small sea-port town, and more so, when one reflects on the price of admission. I suspect the Government must assist them, or I am sure they could not live on the receipts; if so, it is an additional trait in the resemblance of character between the French and Athenians, which is most striking.

10 Up at five o'clock: a choice carriage lined with blue velvet; five horses; a French postilion, a most grotesque figure—cocked hat and jacket, two great wisps of straw tied on his thighs, and a pair of jack-boots as big as two American churns. " Their horses, (*chevauxes* they call them,) ben't quite so nimble as our'n." Set off for Paris; huzza! The country flat and amazingly populous; the houses of the peasantry scattered as thick as they can lie, about a mean between an English cottage and an Irish cabin, or hovel; but if the house be inferior, there is an appearance in the spot of ground about, far beyond what I have seen in England. Every cottage stands in the middle of a parallelogram of perhaps an acre or two, which is planted with trees, and I suppose includes their potagerie, &c.; the quantity of wood thus scattered over the face of the country is immense, and has a beautiful effect: every foot of ground seems to me under cultivation, so there will be no starving, please God, this year. France, D'Aucourt says, in a good year, grows one-third more than she consumes. No enclosures, but all the country open; excepting that circumstance, not unlike Yorkshire, which I look upon as the finest part of England; an orchard to every cottage, besides rows of apple-trees, without intermission, by the road side. Why might it not be so in *other* countries, whose climate differs but very little from that of Normandy? *Think of this.*—The country still flat as a bowling-green, but as interesting as much wood and the most perfect cultivation can make it.

Again and again delighted with the prospect of the abundant harvest which a few months will produce. No streams nor meadows, but all tilled; roads excellent. Arrive at Rouen at two hours after nightfall: a beautiful approach to the town through a noble avenue of trees, I believe, "for it was so dark, Hal, thou couldst not see thy hand." Lodge at the Hotel d'Egalité.

11. Set off at ten o'clock. A hill immediately over Rouen of immense height, and so steep that the road is cut in traverses. When at the top, a most magnificent prospect to look back over Normandy, with Rouen at your feet, and the Seine winding beautifully through the landscape. The face of the country pretty much as yesterday, except that the cottages are not so much detached, but rather collected in small hamlets; a mean appearance, and far inferior in all respects. The little plantations around the cottages set them off and hid all defects; but here they are grouped together and completely exposed; yet still they are far beyond the cottages I have been used to see. Very few towns, and those of a sombre appearance; the manufacturing towns of England beyond all comparison superior. The beauty of France is in the country. Pass two or three *châteaux*, which are very thinly scattered; all shut up and deserted—their masters having been either guillotined, or being now on the right (*viz.* the *wrong*,) bank of the Rhine. In general they are in bad taste: no improvements around them, as in England, but built close on the road; and generally a dirty little

hamlet annexed, the wretched habitation of the slaves of the feudal system. Well! all those things are past and gone, just as if they had never been. I can see the genius of the French noblesse was not adapted to the country. In England, I suppose the seats of the gentry, in the same kind of country, would be as one hundred to one. Pass a beautiful valley, with a stream, the first I have seen, winding through it, and mount a second hill almost as high as that above Rouen. Table-land cultivated as before, that is to say, without one foot of ground wasted. To my utter astonishment, a large flock of sheep! What, sheep in France! I suppose they must have swam over from England.—Another flock—another : " They sear mine eye-balls." I could wish John Bull were here for one half hour, just to look at the fields of wheat that I am passing. It is impossible to conceive higher cultivation: I have seen nothing of a corn country like it in England. The road this day but middling. Sleep at Magny.

12. A most blistering bill for supper, &c. In great indignation; and the more so, because I could not scold in French. Passion is eloquent, but all my *figures* of speech were lost on the landlord. If this extortion resulted from any scarcity, I would submit in silence; but it is downright villany. Well! " 'Tis but in vain," literally. Set off in a very ill humour, but soon reconciled to my losses by the smiling appearance of the country. Still flat, and richly cultivated. Breakfast at Pontoise. The serenity of my temper, which I had

just recovered, ruffled completely by a second bill. "Landlords have flinty hearts; no tears can move them." This comes of riding in fine carriages, with velvet linings! We are downright *Milors Anglais*, and they certainly make us pay for our titles. Several vineyards, the first I have met with. An uninterrupted succession of corn, vines, and orchards, as far as the eye can reach, rich and *riant* beyond description. I see now clearly that John Bull will be able to starve France. *St. Denys*—The building for washing the royal linen turned into an arsenal, and a palace into a barrack for the Gendarmerie: a church, with the inscription—" *Le Peuple Français reconnait l'Etre Suprême, et l'immortalité de l'ame.— Groscaillou*—Several windmills turning, as if they were grinding corn, but, to be sure, they have none to grind: an artful fetch to deceive the worthy Mr. Bull, and make him believe there is still some bread in France. In sight of Paris at last. Huzza! Huzza!

I have now travelled one hundred and fifty miles in France, and I do not think I have seen one hundred and fifty acres uncultivated: the very orchards are under grain. All the mills I have seen were at work, and all the chateaux shut up, without exception. *Paris*—Stop at the *Hotel des Etrangers, Rue Vivienne*, a magnificent house, but, I foresee, as dear as the devil; my apartment in the third story very handsomely furnished, &c. for fifty francs per month, and so in proportion for a shorter time; much cheaper than the Adelphi and other hotels in London; but I will not stay here for all that—I must get into private lodgings. At six o'clock, dinner with D'Aucourt at the *Restaurateur's* in the *Maison Egalité*, formerly the Palais Royal, which is within fifty yards of our hotel. The bill of fare printed, as large as a playbill, with the price of every thing marked. I am ashamed to say so much on the subject of eating, but I have been so often bored with the famine in France, that it is, in some degree, necessary to dwell upon it. Our dinner consisted of soup, roast fowl, fried carp, salads of two kinds, a bottle of Burgundy, coffee after dinner, and a glass of liqueur, with excellent bread—(I forgot, we had cauliflowers and sauce,)—and our bill for the whole, wine and all, was 1,500 livres, in assignats, which, at the present rate, (the louis being 6,500 livres,) is exactly 4*s.* 7½*d.* sterling. What would I have given to have had P. P. with me! Indeed, we would have discussed another bottle of the Burgundy, or, by 'r Lady, some two or three.—" The rogue has given me medicines to make me love him: Yes, I have drunk medicines." I wish to God our bill of fare was posted on the Royal Exchange, for John Bull's edification. I do not think he would dine much better for the money, even at the London Tavern, especially if he drank such Burgundy as we did. The saloon in which we dined was magnificent, illuminated with patent lamps and looking glasses of immense size; the company of a fashionable appearance, full as much so as ever I have seen at the Bedford Coffee House; in short, every thing wore a complete appearance of opulence and luxury. Walked round the Palais Royal, but too dark to see any thing. Ascend a shop kept by J. B. Louvet. Coffee-houses all full as they can hold, but did not go into one of them. D'Aucourt grumbling at the appearance of things not being half so brilliant as formerly; believe he is fibbing a little. Bed!

13. Capt. Sisson, with whom we travelled up, called to breakfast. Settled our account of expenses. From Havre to Paris is 160 miles, or thereabouts. We lay two nights on the road. We were charged once or twice extravagantly. We were driven with four, five, and, during two stages, with six horses, and yet our expense for the whole was but sixty crowns, or 15*l.* sterling, which was 5*l.* a piece. In England, to travel the same distance, with four horses, would have cost us, at the very lowest, double the money. So much for the relative expense of the two countries, which I am fond of comparing, and I think I know England pretty well. Council of war with D'Aucourt. Agree to keep close for a day or two, until we get French clothes made, and then pay my first visit to Monroe (the American Ambassador) and deliver my letters. In the mean time to make inquiries. The *Directoire Executif* have presented General Jourdan with six horses, magnificently caparisoned, a sword, and a case of pistols. What a present for a Republican General! I observe they have given nothing to Pichegru. It looks odd that he should be passed over. Do they intend to fix the public attention on Jourdan? *Mind this.* I

should be sorry if Pichegru were thrown into the shade. In the evening at the Grand Opera, Theatre des Arts; *Iphigénie.* The theatre magnificent, and I should judge, about one hundred performers in the orchestra. The dresses most beautiful, and a scrupulous attention to costume, in all the decorations, which I have never seen in London. The performers were completely Grecian statues animated, and I never saw so manifestly the superiority of the taste of the ancients in dress, especially as regards the women. Iphigénie (*La citoyenne Cheron*) was dressed entirely in white, without the least ornament, and nothing can be imagined more truly elegant and picturesque. The acting admirable, but the singing very inferior to that of the King's Theatre in the Haymarket. The French cannot sing like the Italians. Agamemnon excellent. Clytemnestra still better. Achilles abominable, yet more applauded than either of them. Sang in the old French style, which is most detestable, shaking and warbling on every note: vile! vile! vile! The others sang in a style sufficiently correct. The ballet, *L'Offrande à la Liberté,* most superb. In the centre of the stage was the statue of Liberty, with an altar blazing before her. She was surrounded by the characters in the opera, in their beautiful Grecian habits. The civic air " *Veillons au salut de l'Empire,*" was sung by a powerful base, and received with transport by the audience. Whenever the word, *esclavage* was uttered, it operated like an electric shock. The Marseillaise hymn was next sung, and produced still greater enthusiasm. At the words, "*Aux armes citoyens!*" all the performers drew their swords and the females turned to them as encouraging them. Before the last verse there was a short pause; the time of the music was changed to a very slow movement, and supported only by the flutes and oboes; a beautiful procession entered; first little children like cherubs, with baskets of flowers; these were followed by boys, a little more advanced, with white javelins (the *Hasta pura* of the ancients) in their hands. Then came two beautiful female figures, moving like the Graces themselves, with torches blazing; these were followed by four negroes, characteristically dressed, and carrying two tripods between them, which they placed respectfully on each side of the altar; next came as many Americans, in the picturesque dress of Mexico; and these were followed by an immense crowd of other performers, variously habited, who ranged themselves on both sides of the stage. The little children then approached the altar with their baskets of flowers, which they laid before the goddess; the rest in turn succeeded, and hung the altar and the base of the statue with garlands and wreaths of roses; the two females with the torches approached the tripods, and, just touching them with the fire, they kindled into a blaze. The whole then knelt down, and all of this was executed in cadence to the music and with grace beyond description. The first part of the last verse, "*Amour sacré de la patrie,*" was then sung slowly and solemnly, and the words "*Liberté, Liberté cherie,*" with an emphasis which affected me most powerfully. All this was at once pathetic and sublime, beyond what I had ever seen or could almost imagine; but it was followed by an incident which crowned the whole, and rendered it indeed a spectacle worthy of a free republic. At the repetition of the words, *Aux armes, citoyens!* the music changed again to a martial style, the performers sprung on their feet, and in an instant the stage was filled with National Guards, who rushed in with bayonets fixed, sabres drawn, and the tri-colour flag flying. It would be impossible to describe the effect of this. I never knew what enthusiasm was before; and what heightened it beyond all conception was, that the men I saw before me were not hirelings acting a part; they were what they seemed, French citizens flying to arms, to rescue their country from slavery. They were the men who had precipitated Cobourg into the Sambre, and driven Clairfait over the Rhine, and were, at this very moment, on the eve of again hurrying to the frontiers, to encounter fresh dangers and gain fresh glory. This was what made the spectacle interesting beyond all description. I would willingly sail again from New York to enjoy again what I felt at that moment. *Set the ballets of the Haymarket beside this!* This sublime spectacle concluded the ballet: but why must I give it so poor a name? It was followed by another ballet, which one might call so, but even this was totally different from what such things used to be. The National Guards were introduced again, and, instead of dancing, at least three-fourths of the exhibition consisted of military evolutions, which, it should seem, are now more to the French taste than allemandes and minuets and pas de deux. *So best!* It is curious now to consider at what rate one may see all this. I paid for my seat in the boxes one hundred and fifty livres, in assignats, which, at the present rate, is very nearly sixpence sterling. The highest priced seats were but two hundred livres, which is eightpence. I mention this principally to introduce a conjecture which struck me at Havre, but which seems much more probable here, that the Government supports the theatres privately. And, in France, it is excellent policy, where the people are so much addicted to spectacles, of which there are now about twenty in Paris, and all full every night. What would my dearest love have felt at the " *Offrande à la liberté ?*"

14. Dined at a tavern in a room covered with gilding and looking-glasses down to the floor. Superb beyond any thing I had seen. It was the Hotel of the Chancellor to the Duke of Orleans. There went much misery of the people to the painting and ornamenting of that room, and now it is open to any one to dine in for three shillings. " Make *aristocracy* laugh at that." But Paris now yields so many thousand instances of a similar complexion that nobody minds them. Comedie: ballet, (improperly so called) *Le Chant du Depart.* A battalion under arms, with their knapsacks at their backs ready to march, with their officers and a representative of the people (whom P. P. would call a tyrant)

at their head. On one side of the stage a group of venerable figures, representing the parents of the warriors. On the other, a band of females (who, I can venture to say, were not selected for their ugliness) appeared as their wives and lovers, and a number of beautiful children were scattered over the stage. The representative began the song, which was answered by the soldiers; the next verse was sung by the women, and I leave it to any man with a soul capable of feeling, what the effect of such a song from such beautiful beings must have been. The next was sung by the old men, and, at the end of it, the little boys and girls ran in amongst the soldiery, who caught them up in their arms and caressed them. Some of the little fellows pulled off the grenadiers' caps and put them on their own heads, whilst others were strutting about with great sabres longer than themselves. At length the battalion was formed again and filed off, the representative and officers saluting the audience as they passed, whilst the women and children were placed on an eminence, and waved their hands to them as they went along. Nothing could exceed the peals of applause when the ensign passed with the tri-colour flag displayed. *Here was no fiction*, and that it was which gave it an interest that drew the tears irresistibly into my eyes.—N. B. From all this it is evident that the French are a nation of cannibals, incapable of human feeling, and that John Bull will just begin at the banks of the Wahal, and never stop till he has driven them into the Mediterranean.

15. Went to Monroe's, the Ambassador, and delivered in my passport and letters. Received very politely by Monroe, who inquired a great deal into the state of the public mind in America, which I answered as well as I could, and in a manner to satisfy him pretty thoroughly as to my own sentiments. I inquired of him where I was to deliver my despatches. He informed me, to the Minister for Foreign Affairs, and gave me his address. I then rose and told him that when he had read B——'s letter, (which was in cypher) he would, I hope, find me excused in taking the liberty to call again. He answered, he would be happy at all times to see me, and, after he had inquired about Hamilton Rowan, how he liked America, &c. I took my leave, and returned to his office for my passport. The Secretary smoked me for an Irishman directly. *A la bonne heure.* Went at three o'clock to the Minister for Foreign Affairs, Rue du Bacq, 471. Delivered my passport, and inquired for some one who spoke English. Introduced immediately to the Chef de Bureau, Lamare, a man of exceedingly plain appearance. I showed my letter, and told him I wished for an opportunity to deliver it into the Minister's hands. He asked me, "would it not do if he took charge of it?" I answered, he undoubtedly knew the official form best, but if it was not irregular, I should consider myself much obliged by being allowed to deliver it in person. He then brought me into a magnificent ante-chamber, where a general officer and another person were waiting,

and, after a few minutes delay, I was introduced to the Minister, Charles de la Croix, and delivered my letter, which he opened, and seeing it in cypher, he told me, in French, he was much obliged to me for the trouble I had taken, and that the Secretary would give me a receipt, acknowledging the delivery. I then made my bow and retired with the Secretary, the Minister seeing us to the door. He is a respectable-looking man; (I should judge him near sixty,) with very much the air of a bishop. The Secretary has given me a receipt, of which the following is a translation: " I have received from Mr. James Smith, a letter addressed to the Committee of Public Safety, and which he tells me comes from the Citizen Adet, Minister Plenipotentiary of the French Republic at Philadelphia. Paris, 26th Pluviose, third year of the French Republic. The Secretary-General of Foreign Affairs, Lamare." I have thus broken the ice. In a day or two I shall return for my passport.

I am perfectly pleased with my reception at Monroe's and at the Minister's, but can form no possible conjecture as to the event. The letter being in cypher, he could form no guess as to whom I might be, or what might be my business. All I can say is, that I found no difficulty in obtaining access to him; that his behaviour was extremely affable and polite; and, in a word, that if I have no ground to augur any thing good, neither have I reason to expect any thing bad. All is *in equilibrio.* I have now a day or two to attend to my private affairs, and the first must be that of Mr. W. Browne (my brother Matthew.) Opera in the evening. The " *Chant du Depart*" again. I lose three-fourths of the pleasure I should otherwise feel, for the want of my dear love, or my friend P. P. to share it with. How they would glory in Paris just now!—And then the Burgundy every day at the restaurateurs! Poor P. P.! he is the only possible bearable companion, except the boys. Well "'Tis but in vain," &c.

16. Walked out alone to see sights. The *Thuileries*, the *Louvre*, *Pont Neuf*, &c. superb. Paris a thousand times more magnificent than London, but less convenient for those who go afoot. Saw two companies of grenadiers in the garden of the Thuileries, the first I have met. All very fine fellows, but without the *air militaire* of private sentinels; many in the ranks have the appearance of gentlemen in soldiers' coats, and, on the whole, they exactly resembled two companies of Irish volunteers, as I have seen them in that country, in the days of my youth and innocence. These are the youth of the first requisition. Their uniform blue, faced white, red cape, cuffs and shoulder-knots, plumes in their hats, with white belts, vest and breeches, black stocks and gaiters. I think them equal in figure to any men I have ever seen of their number. The women! only to think what a thing fashion is! The French women have been always remarkable for fine hair, and therefore at present they all prefer to wear wigs. They actually roll and pin up their own beautiful tresses, so that they become invisible, and

over them they put a little shock perriwig. Damn their wigs! I wish they were all burnt; but it is the fashion, and that is a solution for every absurdity. In the evening walked to the Palais Royal; filled with the military, most of them superb figures: — I do not mean as to dress, but air, manners, and gait. I now perceive the full import of the expression, *an armed nation*, and I think I know a country, that (for its extent and population), could produce as many and as fine fellows as France. Well, all in good time! It will be absolutely necessary to adopt measures similar to those which have raised and cherished this spirit here, if ever God Almighty is pleased in his goodness to enable us to shake off our chains. I think Ireland would be formidable as an armed nation.

17. Went at one o'clock to the Minister's bureau, for my passport. A clerk tells me that a person called yesterday in my name and got it. I assured him I knew nobody in Paris, and had not sent any one to demand it, and reminded him that it was on this day he had desired me to call. He looked very blank at this, and just then the principal Secretary coming up, I informed him of what had happened. He recollected me immediately, and told me the Minister wished to see me, and had sent to the Ambassador to learn my address. I answered I should attend him whenever he pleased; he replied "instantly," and accordingly I followed him into the Minister's cabinet, who received me very politely. He told me in French, that he had had the letter I

brought decyphered, and laid instantly before the *Directoire Executif*, who considered the contents as of the greatest importance; that their intentions were, that I should go immediately to a gentleman to whom he would give me a letter, and, as this gentleman spoke both languages perfectly, and was confidential, I could explain myself to him without reserve; that his name was Madgett. I answered that I knew the person by reputation, and had a letter of introduction to him, but did not consider I was at liberty to make myself known to any person without his approbation. He answered that I might communicate with Madgett, without the least reserve; sat down and wrote a note to him, which he gave me: I then took my leave, the Minister seeing me to the door. I mention these minute circumstances of my reception, not that I am one to be too much elevated by the attentions of any man in any station, (at least, I hope so,) but that I consider the respect shown to me by De la Croix as really shown to my mission; and, of course, the readiness of access and extreme civility of reception that I experience I feel, as so many favourable presages. I have been at the bureau twice, and both times have been admitted to the Minister's cabinet without a minute's delay. Surely all this looks well. The costume of the Minister was singular; I have said, already, that he had the presence of a bishop. He was dressed to-day in a grey silk robe-de-chambre, under which he wore a kind of scarlet cassock of satin, with rose-coloured silk stockings, and scarlet ribands in his shoes. I believe he has as much the manners of a gentleman as Lord Grenville. I mention these little circumstances, because I know they will be interesting to her whom I prize above my life ten thousand times. There are about six persons in the world who will read these detached memorandums with pleasure; to every one else they would appear sad stuff. But they are only for the women of my family, for the boys, if ever we meet again, and for my friend P. P. Would to God he were here just now! Well, "if wishes were horses, beggars would ride." And there is another curious quotation, equally applicable, on the subject of wishing, which I scorn to make. Set off for Madgett's and delivered my letter. Madgett delighted to see me; tells me he has the greatest expectation our business will be taken up in a most serious manner; that the attention of the French Government is now turned to Ireland, and that the stability and form it had assumed, gave him the strongest hopes of success; that he had written to Hamilton Rowan, about a month since, to request I might come over instantly, in order to confer with the French Government and determine on the necessary arrangements, and that he had done this by order of the French Executive. He then asked me, had I brought any papers or credentials? I answered, that I only brought the letter from Adet to the Executive, and one to the American Ambassador; that I had destroyed a few others on the passage, including one from Mr. Rowan to himself, as we were chased by a Bermudian; that,

have their attention turned most seriously to Irish affairs; that they feel, unless they can separate Ireland from England, the latter is invulnerable; that they are willing to conclude a treaty offensive and defensive with Ireland, and a treaty of commerce on a footing of reciprocal advantage; that they will supply ten sail of the line, arms, and money, as he told me yesterday; and that they were already making arrangements in Spain and Holland for that purpose. He asked me, did I think any thing would be done in Ireland by her spontaneous efforts? I told him, most certainly not; that if a landing were once effected, every thing would follow instantly, but that was indispensable; and I begged him to state this as my opinion, to such persons in power as he might communicate with; that if 20,000 French were in Ireland, we should in a month have an army of 1, 2, or, if necessary, 300,000 men, but that the *point d'appui* was indispensable. He said it appeared so to him also. He then returned to the scheme of importing stores, &c. through the medium of America. I again mentioned the difficulty from the gunpowder act, and the risk of alarming the Irish Government. He said he still thought it would be possible; and mentioned as a reason, that eighteen brass cannon had, to his knowledge, lately been smuggled to Ireland, through Belfast. If this be true, it surprises me not a little; but I rather judge Madgett is misinformed. I answered, that if the landing were once effected, the measure would be unnecessary; as, in that event, we should soon have all the stores of the kingdom in our hands; and, if it was not effected, the people would not move, unless in local riots and insurrections, which would end in the destruction of the ringleaders. He seemed struck with this, and said he saw that part of the scheme was useless. I then mentioned the necessity of having a man of reputation at the head of the French forces, and mentioned Pichegru or Jourdan, both of whom are well known by character in Ireland. He told me there was a kind of coolness between the Executive and Pichegru, (this I suspected before,) but that, if the measures were adopted, he might still be the General; adding that he was a man of more talents than Jourdan. I answered, "either would do." He then desired me to prepare a memorial in form for the French Executive as soon as possible, which he would translate and have delivered in without delay. We fixed to dine together at his lodgings, and so parted. There is one thing here I wish to observe; Madgett showed me the Minister's note, which appeared to me completely confidential, and in which he mentions his own desire to forward the business as much as possible, as a friend to liberty and to humanity. The Minister also desired me to explain myself to Madgett without reserve. Am I too sanguine in believing what I so passionately wish, that the French Executive will seriously assist us?

18, 19, 20. At work in the mornings at my memorial. Call on Madgett once a day to confer with him. He says there will be a person sent to Ireland immediately, with whom I shall have a conference; and that it would be desirable he should bring back an appointment of Minister Plenipotentiary for me, in order to conclude an alliance offensive and defensive with the Republic; in which case I should be acknowledged as such by the French Government. Certainly nothing could be more flattering to me; however, I answered that such an appointment could not be had without communicating with so many persons as might endanger the betrayal of the secret to the Irish Government; that I only desired credit with the *Directoire Executif*, so far as they should find my assertions supported by indisputable facts; that the information I brought was the essential part, and the credential, though highly gratifying to my private feelings, would be, in fact, but matter of form. That when a government was formed in Ireland, it would be time enough to talk of embassies; and then, if my country thought me worthy, I should be the happiest and proudest man living to accept the office of Ambassador from Ireland. So there was an end to my appointment. I must wait till the war at least is commenced, if ever it commences, or perhaps until it is over, if I am not knocked on the head meantime. I should like very well to be the first Irish Ambassador; and if I succeed in my present business, I think I shall have some claim to the office. "Oh, Paris is a fine town and a very charming city." If Ireland were independent, I could spend three years here with my family, especially my dearest love, very happily. I dare say P. P.* would have no objection to a few months in the year à l'Hotel d'Irlande. He is a dog. Indeed, we would discuss several bottles of diplomatic Burgundy. But all this is building castles in the air: let me finish my memorials, which Madgett tells me this day (the 20th) the Minister has written to him about. I am glad of that impatience. He, Madgett, says, if we succeed, it is part of the plan (but I believe he means *his own* plan) to demand Jamaica for Ireland, by way of indemnity. I wish we had Ireland without Jamaica. My memorial filled with choice facts. Dine alone every day; D'Aucourt leaving me very much to myself, of which I am glad. Military in the Palais Royal, superb figures (but this I said already). Many fine lads of twenty, who have sacrificed an arm or a leg to the liberty of their country: I could worship them. " The Baronet can ca' for aught he needs, but he is not yet quite maister o' the accent." Very wise memorandums for a Minister Plenipotentiary planning a revolution. Oh Lord! Oh Lord! Well, " 'Tis but in vain," &c.

21. Bought the *Constitution Française* at the shop of J. B. Louvet, in the Palais Royal, and received it from the hands of his wife, so celebrated under the name of Lodoïska. I like her countenance much: she is not handsome, but very interesting. Louvet is one of those who escaped the 31st May, and after a long concealment and a thousand perils, in which Lodoïska conducted herself like a heroine, returned

* A conventional term for the Author's particular friend, Mr. T. Russell.

on the fall of Robespierre, whom he had been the first to denounce, and resumed his place in the Convention. He is now a distinguished member of the *Conseil des Cinq Cent;* supports a newspaper, *La Sentinelle,* and keeps a bookseller's shop in the Palais Royal. I am glad I have seen Lodoïska; I wish my dearest love could see her. I think she would behave as well in similar circumstances. Her courage and her affection have been tried in some, very nearly as critical. Well! I must go finish my memorial. N. B. Stone has been acquitted in England, I believe very justly. He will never set the Thames in a blaze.

22. Finished my memorial, and delivered a fair copy, signed, to Madgett, for the Minister of Foreign Relations. Madgett in the horrors. He tells me he has had a discourse yesterday for two hours with the Minister, and that the succours he expected will fall very short of what he thought. That the marine of France is in such a state that Government will not hazard a large fleet; and, consequently, that we must be content to steal a march: that they will give 2000 of their best troops, and arms for 20,000; that they cannot spare Pichegru nor Jourdan; that they will give any quantity of artillery; and, I think he added, what money might be necessary. He also said they would first send proper persons among the Irish prisoners of war, to sound them, and exchange them on the first opportunity. To all this, at which I am not disappointed, I answered, that as to 2000 men, they might as well send 20. That with regard to myself, I would go, if they would send but a corpo-

ral's guard; but that my opinion was, that 5000 was as little as could be landed with any prospect of success, and that that number would leave the matter doubtful; that if there could be an imposing force sent in the first instance, it would overbear all opposition, the nation would be unanimous, and an immense effusion of blood and treasure spared; the law of opinion would at once operate in favour of the Government which, in that case, would be instantly formed—and I pressed particularly the advantages resulting from this last circumstance. He seemed perfectly satisfied with my arguments, but equally satisfied that it would not, or rather could not, be done. I then bade him remember that my plan was built on the supposition of a powerful support in the first instance; that I had particularly specified so in my memorial; and begged him to apprize the Minister that my decided opinion was so; that, nevertheless, with 5000 men, the business might be attempted, and I did believe would succeed; but that, in that case, we must fight hard for it; that, though I was satisfied how the militia and army would act in case of a powerful invasion, I could not venture to say what might be their conduct under the circumstances he mentioned; that, if they stood by the Government, which it was possible they might, we should have hot work of it; that, if 5000 men were sent, they should be the very flower of the French troops, and a considerable proportion of them artillerymen, with the best General they could spare. He interrupted me to ask who was known in Ireland after Pichegru and Jourdan. I answered Hoche, especially since his affair at Quiberon. He said he was sure we might have Hoche. I also mentioned, that if they sent but 5000 men, they should send a greater quantity of arms; as in that case we could not command, at once, all the arms of the nation, as we should if they were able to send 20,000, or even 15,000. I added, that as to the prisoners of war, my advice was to send proper persons among them, but not to part with a man of them until the landing was effected, and then exchange them as fast as possible. He promised to represent all this, and that he hoped we should get 5000 men at least, and a greater quantity of arms. We then parted. Now what is to be my plan? Suppose we get 5000 men, and 30, or even 20,000 stand of arms, and a train of artillery: I conceive, in the first place, the embarkation must be from Holland; but in all events the landing must be in the North, as near Belfast as possible. Had we 20,000, or even 15,000, in the first instance, we should begin with the capital, the seizing of which would secure everything; but, as it is, if we cannot go large we must go close-hauled, as the saying is. With 5000 we must proceed entirely on a revolutionary plan, I fear, (that is to say, reckon only on the Sansculottes;) and, if necessary, put every man, horse, guinea, and potatoe, in Ireland in requisition. I should also conceive that it would be our policy at first to avoid an action, supposing the Irish army stuck to the Government. Every day would strengthen and discipline us, and give us opportunities to work upon them. I doubt whether we could, until we had obtained some advantage in the field, frame any body that would venture to call itself the Irish Government, but if we could, it would be of the last importance. "Hang those who talk of fear!" With 5000 men, and very strong measures, we should ultimately succeed. The only difference between that number and 20,000, is that, with the latter there would be no fighting, and with this we may have some hard knocks. "Ten thousand hearts are swelling in my bosom!" I think I will find a *dozen* men who will figure as soldiers.—O good God! good God! what would I give to-night that we were safely landed, and encamped on the Cave Hill. If we can find our way so far, I think we shall puzzle John Bull to work us out. Surely we can do as much as the Chouans or people of La Vendée.

23. Looked over Paine's " Age of Reason, second part." D——d trash! His wit is, without exception, the very worst I ever saw. He is discontented with the human figure, which he seems to think is not well constructed for enjoyment. He lies like a dog. Ask P. P. whether it is not possible to be most exquisitely happy, even under the incumbrance of that shape so awkward in Mr. Paine's eyes? I beg the gentleman may speak for himself. I suppose he includes the female shape also. He seems to have some hopes that he shall enjoy immortality in the shape of a butterfly. "Say, little foolish fluttering thing." D—n his nonsense! I wish he was a butterfly, with all my soul. He has also discovered that

a spider can hang from the ceiling by her web, and that a man cannot; and this is *Philosophy!* I think Paine begins to dote; but d—n his trash! as I said with great eloquence already, and let me mind my business. I must now write my own credentials to the French Government. Awkward enough for a man to trumpet himself; however, it must be. " 'Tis but in vain," &c. This is an invaluable quotation, and wears like steel; for it, amongst other obligations, I am indebted to the witty and ingenious lucubrations of my friend P. P. Apropos! I never wanted the society, assistance, advice, comfort, and direction of the said P. P. half so much as at this moment. I have a pretty serious business on my hands, with a grand responsibility; and here I am, alone, in the midst of Paris, without a single soul to advise or consult with, and nothing in fact to support me but a good intention. Sad! sad! well, hang fear—" 'Tis but in vain, for soldiers to complain." *Dacapo.* A busy day! Called on Madgett, in order to explain farther to him that all I had said relative to the support to be expected from the people of Ireland, and the conduct of the army, was on the supposition of a *considerable* force being landed in the first instance. This I had pressed upon him yesterday; but I cannot make it too clear, for my own credit. My theory, in three words, is this: With twenty thousand men there would be no possibility of resistance for an hour, and we should begin by the capital; with five thousand I should have no doubt of success, but then we should expect some fighting, and we should begin near Belfast;

with two thousand I think the business utterly desperate, for, let them land where they would, they would be utterly defeated before any one could join them, or, in fact, before the bulk of the people could know that they were come. This would be a mere Quiberon business in Ireland, and would operate but as a snare for the lives of my brave and unfortunate countrymen, to whose destruction I do not wish, God knows, to be accessory. Nevertheless, I concluded, that if they sent but a sergeant and twelve men, I would go, but wished them to be fully apprised of my opinion, that, in case of a failure, they might not accuse me of having deceived them. He agreed with me in every word of the statement, and desired me to insert part of it in my letter to the Minister. He also promised, positively, to have a letter written from the proper office to Guise, to inquire after Mr. William Browne, (my brother Matthew,) though he assures me the order for his liberation was expedited about the first of May last. If we can find the said Mr. Browne, he may be very serviceable amongst the prisoners of war, both soldiers and seamen being chiefly Irish. I have not pressed my inquiries about him, as my wishes prompt, lest I should appear to prefer the dearest affections of my heart, which God and my dearest love know I do not, to the public business with which I am charged. Quit Madgett, whom I believe *honest*, and whom I feel *weak;* go to Monroe; received very favourably. He has had my letter decyphered, and dropped all reserve. I told him I felt his situation was one of considerable delicacy, and therefore I did not wish to press upon him any information, relative either to myself or to my business, farther than he might desire. He answered that the letters had satisfied him, particularly that from H. R. of whom he spoke in terms of great respect; and that, as he was not responsible for what he might hear, but for what he might do, I might speak freely. I then opened myself to him without the least reserve, and gave him such details as I was able of the actual state of things, and of the grounds of my knowledge from my situation. I also informed him of what I had done thus far. He then addressed me in substance as follows: "You must change your plan; I have no doubt whatsoever of the integrity and sincerity of the Minister De la Croix, nor even of Madgett, whom I believe to be honest. But, in the first place, it is a subaltern way of doing business, and, in the next, the vanity of Madgett will be very likely to lead him (in order to raise his importance in the eyes of some of his countrymen who are here as patriots, and of whom I have by no means the same good opinion as to integrity that I have of him,) to drop some hint of what is going forward. Go at once to the *Directoire Executif*, and demand an audience; explain yourself to them; and, as to me, you may go so far as to refer to me for the authenticity of what you may advance, and you may add that you have reason to think that I am, in a degree, apprised of the outline of your business." I mentioned Carnot, of whose reputation we had been long apprised, and who, I understood, spoke English. He said, "Nobody fitter, and that La Reveilliere Lepaux also spoke English: that either would do." I then expressed a doubt whether, as I was already in the hands of Charles de la Croix, there might not be some indelicacy in my going directly to the *Directoire Executif*, and, if so, whether it might not be of disservice. He answered " By no means; that in his own functions the proper person for him to communicate with was De la Croix, but that, nevertheless, when he had any business of consequence, he went at once to the fountainhead." He then proceeded to mention that, in all the changes which had taken place in France, there never was an abler or purer set of men at the head of affairs than at present; that they were sincere friends to liberty and justice, and in no wise actuated by a spirit of conquest; that, consequently, if they took up the business of Ireland on my motion, I should find them perfectly fair and candid; that not only the Government, but the whole people, were most violently exasperated against England, and that there was no one thing that would at once command the warmest support of all parties so much as any measure which promised a reduction of her power. He then examined me pretty closely on the state of Ireland, on which I gave him complete information, as far as I was able; and we concluded by agreeing that to-morrow I should go boldly to the Luxembourg, and demand an audience of Carnot or La Reveilliere Lepaux. Monroe tells me that

Barrere (for I inquired) is yet in France, and he thought would not quit it. I told him Barrere would be very acceptable in Ireland, as a deputy with the army. He answered that he did not at all doubt but it might so happen; that he would not advise me to begin by bolting out the name of Barrere, but that I might take an opportunity to mention him. I remarked that it had fallen to Barrere's lot to make some of the most splendid reports in the Convention, which made him well known to us; and that the people were used, in a degree, to associate the ideas of Barrere and victory, which, trifling as it was, was of some consequence. On the whole, I am glad to find my lover Barrere, as I hope, in no danger. It would be a most extraordinary thing if I should happen to be an instrument in restoring his talents to the cause of liberty. I have always had a good opinion of him. Monroe tells me the ground of the coolness between Pichegru and the Government is, that he is supposed to be attached too much to the party of the Moderés. I am glad of this; (not that there is a coolness, but that the Government is not of that party.) We talked of the resources of France and England. I mentioned that, in my judgment, France had one measure which sooner or later she must adopt, and the sooner the better,—and that was a bankruptcy; that she would then start forth with her immense resources against England, staggering under 400,000,000 of debt. Monroe took me by the hand and said, "You have hit it; and I will tell you it is a thing decided upon." If it be so, look to yourself, Mr. John Bull, "Look to your house, your daughter, and your ducats." Take my leave of Monroe, with whom I am extremely pleased. There is a true republican frankness about him, which is mighty interesting. And now am not I a pretty fellow to go to the *Directoire Executif?* It is very singular that so obscure an individual should be thrown into such a situation. I presume I do not write these memorandums to flatter myself; and I here solemnly call God to witness the purity of my motives, and the uprightness with which I shall endeavour to carry myself through this most arduous and critical situation. I hope I may not ruin a noble cause by any weakness or indiscretion of mine. As to my integrity, I can answer for myself. What shall I do for the want of P. P.? I am in unspeakable difficulty for the want of his advice and consolation. Well, if ever we meet again, it will amuse him to read these hints; but he is a dog, and so " 'Tis but in vain," &c.

24. Went at 12 o'clock, in a fright, to the Luxembourg; conning speeches in execrable French, all the way. What shall I say to Carnot? Well, " whatsoever the Lord putteth in my mouth, that surely shall I utter." Plucked up a spirit as I drew near the Palace, and mounted the stairs like a lion: —Went into the first Bureau that I found open, and demanded at once to see Carnot. The clerks stared a little, but I repeated my demand with a courage truly heroic; on which they instantly sub-

mitted, and sent a person to conduct me. This happened to be his day for giving audience, which each member of the Executive Directory does in his turn. Introduced by my guide into the ante-chamber, which was filled with people; the officers of state, all in their new costume. Wrote a line in English, and delivered it to one of the Huissiers, stating that a stranger just arrived from America wished to speak to Citizen Carnot, on an affair of consequence. He brought me an answer in two minutes, that I should have an audience. The folding-doors were now thrown open, a bell being previously rung to give notice to the people that all who had business might present themselves, and Citizen Carnot appeared, in the petit-costume of white satin with crimson robe, richly embroidered. It is very elegant, and resembles almost exactly the draperies of Vandyke. He went round the room receiving papers and answering those who addressed him. I told my friend the Huissier, in marvellous French, that my business was too important to be transacted there, and that I would return on another day, when it would not be Carnot's turn to give audience, and when I should hope to find him at leisure. He mentioned this to Carnot, who ordered me instantly to be shown into an inner apartment, and said he would see me as soon as the audience was over. That I thought looked well, and I began accordingly to con my speech again. In the apartment were five or six personages, who being, like myself, of great distinction, were admitted to a private audience. I allowed them all precedence, as I wanted to have my will of Carnot; and while they were in their turns speaking with him, I could not help reflecting how often I had wished for the opportunity I then enjoyed; what schemes I had laid, what hazards I had run! When I looked round and saw myself actually in the cabinet of the Executive Directory, vis-à-vis Citizen Carnot, the "organizer of victory," I could hardly believe my own senses, and felt as if it were all a dream. However, I was not in the least degree disconcerted, and when I presented myself, after the rest were dismissed, I had all my faculties, such as they were, as well at my command as on any occasion in my life. Why do I mention those trifling circumstances? It is because they will not be trifling in her eyes, for whom they were written. I began the discourse by saying, in horrible French, that I had been informed he spoke English.—"A little, Sir; but I perceive you speak French, and if you please, we will converse in that language." I answered, still in my jargon, that if he could have the patience to endure me, I would endeavour, and only prayed him to stop me whenever I did not make myself understood. I then told him I was an Irishman; that I had been Secretary and Agent to the Catholics of that country, who were about 3,000,000 of people; that I was also in perfect possession of the sentiments of the Dissenters, who were at least 900,000, and that I wished to communicate with him on the actual state of Ireland. He stopped me here to express a doubt as to the numbers being so great as I represented. I answered, a calculation had been made within these few years, grounded on the number of houses, which was ascertained for purposes of revenue; that, by that calculation, the people of Ireland amounted to 4,100,000, and which was acknowledged to be considerably under the truth. He seemed a little surprised at this, and I proceeded to state, that all those people were unanimous in their sentiments in favour of France, and eager to throw off the yoke of England. He asked me then, "What they wanted?" I said, "An armed force in the commencement, for a *point d'appui*, until they can organize themselves; and undoubtedly a supply of arms, and some money." I added, that I had already delivered in a memorial on the subject to the Minister of Foreign Relations, and that I was preparing another, which would explain to him, in detail, all that I knew, better than could be done in conversation. He then said, "We shall see those memorials." The "Organizer of Victory" proceeded to ask me, "Are there not some strong places in Ireland?" I answered, I knew of none, except some works to defend the harbour of Cork. He stopped me here, exclaiming, "Ay, Cork! But may it not be necessary to land there?"—By which question I perceived he had been *organizing* a little already, in his own mind. I answered, I thought not. That if a landing in *force* were attempted, it would be better near the capital, for obvious reasons; if with a small army, it should be in the North rather than the South of Ireland, for reasons which he would find in my memorials. He then asked me, "Might there not be some danger or delay in a longer navigation?" I answered, it would not make a difference of two days, which was nothing in comparison of the advantages. I then told him that I came to France by direction and concurrence of the men who (and here I was at a loss for a French word, with which, seeing my embarrassment, he supplied me,) *guided* the two great parties I had mentioned. This satisfied me clearly, that he attended to and understood me. I added, that I had presented myself in August last, in Philadelphia, to Citizen Adet, and delivered to him such credentials as I had with me; that he did not at that juncture think it advisable for me to come in person, but offered to transmit a memorial, which I accordingly delivered to him. That about the end of November last, I received letters from my friends in Ireland, repeating their instructions in the strongest manner, that I should, if possible, force my way to France, and lay the situation of Ireland before its Government. That, in consequence, I had again waited on Citizen Adet, who seemed eager to assist me, and offered me a letter to the *Directoire Executif*, which I accepted with gratitude. That I sailed from America in the very first vessel, and had arrived about a fortnight; that I had delivered my letter to the Minister for Foreign Affairs, who had ordered me to explain myself without reserve to Citizen Madgett, which I had accordingly done. That by his advice I had prepared and delivered one memorial on the actual state of Ireland, and was then at work on another, which would comprise the whole of the subject. That I had the highest respect for the Minister; and that as to Madgett, I had no reason whatsoever to doubt him; but, nevertheless, must be permitted to say, that in my mind, it was a business of too great importance to be transacted with a mere *Commis*. That I should not think I had discharged my duty, either to France or Ireland, if I left any measure unattempted which might draw the attention of the Directory to the situation of the latter country; and that, in consequence, I had presumed to present myself to him, and to implore his attention to the facts contained in my two memorials. That I should also presume to request, that, if any doubt or difficulty arose in his mind on any of those facts, he would have the goodness to permit me to explain. I concluded by saying, that I looked upon it as a favourable omen, that I had been allowed to communicate with him, as he was already perfectly well known by reputation in Ireland, and was the very man of whom my friends had spoken. He shook his head and smiled, as if he doubted me a little. I assured him the fact was so; and, as a proof, told him that in Ireland we all knew, three years ago, that he could speak English; at which he did not seem displeased. I then rose, and after the usual apologies took my leave; but I had not cleared the antechamber, when I recollected a very material circumstance, which was, that I had not told him in fact *who*, but merely *what* I was; I was, therefore, returning on my steps, when I was stopped by the sentry, demanding my card; but from this dilemma, I was extricated by my lover the Huissier, and again admitted. I then told Carnot that, as to my situation, credit, and the station I had filled in Ireland, I begged leave to refer him to James Monroe, the American Ambassador. He seemed struck with this, and then for the first time asked my name. I told him that in fact I had just now two names, my real one and that under which I travelled and was described in my passport. I then took a slip of paper, and wrote the name " James Smith, citoyen Americain," and under it, Theobald Wolfe Tone, which I handed him, adding that my real name was the undermost. He took the paper, and looking over it, said, " Ha! Theobald Wolfe Tone!" with the expression of one who has just recollected a circumstance, from which little movement I augur good things. I then told him I would finish my memorial as soon as possible, and hoped he would permit me in the course of a few days after to present myself again to him; to which he answered, " By all means;" and so I again took my leave. Here is a full and true account of my first audience of the Executive Directory of France, in the person of Citizen Carnot, the " Organizer of Victory." I think I came off very clear. What am I to infer from all this? As yet I have met with no difficulty nor check, nothing to discourage me; but I wish with such extravagant passion for the emancipation of my country, and I do so abhor and detest the very name of England, that I doubt my own judgment, lest I see things in too favourable a light. I hope I am doing my duty. It is a bold measure; after all if it should succeed, and my visions be realized—Huzza! *Vive la Republique!* I am a pretty fellow to negotiate with the Directory of France; to pull down a monarchy and establish a republic; to break a connection of 600 years standing, and contract a fresh alliance with another country." By 'r Lakin, a parlous fear!" What would my old friend Fitzgibbon say, if he was to read these wise memorandums? " He called me dog, before he had a cause;" I remember he used to say that I was a *viper* in the bosom of Ireland. Now that I am in Paris, I will venture to say that he lies, and that I am a better Irishman than he and his whole gang of ———, as well as the gang who are opposing him *as it were.* But this is all castle-building. Let me finish my memorial, and deliver it to the Minister. Nothing but *Minister and Directoire Executif and revolutionary memorials.* Well, my friend Plunket (but I sincerely forgive him,) and my friend Magee, (whom I have not yet forgiven,) would not speak to me in Ireland, because I was a Republican. Sink or swim, I stand *to-day* on as high ground as either of them. My venerable friend, old Captain Russell, always had hopes of me in the worst of times: Huzza! I would give five louis-d'ors, for one day's conversation with P. P. What shall I do for want of his advice and assistance? Not but what I think

I am doing pretty well, considering I am quite alone, with no papers, no one to consult or advise with, and shocking all Christian ears with the horrible jargon which I speak, and which is properly no language. I see I have grand diplomatic talents, and by-and-by I hope to have an opportunity of displaying my military ones, and showing that I am equally great in the cabinet and the field. This is sad stuff! except for my love, who will laugh at it, or P. P. who will enjoy it. I have to add to this day's journal, that I saw yesterday at the Luxembourg, besides my friend Carnot, the Citizens Letourneur, the President, Barras, and La Reveilliere Lepaux. Barras looks like a soldier, and put me something in mind of James Bramston. La Reveilliere is extremely like Dr. Kearney. Mem. I saw two *poissardes* admitted to speak to Carnot, who gave them money, whilst a General officer in his uniform was obliged to wait for his turn. Oh Lord! Oh Lord! shall I ever get to finish my memorial? But when I begin to write these ingenious memorandums, I feel just as if I were chatting with my dearest love, and know not when to leave off. By the by, there is a good deal of vanity in this day's journal. No matter! there is no one to know it, and I believe that wiser men, if they would speak the truth, would feel a little elevated in my situation; hunted from my own country as a traitor, living obscurely in America, as an exile, and received in France, by the Executive Directory, almost as an Ambassador! Well, murder will out! I am as vain as the devil; and one thing which makes me wish so often for P. P. (not to mention the benefit of his advice) is to communicate with him the pleasure I feel at my present situation. I know how sincerely he would enjoy it, and also how he would plume himself on his own discernment, for he always foretold great things. So he did, sure enough; but will they be verified? Well, if all this be not vanity, I should be glad to know what is! But nobody is the wiser, and so I will go finish my memorial. (Sings, "*Allons, enfans de la patrie,*" &c.)

25. Finished the draft of my second memorial, and read it over with Madgett.

26. This morning finished an awkward business, that is to say, wrote a long letter to the Minister, all about myself: very proper in an ambassador to frame his own credentials. "My commission was large, for I made it myself." Read it over carefully; every word true, and not exaggerated. Resolved to go at once to the Minister, and deliver my letter, like a true Irishman, with my own hands. Went to his bureau, and saw Lamare, the Secretary, whom I sent in to demand an audience. Lamare returned with word that the Minister was just engaged with Neri Corsini, Ambassador from the Grand Duke of Tuscany, and would see me the moment he was at leisure. Waited accordingly in the antechamber. A person came in, and after reconnoitring me for some time, pulled out an English newspaper and began to read it. Looked at him with the most interesting indifference, as if he was reading a chapter in the

Koran. Did the fellow think I would rise at such a bait as that? Neri Corsini being departed, I was introduced, leaving my friend in the antechamber to study his newspaper. I began with telling the Minister, that though I spoke execrable French, I would, with his permission, put his patience to a short trial. (Once for all, I am thus minute for the sake of my wife, whom I love ten thousand times more than all the universe, and who will consider every circumstance, even the most trifling, which relates to me, of consequence.) I then told him that, in obedience to his orders, I had finished a memorial on the actual state of Ireland, which I had delivered to Madgett; that I had finished the draft of another, which I would deliver to-morrow, on the means necessary to accomplish the great object of my mission, the separation of Ireland from England, and her establishment as an independent Republic in alliance with France. De la Croix interrupted me here by saying, that I might count upon it; there was no object nearer the heart of the Executive Directory; they had that business, at that very moment, before them, and would leave no means consistent with their utmost capacity untried to accomplish it. And he repeated with earnestness, " that I might count upon it." These are strong expressions from a man in his station. I then said, that this information gave me the most sincere pleasure, not only on account of my own country, but of France, to whom the independence of Ireland was scarcely less an object than to Ireland itself. He answered, "We know that perfectly; and, for myself, I can assure you, that for the sake of both countries, as well as for the sake of liberty and humanity, you may depend on my most sincere and hearty co-operation in every measure likely to accomplish that end." I then returned to the business which brought me to him, that is to say, my credentials. I told him, in as few words as possible, the station I had filled in Ireland, and added that I had thrown a few facts relative to myself on paper, which I delivered to him, and that as to my credit or veracity I could refer him to James Monroe, who had allowed me to mention his name, as a voucher for my integrity. He said it was unnecessary, and as to applying to Monroe, he would not wish to take any step relating to the business, which could in the least by possibility take wind; that Madgett was the only person whatsoever, to whom he confided the affair; that his principal Secretary, and those who were most confidential with him, knew nothing of it; and he recommended to me to be equally cautious. I assured him, as the fact was, that I kept the most rigid guard on myself; that I did not know a soul in Paris, nor desired to know any one; that I formed no connections, nor intended to form any; and that, in short, I kept myself purposely in solitude, that I might escape notice as much as possible. He said I was very right, and asked me, did I know the person I saw in the antechamber? I answered, I did not. He said he was an Irish patriot, named Duchet, (as he pronounced it,) who was persecuted into exile for some writing under the signature of *Junius Redivivus*. I said, it might be so, but that I knew nothing of him, or of the writings, and if such an event had taken place, it must have been since June last, when I left Ireland. I then mentioned the circumstance of his pulling out an English newspaper, and setting a trap for me therewith, and how I avoided falling into his snare. The Minister said again, I was quite right, but that that person had delivered in several memorials on the state of Ireland. This is very odd! I never saw the man in my life, and yet I rather imagine he knew my person. Who the devil is Junius Redivivus? or who is Duchet, if his name be Duchet? I must talk a little to Madgett of this resurrection of Junius, of which, to speak the truth, I have no good opinion.—The Minister then asked me what we wanted in Ireland? I answered, that we wanted a force to begin with, arms, ammunition, and money. He asked me, what quantities of each would I think sufficient? I did not wish to go just then into the detail, as I judged, from Madgett's discourse, that the Minister's plan was on a smaller scale than mine, and I did not desire to shock him too much in the outset. I therefore took advantage of my bad French, and mentioned that I doubted my being able sufficiently to explain myself in conversation, but that he would find my opinions at length in the two memorials * I had prepared; and when he had considered them, I hoped he would allow me to wait on him, and explain any

* See Appendix.

point which might not be sufficiently clear. He then proceeded to give me his own ideas, which were, as I suspected, upon a small scale. He said he understood Ireland was very populous and the people warlike, so as soon to be made soldiers, and that they were already in some degree armed. I answered, not so much as to be calculated upon in estimating the quantity of arms wanted, as most of the guns which they had were but fowling-pieces. He then said, he knew they had no artillery nor cannoniers, and that, consequently, it would be necessary to supply them with both; that field-pieces would be sufficient, as we had no strong places; that we should have thirty pieces of cannon, (*une trentaine,*) half eight-pounders, and half sixteen-pounders, properly manned and officered, and twenty thousand stand of arms. I interrupted him, to say, twenty thousand *at least,* as the only limitation to the numbers we could raise would be the quantity of arms we might have to put into their hands. He then went on to say, that these should be landed near Belfast, where he supposed they would be most likely to meet with early support. I answered, " Certainly, as that province was the most populous and warlike in the kingdom." He then produced a map of Ireland, and we looked over it together. I took this advantage to slide in some of my own ideas, by saying that if we were able to begin in considerable force, we should commence as near the capital as possible, the possession of which, if once obtained, would, I thought, decide the whole business; but, if we began with a smaller force, we should commence as near Belfast as we could, and then push forward, so as to secure the mountains of Mourne and the Fews, by means of which and of Lough Erne, we could cover the entire province of Ulster, and maintain ourselves until we had collected our friends in sufficient force to penetrate to Dublin. He liked my plan extremely, which certainly appears to be the only feasible one, in case of a small force being landed. He then mentioned the Irishmen serving in the British navy, and asked me what I thought of sending proper persons amongst them to insinuate the duty they owed to their country; and whether, in such case, they would act against us or not? This is Madgett's scheme; and, if it is not followed by very different measures, is nonsense. I answered, that undoubtedly the measure was a good one, if accompanied properly; but, to give it full effect, it was absolutely necessary there should be a government established in Ireland, for reasons which he would find detailed in my memorials, and of which I gave him an imperfect abstract. I think he seemed satisfied on that head. I added, that great caution ought to be used in sending these persons, lest it might take wind in some shape, and alarm the British Government. On the whole, I fancy the scheme of sending apostles among the Irish seamen will be given up; for, certainly, if there be once a government established in Ireland, it would, in my mind, be unnecessary, and if there be not, it would be useless. The Minister then repeated, in the plainest and most unequivocal terms, his former assurances, as well of his personal support as of the positive and serious determination of the Executive Directory to take up the business of Ireland in the strongest manner that circumstances would possibly admit. He added, that he hoped if France made the sacrifices she was inclined to do of men and money, to enable us to establish our freedom, and even delayed to make peace on our account, we should, in return, manifest more gratitude and principle than other nations had done in similar cases; and desired me, as to any part of the business whose preparations might rest with me, not to lose a minute. He also desired me to press Madgett to expedite the translations as much as possible, and, on the whole, certainly appeared to be nearly as earnest and anxious in the business as myself. I then took my leave. The result of this conversation, the principal circumstances of which I have substantially related, is, that the Executive Directory at present are determined to take us up, but on a small scale; that they will give us thirty pieces of cannon, properly manned, and twenty thousand stand of arms, with some money, of course, to begin with; but I did not collect from the Minister that they had an idea of any definite number of troops, at least he mentioned none, and I did not press him on that head, as I wish they should first read and consider my memorials; perhaps what is said in them may induce them to reconsider the subject; and, if so, I shall have done a most important service both to France and Ireland. If they act on the plan mentioned to me by De la Croix, as above related, I, for one, am ready and willing, most cheerfully, to stake my life on the hazard: but the measure is against my judgment; not from any doubt of the people at large, but from the difficulty, perhaps the impossibility, of having a proper organized Government. Do I say, therefore, that the measure ought not to be attempted on the present scale? By no means: I am clear it ought. As to France, it is but the risk of the outfit, which is nothing; and, as to Ireland, she is in that situation that she ought to hazard every thing on the chance of bettering her condition. I speak of the people at large, and not of the aristocracy. For one, then, I am decided. We have, at all events, the strength of numbers, and if our lever be too short, we must only apply the greater power. If the landing be effected on the present plan, we must instantly have recourse to the strongest revolutionary measures, and put, if necessary, man, woman, and child, money, horses, and arms, stores and provisions, in requisition: "The King shall eat, though all mankind be starved." No consideration must be permitted to stand a moment against the establishment of our independence. I do not wish for all this, if it can be avoided, but liberty must be purchased at any price; so "Lay on Macduff, and damned be he who first cries—Hold, enough!" We must strike the ball hard, and take the chance of the tables. I think P. P. will shine in the character of a "youth of the first requisition." I should have observed, that in the course of the conversation, De la Croix mentioned that, on the receipt of Adet's letter enclosing the memorial which I delivered to him on my arrival in Philadelphia in August last, he had written to him that the subject was too important to be discussed at 3,000 miles distance, and, therefore, desired I should come over. I was very glad to hear this, and answered, I was happy to have anticipated his desire. So, it seems, I was written for, as Madgett said. I should be glad to see that memorial now, for I remember it was written in the burning summer of Pennsylvania, when my head was extremely deranged by the heat. Bad as I dare say it was, it caught the attention of people here. Well—vanity again!

27. At work at my memorial, which begins to look very spruce on paper.

28. Went to Monroe's about my passport, and had an hour's conversation with him; I like him very much; he speaks like a sincere republican; he praises the Executive Directory to the skies, and Charles De la Croix;—all for the better. Carnot, he tells me, is a military man, and one of the first engineers of Europe. (*Vide* my observation touching his organizing about Cork harbour.) Le Tourneur is also a military man, so that, with Barras, there are three soldiers in the *Directoire*. I am very glad of that.

29. Finished my second memorial, and delivered it to Madgett for translation. Madgett has the slowness of age, and at present of the gout, about him. Judge! O ye Gods, how that suits with my

impatience! Well, the Minister gave me directions to expedite him, so, please God, I will levee him at least once a day. We have not a minute to spare, for in a little time the channel fleet will probably be at sea, and the camps formed in Ireland, and of course the Government there will have the advantage of a force ready concentred and prepared to act instantly, and perhaps they may happen to take the wrong side, which would be very bad. (Mem. To *insense* Carnot on this head.) I must allow two or three days for translation, and two or three more for reflection on the subject of my memorials, before I go again to the Luxembourg. It is very singular! In cool blood, I can hardly frame a single sentence in French, and yet, both with Carnot and De la Croix I run on without the least difficulty. I screw my mind up, and I do not know how it is, but expressions flow upon me; I dare say I give them abundance of bad language, but no matter for that; they understand me, and that is the main point. I have now six days before me, and nothing to do. Huzza! Dine every day at Beauvillier's for about half a crown, including a bottle of choice Burgundy, which I finish regularly. Beauvillier has a dead bargain of me for *water;* I do not think I consume a spoonful in a week. A bottle of Burgundy is too much, and I resolve every morning regularly to drink but the half, and every evening regularly I break my resolution. I wish I had P. P. to drink the other half, and then perhaps I should live more soberly. Oh Lord! Oh

Lord! Soberly! Yes, we should be a sober pair; patriots, as Matty says. Well, "It is the squire's custom every afternoon, as soon as he is drunk," to begin thinking of his wife and family. I have, to be sure, sometimes most delightful reveries. If I succeed in my business here, and ever return to Ireland, and am not knocked on the head, there will not be on earth so happy a circle, as round my fireside. Well, huzza! "I hope to see a battle yet before I die." The French have an abominable custom of adulterating their Burgundy with water. (Mem. Mr. Nisby's opinion thereon.) I cannot but respect the generous indignation which P. P. would feel at such a vile deterioration of that noble liquor, and the glorious example he would hold up for their imitation. He would teach them how, and in what quantities, generous Burgundy ought to be drunk; I would gladly pay his reckoning to-day *en numeraire*, which would be no small sum, for the pleasure of his company. Well, "'tis but in vain!" I think it right for my credit to mention, that all these wise reflections are written before dinner. So now I will go to Beauvilliers'. (Sings, "When generous wine," &c.)

## March 1796.

1. This day I got an English newspaper from Madgett, dated the 2d of last month, in which there is a paragraph alluding to the death of "the late unfortunate Major Sweetman," in a duel. I do not think I ever received such a shock in my life!

Good God! if it should be my friend! The only chance I have is, that there may be another person of that name; but I fear the worst. I had the sincerest and most affectionate regard for him; a better and a braver heart blood never warmed; I have passed some of the pleasantest hours of my life in his society. If he be gone, my loss is unspeakable, but his country will have a much severer one; he was a sincere Irishman, and if ever an exertion was to be made for our emancipation, he would have been in the very foremost rank; I had counted upon his military talents, and had amused myself often in making him a General; poor fellow! If he be gone, there is a chasm in my short list of friends, that I shall not find it easy to fill. After all, it may be another, but I fear, I fear. I cannot bear to think of it.

6. I have not had spirits, since the news of poor Sweetman's death, to go on with my memorandums. As it happens, I have no serious business; and I am glad of it, for my mind has been a good deal engaged on that subject. It seems the quarrel arose about treading on a lady's gown, in coming out of the opera;—a worthy cause for two brave men to fight about! They fought at four yards' distance, which was Sweetman's choice: they were both desperately wounded, but Captain Watson (an Irishman also) is likely to recover; my poor friend is gone. When he received the shot, which went through his body, he cried out to Watson, "Are you wounded?" —"Yes," replied the other, "I believe mortally."—

"And so am I," replied Sweetman, instantly falling. I certainly did not think I could have been so much affected on his account, as I have been. Independently of my personal regard for him, I reckoned much upon his assistance, in case of the French Government affording us any aid. His courage, his eloquence, his popular talents, his sincere affection for his country, would have made him eminently serviceable: all that is now lost; we must supply his place as we can. I will write no more about him, but shall ever remember him with the most sincere regret.

Madgett has not yet finished the translation; hell! hell! However he tells me he has written to the Minister on the subject of Bournonville's being appointed to the command, in case the expedition takes place. I have been reading the report of Camus, and it has satisfied me that I could not have wished for a General fitter for the station; I hope we may get him. One thing I see: Madgett must appear to do every thing himself; he pleases himself with the idea that it was he who thought of Bournonville. I am sure, at present, I care little who has the credit of proposing any measure, provided the business be done; but the truth and fact is, that it was I who mentioned him. Madgett has lost two or three days in hunting for maps of Ireland; certainly maps are indispensable, but not in this stage of the business. He had been much better employed in translating; his slowness provokes me excessively, but I keep it all to myself: this day, however, he promises me he will have finished, and given in my last memorial to the Minister; if he does, I will see De la Croix the day after to-morrow, and Carnot, if possible, the day after that. In the mean time I am idle. I have been at the Museum, where there is, I suppose, the first collection of paintings in the world; all France and Flanders have been ransacked to furnish it. It is a school where the artists are permitted to go and copy the best works of the best masters. The day I called, it was not open to the public, but when the porter perceived I was a foreigner, he admitted me directly; it would not be so in England. I like the works of Guido best: there are some portraits incomparably executed by Vandyke, Rubens, Rembrandt, and Raphael; but the Magdalen of Le Brun is, in my mind, worth the whole collection. I never saw any thing in the way of painting that came near to it; I am no artist, but it requires no previous instruction to be struck with the numberless beauties of this most enchanting picture: it is a production of consummate genius. I have been likewise at the Hotel des Invalides, where I had the pleasure of seeing the veterans at their dinner: they are very well accommodated, and it was a spectacle which interested me much. It put me in mind of the Royal Hospital and my old friend Captain Russell; and that brought a thousand other ideas to my mind. Well, I hope I shall get back to Ireland yet. *Utinam.*

7. Spent this day with Dupetit Thouars, an ex-lieutenant of the marine, who came over with me in

the Jersey, and Roussillon, an ex-lieutenant also; they are both of the *ci-devant noblesse*. Dupetit Thouars is a great original: he has a good deal of talent, and still more humour, and is the most complete practical philosopher I ever saw; nothing can ruffle him; but it is his *temperament*. Roussillon is a young man of very elegant manners, and adversity, I am sure, has improved him. It is a pity they should be aristocrats; yet I can hardly be angry with them. Aristocracy has been most terribly humbled in France, and this reverse of fortune is too much for them. It is not only their own downfall, but the exultation of others whom they were accustomed to despise, which mortifies them. But when I come to analyse their complaints, there is so much fanciful grievance mixed with severe actual suffering, that it abates a good deal of the compassion I should otherwise feel for them; and I must add, that much of what they regret they are deprived of most meritoriously, and many of the pleasures they have lost were pleasures of the most depraved luxury; splendid, indeed, but abominably vicious. It is not fair, however, to judge too hardly of them, now they are down; but I confess I should be most sincerely sorry to be a witness of their resurrection: there is, however, no great danger of that, and they seem to be sufficiently sensible of it. They had quitted the service some time back, I dare say in great disdain, and are now suing unsuccessfully to be readmitted. I cannot blame the Republic for being doubtful of the ancient marine, since the affair at Toulon. Apropos! Roussillon tells me that Trogoff, the admiral who betrayed the French fleet, and delivered it into the hands of Lord Hood, died in an hospital at Leghorn, where the English generously paid *one shilling* a day for his maintenance. The scoundrel! it was just one shilling too much;—and Dumourier, an exile on the face of the earth, ordered to quit England in six hours after his arrival, and expelled from Brabant by the Emperor, whom he had served, or endeavoured to serve, by his treachery. If men had common sense, (not to say common honesty,) they would not be traitors to their country, with such examples before their eyes. But I am preaching about aristocracy, and God knows what! To return: I pity sincerely my two *ci-devant* lieutenants, for "Cot knows I have had afflictions and trouples enough upon my own pack, and as for a gentleman in distress, I lofe him as I lofe my own powels." We spent the day in seeing sights, viz.—the Pantheon, which will be most superb when it is finished, but far inferior to St. Paul's, either in size or magnificence. We descended into the catacombs, where were the cenotaphs of Voltaire, Rousseau, and (what interested me much more) of Dampierre, who was killed at Famars. Certainly nothing can be imagined more likely to create a great spirit in a nation than a depository of this kind, sacred to every thing that is sublime, illustrious, and patriotic. The French have, however, a little overshot the mark; for they have had occasion already to displace two, at least, of their mighty dead;—I mean Marat, whom I believe to have been a sincere enthusiast, incapable of feeling or remorse, and Mirabeau, whom I look upon to have been a most consummate scoundrel. If we have a Republic in Ireland, we must build a Pantheon; but we must not, like the French, be in too great a hurry to people it. We have already a few to begin with: Roger O'Moore, Molyneux, Swift, and Dr. Lucas, all good Irishmen. Mounted to the top of the Pantheon, from whence we could see all Paris, as in a ground-plan, together with the country for several leagues round. It was the most singular spectacle I had ever witnessed. Went from thence to the Botanic Garden, where there was not much vegetation to be seen, there being a foot deep of snow upon the ground: walked, however, through the green-houses, where there is a vast collection of curious exotics. I felt my ancient propensities begin to revive, for I love botany, though I do not understand it. It reminded me of my walks round Chateauboue,* with my dearest love and our little babies, when I used to be gathering my *vetches*. Well, I hope I shall be there yet before I die. Crossed the Seine, and saw the Place Royale, formerly the principal square of Paris, and built by Richelieu; his hotel is on one side of the quadrangle: it is now a park of artillery for the Republic, and filled with cannon. Saw the spot where the Bastille once stood, and where there is now a statue of Liberty. Traversed that great ly-

* My father's cottage in county Kildare.—*Author*.

ceum of French politics, the Faubourg St. Antoine; arrived at the Temple, where Louis the XVIth was imprisoned, from whence Marie Antoinette was led to execution, and where Louis the XVIIth (if I may so call him) died. Nothing can be imagined more gloomy than the appearance of this prison. It made me melancholy to look at it.

8. Went to Madgett, in consequence of a report which I saw in the papers relative to a general peace. He assures me there is nothing in it:—a peace would ruin all. He tells me also that he finished and delivered yesterday my second memorial to the Minister, who had read the first with great attention, and was extremely edified thereby, as may well be imagined. Madgett tells me that De la Croix assures him, the Executive Directory are determined on the measure; that is to say, on the principle of it. All that is very good; but, please God, I will have it from the Minister's own mouth; after which I will indulge myself with a short interview with Carnot. I have not seen him since February 24th, a fortnight ago; but that has not been my fault, and the time has been employed in writing, copying, and translating my memorials. The day after to-morrow I will go to the Minister, and the day after that to the Luxembourg. Madgett tells me Bournonville is appointed to the command of the army in Holland. That is bad; nevertheless, from the idea I have formed of his character, I should hope that, if he was properly *insensed* on the subject of Irish affairs, he would prefer that

command, supposing the expedition to be once undertaken. There would be glory; and, if we succeeded, which I cannot for a moment doubt, the Irish are a generous people, even to a fault, and would reward his services most liberally. Desired Madgett, if he had an opportunity, and could do it with security as to secrecy, to explain all this to Bournonville. Dined at the Restaurateur, with Roussillon, whom I like very much. In the evening, the Theatre Italien.

9, 10. Strolling about: the Museum again, and the inimitable Magdalen of Le Brun; spent near an hour looking at it.

11. Went to the Minister, De la Croix, and had a long conversation. He began by saying, that he had read my two memorials carefully, and that I seemed to insist on a considerable force, as necessary to the success of the measure; that, as to that, there were considerable difficulties to be surmounted, arising from the superiority of the English fleet. That, as to 20,000 men, they could not possibly be transported, unless the French were masters of the channel, in which case they could as easily send 40,000, or 60,000, and march at once to London. (N. B. In this De la Croix is much mistaken. It would be, in my mind, just as impossible for France to conquer England, as for England to conquer France. He does not know what it is to carry on war in a country where every man's hand is against you, and yet his own country might have given him a lesson; however, it was not my business

to contest the point with him, so I let him go on.) As to 20,000 men, it was thus out of the question. As to 5000, there would be great difficulties: they would require, for example, 20 ships to convey them; it would not be easy to equip 20 sail in a French port, without the English having some notice; and, in that case, they would instantly block up the port with a force double to any that could be sent against them. To this I answered, that I was but too sensible of the difficulty he mentioned; that, however, all great enterprises were attended with great difficulties; and I besought him to consider the magnitude of the object. That as to 5000, when I mentioned that number, it was not that I thought it necessary for the people at large, but for those men of some property, whose assistance was so essential in framing a government in Ireland without loss of time, and who might be deterred from coming forward at first, if they saw but an inconsiderable force to support them; that I begged leave to refer to my second memorial, where he would find my reasons on this subject detailed at length; that I had written those memorials under a strong sense of duty, not with a view to flatter or mislead him, or to say what might be agreeable to the French Government; but to give them such information as I thought essential for them to know: that, as to the truth of the facts contained in them, I was willing to stake my head on their accuracy.—He answered, he had no doubt as to that; that he saw as well as I the convenience of an immediate government, but was it not feasible on a smaller scale than I had mentioned? For example, if they gave us a General of established reputation, an Etat Major, thirty pieces of artillery, with cannoniers, and 20,000 stand of arms, would not the people join them, and, if so, might we not call the clubs that I had mentioned in my memorials, (meaning the Catholic Committee and the United Irishmen of Belfast) and frame of them a provisory government, until the national convention could be organized?—I replied, that, as to the people joining them, I never had the least doubt; that my only fear was lest the men who composed the clubs of which he spoke, might be at first backward, from a doubt of the sufficiency of the force; that I hoped they would act with spirit and as became them, but that I could not venture to commit my credit with him on any fact of the certainty of which I was not positively convinced. "Well, then," continued he, "supposing your patriots should not act at first with spirit; you say you are sure of the people. In that case, you must only choose delegates from the army, and let them act provisorily, until you have acquired such a consistency as will give courage to the men of whom you make mention." I answered, that, by those means, we might undoubtedly act with success; that a sort of military government was not, however, what I should prefer to commence with, if I saw any other, but that the necessity of the case must justify us in adopting so strong a measure in the first instance.* I added, that the means which he then mentioned undoubtedly weakened my argument as to the necessity of numbers, considerably. He then said, that from Madgett's representations, he had been induced to think that men were not at all wanting. I answered, that was very compatible with my theory, for that certainly, if there were any idea of national resistance, 5000 might be said to be no force at all for a conquest. I then shifted the discourse by observing that, as to the embarkation, on whatever scale it was made, it might be worth consideration whether it could not be best effected from Holland: that the harbours of that country were, I believed, less closely watched than the French, and that at any rate England had no port for ships of war to the northward of Portsmouth; so that, even if she had a fleet off the coasts of Holland, it must return occasionally to refit, and, during one of these intervals, the expedition might take place. He asked me, " Are you sure England has no port northward of Portsmouth?" I answered " certainly."— " Not in Scotland?" inquired he. I referred him to

* N.B. In this I lied a little, for my wishes are in favour of a very strong, or, in other words, a military government, in the outset; and if I had any share or influence in such government, I think I would not abuse it; but I see the handle it might give to demagogues, if we had any such among us. It is unnecessary here to write an essay on the subject; but the result of my meditations is, that the advantages, all circumstances considered, outweigh the inconveniences and hazard; and I, for one, am ready to take my share of the danger and the responsibility: I was therefore glad when De la Croix proposed the measure.— *Author.*

the map. (I was a little surprised he did not know this.) This brought on the old subject of debauching the Irish seamen in the British navy, which seems a favourite scheme of De la Croix, and is, in my mind, flat nonsense. He questioned me as before, whether by preparing a few of them and suffering them to escape, they might not rouse the patriotism of the Irish seamen, and cause a powerful revulsion in the navy of England. I answered, as I had done already, that the measure was undoubtedly good, if properly followed up, at the same time that there was great hazard of alarming the British Government; that he would find my plan on the subject in my second memorial, where he would see that an Irish government was, in my mind, an indispensable requisite; that I did not build on the patriotism of the Irish seamen, but on their passions and interests; that we could offer them the whole English commerce as a bribe, whilst England had nothing to oppose in return but the mere force of discipline; and I pressed this as strongly on the Minister as my execrable French would permit. He then mentioned that it would be necessary to send proper persons to Ireland to give notice to the people there of what was intended. I answered, one person was sufficient. He asked me, " O, you know one Ducket?" (the fellow who pulled out the English newspaper to decoy me.) I answered, I knew nothing at all about him. He then asked me, " O, you know one Simon, a priest?" I answered, I had some recollection of one Fitzsimon, a priest, in Ireland, but that I was not personally acquainted with him. I also added that I had a strong objection to letting priests into the business at all; that most of them were enemies to the French Revolution, and, if it were possible to find a military man, he would be the properest person; the more so, as it would encourage those to whom he might address himself, by showing that the French Government were serious in their intentions. He then said he would look out for such a person. I took this occasion to observe, that there was not an hour to lose, that the season was approaching fast when the British channel fleet would be at sea, and the various encampments formed in Ireland, which generally took place about the middle of May or beginning of June. He said, the necessary preparations, on the smallest scale, could not be ready sooner than one month. I replied, that one month would be time enough; but added again, that there was not a minute to lose. I then took my leave, having been closeted nearly an hour and a half.—On the whole, I do not much glory in this day's conversation. If I have not lost confidence, I certainly have not gained any. I see the Minister is rooted in his narrow scheme, and I am sorry for it. Perhaps imperious circumstances will not permit him to do otherwise; but, if the French Government have the power effectually to assist us, and do not, they are miserable politicians. It is now one hundred and three years since Lewis XIV. neglected a similar opportunity of separating Ireland from England, and France has had reason to lament it ever since. He, too, went upon the short-sighted policy of merely embarrassing England, and leaving Ireland to shift as she might. I hope the Republic will act on nobler motives, and with more extended views. At all events, I have done my duty in submitting the truth to them, and I shall continue so to do, and to press it upon them in all possible modes that I can compass. If they will give us 5000 men, so ;—if not, " Let the sheriff enter; if I become not the gallows as well as another, a plague o' my bringing up."

Seriously. I would attempt it with *one hundred* men. My life is of little consequence, and I should hope not to lose it neither. " Please God, the dogs shall not have my poor blood to lick." In that case, as I have pleasantly said already, if our lever be short, we must apply the greater power. Requisition! Requisition! Our independence must be had at all hazards. If the men of property will not support us, they must fall; we can support ourselves by the aid of that numerous and respectable class of the community, *the men of no property.*

12. Called on Madgett. He tells me that the business is going forward, but that the French Government is in the greatest difficulty from want of money; that the Executive Directory was, within these few days, on the point of resigning, and that they had signified to the Legislature that they would do so, if they were not properly supported. I should be sincerely sorry if this were the case, as well for the sake of France as of Ireland, for I believe they

are both able and honest. Madgett told me farther, that he expected we were on the eve of some considerable change, not of measures, but of men; that the party who wanted to come in were throwing difficulties in the way of the present administration, in order to force them to resign; that if the change took place, it would not extend to the Directors, but only to the Ministers; that with regard to the affairs of Ireland, these would be bettered rather than injured by the alteration; that it was the jacobin party who expected to come in,—not the terrorists, but the true original jacobins who had begun the Revolution; that if they were in power, he was sure they would give us 10,000 men; that, however, as to Bournonville, he was obnoxious to them, and of course would not be appointed to the command. If there is to be any change, I confess I should be glad the jacobins were to come again into play, for I think a little more energy just now would do the French Government no harm. On the whole, I am not much delighted with our present prospects.

13. Went, as is my custom, to the opera. *Serment de la Liberté.* The scene represented the Camp de Mars on the day of the confederation. As usual, the spectacle all military. In the procession, was a band of young men in regimentals, but without arms. At a particular verse of the hymn which was chanted before the altar of liberty, they approached the grenadiers, who were under arms, and received from them their firelocks, which they shouldered, and took their places in the line; several evolutions,

and the manual exercise, were then performed by the whole body, for, as I have already remarked, these are the ballets of the French nation at present. At the conclusion, a band of beautiful young women, equal in number to the young men, entered, carrying drawn sabres in their hands, and ranged themselves on one side of the stage; the young men being drawn up in a line on the other. Each of the youths advanced in his turn to the centre of the stage, when he was met by his mistress, who presented him with his sabre with one hand, and with the other pointed to the altar of liberty; the youth kissed the hilt of the sabre, and returned it to the scabbard; they then fell back into their places, and were succeeded by the next pair, until all had received their arms and saluted their mistresses. I do not know what Mr. Burke may think, but I humbly conceive from the effect all this had on the audience, that the age of chivalry is not gone in France. I can imagine nothing more suited to strike the imagination of a young Frenchman than such a spectacle as this; and indeed, though I am no Frenchman, nor at present over and above young, it affected me extremely. I am sure nothing on earth has such an influence on me as my wife's opinion; every action of my life has a reference more or less to that, and in the very business wherein I am now engaged, if I succeed, I look for, and shall find the reward dearest to my heart, in her commendation. It is inconceivable, (I lie, I lie, it is not at all inconceivable) the effect which the admiration or contempt of a

woman has on the spirit of a man. Hector, when he is balancing in his mind whether he shall stand or fly before Achilles, is determined by the consideration of what the Trojan ladies will say of him :—
" Troy's proud dames, whose garments sweep the ground." From hence I infer that human nature is pretty much now what it was 3,000 years ago, and that Homer knew it well, as did Shakspeare, and Fielding also, who has hit off the same point admirably, when Lady Bellaston is working upon Lord Fellamar. To return, I owe so much to my wife for her incomparable behaviour on ten thousand different occasions, that I feel myself bound irresistibly to make every effort to place her and her dear little babies in a situation in some degree worthy of her merit, and suitable to my sense of it. I am not without ambition or vanity, God knows ! I love fame, and I suppose I should like power; but I declare here most solemnly, that I prefer my wife's commendations to those of the whole world. Well, if I succeed here, I shall stand on high ground, and I must be allowed to say, I shall deserve it, and then she will be proud of me, as I am of her, and with that sentiment, I conclude this day's journal.

14. Went this day to the Luxembourg; I have the luck of going on the days that Carnot gives audience, and of course is most occupied; waited, however, to the last, when only one person remained besides myself. Carnot then called me over, and said, " You are an Irishman." I answered I was; " Then," said he, " here is almost a countryman of

yours, who speaks English perfectly. He has the confidence of Government; go with him and explain yourself without reserve." I did not much like this referring me over; however, there was no remedy: so I made my bow, and followed my new lover to his hotel. He told me on the way that he was General Clarke;* that his father was an Irishman; that he had himself been in Ireland, and had many relations in that country; he added, (God forgive him if he exaggerated,) that all the military arrangements of the Republic passed through his hands, and in short, gave me to understand that he was at the head of the War Department. By this time, we arrived at the hotel where he kept his bureau, and I observed in passing through the office to his cabinet, an immense number of boxes labelled, *Armée du Nord, Armée des Pyrenées, Armée du Rhin*, &c. &c. so that I was pretty well satisfied that I was in the right track. When we entered the cabinet I told him in three words who and what I was, and then proceeded to detail, at considerable length, all I knew on the state of Ireland, which, as it is substantially contained in my two memorials (to which I referred him, and now refer the reader,) I need not here recapitulate. This took up a considerable time—I suppose an hour and a half. He then began to interrogate me on some of the heads, in a manner which showed me

---

* Since notorious, both under the Imperial and restored Royal Governments, as Duke of Feltre, and Minister of War.

that he was utterly unacquainted with the present state of affairs in Ireland, and particularly with the great internal changes which have taken place there within the last three or four years, which, however, is no impeachment of his judgment or talents; there were, however, other points on which he was radically wrong. For example, he asked me, would not the aristocracy of Ireland, some of which he mentioned, as the Earl of Ormond, concur in the attempt to establish the independence of their country? — I answered: " Most certainly not;" and begged him to remember that if the attempt were made, it would be by the *people*, and the people only; that he should calculate on all the opposition that the Irish aristocracy could give; that the French Revolution, which had given courage to the people, had, in the same proportion, alarmed the aristocracy, who trembled for their titles and estates; that this alarm was diligently fomented by the British Minister, who had been able to persuade every man of property, that their only security was in supporting him implicitly in every measure calculated to oppose the progress of what were called French principles; that, consequently, in any system he might frame in his mind, he should lay down the utmost opposition of the aristocracy as an essential point. At the same time I added that, in case of a landing being effected in Ireland, their opposition would be of very little significance, as their conduct had been such as to give them no claim on the affections of the people; that their own tenants and dependants would, I was satisfied, desert them, and they would become just so many helpless individuals, devoid of power and influence.—He then mentioned that the Volunteer Convention in 1783 seemed to be an example against what I now advanced; the people then having acted through their leaders. I answered they certainly had, and as their leaders had betrayed them, that very convention was one reason why the people had for ever lost all confidence in what were called leaders. He then mentioned the confusion and bloodshed likely to result from a people such as I described, and he knew, the Irish to be breaking loose without proper heads to control and moderate their fury.— I answered it was but too true; that I saw as well as he, that, in the first explosion, it was likely many events would take place in their nature very shocking; that revolutions were not made without much individual suffering; that, however, in the present instance, supposing the worst, there would be a kind of retributive justice, as no body of men on earth were more tyrannical and oppressive in their nature than those who would be most likely to suffer in the event he alluded to; that I had often in my own mind, (and God knows the fact to be so,) lamented the necessity of our situation, but that Ireland was so circumstanced, that she had no alternative but unconditional submission to England, or a revolution, with a chance of all the concomitant sufferings; and that I was one of those who preferred difficulty, danger, and distress, to slavery, especially where I saw clearly there were no other means. " It is very true," replied he, "there is no making an *omelette*, without breaking of eggs." He still seemed, however, to have a leaning towards the co-operation of our aristocracy, which is flat nonsense. He asked me, was there no one man of that body that we could not make use of, and again mentioned, " for example, the Earl of Ormond?" I answered, " not one;" that as to Lord Ormond, he was a mere voluptuary, without a character of any kind, but that of a blockhead; that I did believe, speaking my own private opinion as an individual, that perhaps the Duke of Leinster might join the people, if the revolution was once begun, because I thought him a good Irishman; but that for this opinion, I had merely my own conjectures, and that, at any rate, if the beginning were once made, it would be of very little consequence what part any individual might take. I do not know how Fitzgibbon's name happened to come in here, but he asked me would it not be possible to make something of him? Any one who knows Ireland will readily believe that I did not find it easy to give a serious answer to this question. Yes, Fitzgibbon would be very likely, from his situation, his principles, his hopes and his fears, his property, and the general tenor of his conduct, to begin a *revolution* in Ireland! At last, I believe I satisfied Clarke on the subject of the support to be expected from our aristocracy. He then asked me what I thought the revolution, if begun, would terminate in? I answered, undoubtedly, as I thought, in a Republic allied to France. He proceeded to inquire what security I could give, that in twenty years after our independence, we might not be found engaged as an ally of England against France? I thought the observation a very foolish one, and only answered that I could not venture to foretell what the combination of events for twenty years might produce; but that, in the present posture of affairs, there were few things which presented themselves to my view under a more improbable shape. He then came to the influence of the Catholic clergy over the minds of the people, and the apprehension that they might warp them against France. I assured him, as the fact is, that it was much more likely that France would turn the people against the clergy; that within these last few years, that is to say, since the French Revolution, an astonishing change, with regard to the influence of the priests, had taken place in Ireland. I mentioned to him the conduct of that body pending the Catholic business, and how much and how justly they had lost character on that account. I told him the anecdote of the Pope's legate, (who is also Archbishop of Dublin,) being superseded in the actual management of his own chapel; of his endeavouring to prevent a political meeting therein, and of his being forced to submit and attend the meeting himself; but, particularly, I mentioned the circumstance of the clergy excommunicating all Defenders, and even refusing the sacraments to some of the poor fellows *in articulo mortis*, which to a Catholic is a very serious affair, and all to no purpose. This last circumstance seemed to strike him a good deal. He then said that I was not to augur any thing either way, from what had passed on that day; he would read and consider my memorials very attentively, but I must see that a business of such magnitude could not be discussed in one conversation, and that the first; that I was not, however, to be discouraged because he did not at present communicate with me more openly. I answered I understood all that; that undoubtedly, on this occasion, it was my turn to speak, and his to hear, as I was not to get information, but to give it. I then fixed with him to return in six days, (on the 1st of Germinal,) and having requested him to get the original memorials, as he was perfect master of English and I could not answer for a translation which I had never seen, I took my leave.

I see clearly that all Clarke's ideas on Irish politics are at least thirty years behind those of the people, and I took pains to impress him with that conviction as delicately as I could. We should, according to his theory, have two blessed auxiliaries to begin with, the noblesse and the clergy. I hope, however, that I have beat him a little out of that nonsense, and that, when he reads the memorials in cool blood, he will be satisfied of its absurdity. By-the-by, my memorials I find have never been laid before the Executive; that is bad; I trust they are now in train. When I mentioned that De la Croix had referred me to Madgett, I found, with some little surprise, that Clarke did not know Madgett. To hear the latter speak, one would suppose it impossible such could be the case. This comes of being a stranger. I must grope my way here as well as I can. Carnot has positively referred me to Clarke, and if he be as confidential as he gives me to understand, I have no reason to complain; but suppose he is not, where is my remedy? and how am I to ascertain that fact? I know nobody here, of whom I can inquire. If I rest in the hands of subalterns, I risk the success of my plans, and act against my wishes and my judgment. If I go back to the principals, I risk the making an enemy of the subalterns, and there is no animal so mean, but has the power to do mischief. I would rather stick to Carnot, but what can I do when he has handed me over to Clarke? " Suffolk, what remedy?" At any rate, I must let things go on in the present track, until I see some other open, or until I conceive myself neglected. As yet, I certainly have no reason to complain. " A pize upon thee for a wicked La'yer, Tom Clarke," I would rather deal with your master, but that can't be for the present, and so " 'Tis but in vain," &c. We shall see what the first of Germinal will produce, and, in the mean time, I will, as Matty says, " let the world wag." It is unnecessary to observe that I only give the outlines of the various conversations related in these memorandums. There are a thousand collateral points, which it is impossible to detail. The general tenor of my discourse was grounded on the facts contained in my two memorials, which I endeavoured to state and support in the strongest manner I could, dwelling particularly on the Defenders, the Dissenters, the recent union between the sects, (which I mentioned as a circumstance of the last importance,) the probable consequences to the naval power of England, and the effects to be hoped for from the proclamations mentioned in my second memorial, which seemed to strike Clarke very forcibly; though he combated them at first, until I asked him how he would like to be an English Admiral leaving Portsmouth under the circumstances I had described? on which he submitted as became him. I do not detail all this, for in fact it would be amplifying my memorials. One thing I must observe here; though I told Carnot that I had been with the Minister, I never told the Minister I had been with Carnot. In like manner, Clarke knows I have seen Madgett, but Madgett does not know I have ever been at the Luxembourg. There is something like duplicity in this; if there be, my situation must excuse it. I am acting to the best of my judgment, and I have not a soul to advise with. P. P., P. P., what would I give that you were here to-day! Mem. Beauvilliers' Burgundy, &c.

15. Went to breakfast with Madgett, in consequence of a note which I received from him. Madgett in high spirits; tells me every thing is going on as well as possible; that our affair is before the Directory; that it is determined to give us 50,000 stand of arms, artillery for an army of that force, 672 cannoniers, and a demi-brigade, which he tells me is from 3,000 to 4,000 men; that the Minister

desires my opinion in writing as to the place of landing. All this is very good and precise. I told him with that force we must land near Belfast, and push on immediately to get possession of the Fews Mountains, which cover the province of Ulster, until we could raise and arm our forces; that, if possible, a second landing should be made in the Bay of Galway, which army should cover itself, as soon as possible, by the Shannon, breaking down most of the bridges, and fortifying the remainder; that we should thus begin with the command of one half of the nation, and that the most discontented part; that, as to the port of embarkation, which the Minister had also mentioned, I suggested some of the Dutch ports, for reasons which have already been explained. If, however, the Dutch ports were too strongly watched, we might go from any of the French harbours on the ocean, and coast round by the West of Ireland into the Loch of Belfast. Madgett reduced this to writing in French, and we went together to the Minister, where he delivered it to him before my eyes. Madgett tells me that Prieur de la Marne is in the secret, and has recommended and guarantee'd a Capuchin friar, of the name of Fitzsimons, to go to Ireland. I told Madgett I had the most violent dislike to letting any priest into the business at all. He said he did not like it neither; but that Prieur de la Marne had known this man for twenty years, and would stake his life on his honesty. I do not care for all that; I will give my opinion plump against his being sent. Madgett mentioned that the fellow had some notion of a resumption of the forfeited lands. That would be a pretty measure to begin with! Besides, he has been out of the country twenty or thirty years, and knows nothing about it, and I dare say hates a Presbyterian like the devil. No! No! If I can help it, he shan't go; if I can't, why I can't. I want a military man. I must see whoever is sent, I presume, and how can I commit the safety of my friends in Ireland to a man in whom I have no confidence myself? And, indeed, I have some doubts whether I have any right to commit the safety of any person but myself. However, the way that I answer that objection, is, that it is absolutely necessary; that I am acting by their own advice and direction, and with their concurrence; that I have not myself shrunk from any trouble, labour, or danger; that it is but just they should take their share, especially when it is essential for the success of the measure; and, finally, that I rely very much upon their discretion to avoid all unnecessary hazard, and conduct themselves properly through this arduous business. These reasons are with me of sufficient weight to decide me in giving the names of five or six men in Ireland, in order that, whoever is sent (if any one is sent by the French Government,) may see them. At the same time, I give my advice that the messenger see but one of them, and leave it to him to communicate with the others. And that one shall be P. P.: I will put him in the post of danger and honour, though I love him like a brother. I wish Ireland to come under obligations to the said P. P. And now I must observe that it is very odd, if the business be, as Madgett says, before the Directory, and so far advanced, that Clarke should know nothing about it. Carnot did not appear to me yesterday to have even seen my memorials, and I rather believe that to be the case. Madgett is much more sanguine than I am, for I preserve in all this business a phlegm which is truly admirable. I have resolved never to believe that the expedition will be undertaken until I see the troops on board, nor that it will succeed until I have slept one night under canvass in Ireland. Then I shall have hopes. At present, I keep my mind under a strict regimen, and, without affectation, I think it must be an extraordinary circumstance which would much elevate or depress me. All which is truly edifying and extremely philosophical. Madgett tells me that Rewbell is the member of the Directory who is the most sanguine and earnest in support of the measure. Well! the first of Germinal, I suppose, I shall know more of the matter. Clarke, after all, must be better authority than Madgett. One thing I see, that Madgett wishes to keep me out of sight as much as possible, which is very natural, and I am sure I am not angry with him for it. Nevertheless, I will smuggle an odd visit now and then to the Luxembourg, "just to see things a little." "Wheels within wheels!" "Business, business," says I, "Mr. Secretary, must be done." Wise memorandums. I had like to have forgotten: I have not neglected Mr. Wm. Browne's (my bro ther Matthew's) affair. Lamare has written to Guise by this day's post, on that subject, having received no answer to a letter which he wrote on the same head about a fortnight since. I wish the said Mr. Browne were here, for a vast multiplicity of reasons.

16. Blank. Dined alone in the Champs Elysées. A most delicious walk. The French know how to be happy (or at least gay) better than all the world besides. The Irish come near them, but the Irish all drink more or less, (except P. P., who never drinks,) and the French are very sober. I live very soberly at present, having retrenched my quantity of wine one half; I fear, however, that if I had the pleasure of P. P.'s company to-morrow, being St. Patrick's Day, we should, indeed, " take a sprig of watercresses with our bread." Yes! we should make a pretty sober meal of it. Oh, Lord! Oh, Lord!

17. St. Patrick's Day. Dined *alone* in the Champs Elysées. Sad! Sad!

18. Blank! Theatre in the evening.

19. Madgett called on me this morning to tell me the Directory have resolved to give us an entire brigade (viz. 8,000 men instead of 4,000). He told me, also, that the Minister had asked him whether I had ever been to the Directory, and that he had said he was sure I had not. (*Mem.* I rather believe that honesty is always the best policy in *every* affair, public and private; for though I am sure it was from the purest motives that I had not told Madgett

of my visits to the Luxembourg, yet I felt very awkward at the question.) I answered that, in consequence of the extreme anxiety which I felt for the success of the business, as well as in pursuance of the directions I had received to omit nothing likely to bring the state of Ireland before the French Government, I had thought it my duty to go, in person, to the Executive, and obtain, if possible, an audience; the more so, as Carnot, who is now one of the Directory, was well known by reputation in Ireland; and I was particularly charged, if possible, to find him out. Madgett seemed quite satisfied at this, and, having fixed to breakfast with him to-morrow, we parted.

20. Breakfast with Madgett. The Minister wants to know our plan of conduct, supposing the landing effected. This has been already detailed in my memorial, but it is necessary to go over the same ground again and again. "Put it to him in other words," viz. The Catholic Committee is already a complete representation of that body, and the Dissenters are so prepared that they can immediately choose delegates. That these two bodies, when joined, will represent, numerically, nine-tenths of the people, and, of course, under existing circumstances, must be the best Government that we can form at the moment. This Madgett reduced to writing, but I have no copy, which is of the less consequence, as the paper is only a paraphrase of part of my last memorial. Desired Madgett to explain to the Minister that my visit to the Luxem-

bourg was in consequence of positive directions I had to communicate with Carnot, whether in or out of power; that I had the highest respect for the Minister's talents and patriotism, and, if there was any irregularity in my applying to Carnot, it was merely an error in judgment, as he must be convinced that, circumstanced as I was, I could never dream of doing any thing which might be disagreeable to a person in his station, &c. I believe this will satisfy De la Croix; but I fancy, between friends, that Madgett, rather than the Minister, is a little piqued; for, with great sincerity, and, I am sure, an honest anxiety for the success of the measure, I can see a little desire in his mind of doing every thing himself; for which, as I have already said with a laudable magnanimity, I am not at all angry with him; nevertheless, I shall take the liberty, under the rose, to follow my own plan a little: I am not aware of having made a blunder yet, unless (which I do not think) my going to Carnot, without informing the Minister, was one. Took a delightful walk in the Champs Elysées, and dined alone, as usual, at a very retired Restaurateur's. I live here in Paris absolutely like a hermit.

21. Went by appointment (this being the 1st Germinal) to the Luxembourg, to General Clarke; "d——n it and rot it for me"—he has not yet got my memorials; only think how provoking. I told him I would make him a fair copy, as I had the rough draft by me. He answered it was unnecessary, as he had given in a memorandum, in writing,

to Carnot, to send for the originals, and would certainly have them before I could make the copy. We then went into the subject as before, but nothing new occurred. He asked me, as before, what form of Government I thought would be likely to take place in Ireland, in case of the separation being effected; adding that, as to France, though she would certainly prefer a Republic, yet her great object was the independence of Ireland under any form? I answered, I had no doubt whatever that, if we succeeded, we should establish a Republic; adding, that it was my own wish, as well as that of *all* the men with whom I co-operated. He then talked of the necessity of sending some person to Ireland to examine into the state of things there, adding, "you would not go yourself." I answered, certainly not; that, in the first place, I had already given in all the information I was possessed of, and for me to add any thing to that would be, in fact, only supporting my credit by my own declaration; that he would find, even in the English papers, and I was sure much more in the Irish, if he had them, sufficient evidence of the state of the country to support every word I had advanced, and evidence of the most unexceptionable nature, as it came out of the mouths of those who were interested to conceal it, and would conceal it, if they could; that for me to be found in Ireland now, would be a certain sacrifice of my life to no purpose; that, if the expedition was undertaken, I would go in any station; that I was not only ready and willing, but should most earnestly supplicate and entreat the French Government to permit me to take a part, even as a private volunteer with a firelock on my shoulder, and that I thought I could be of use to both countries. He answered, " as to that, there could be no difficulty or doubt on the part of the French Government." He then expressed his regret at the delay of the memorials, and assured me he would use all diligence in procuring them, and would not lose a moment after they came to his hands. I intreated him to consider that the season was now advancing fast when the Channel fleet would be at sea and the camps in Ireland formed, and, of course, that every hour was precious, which he admitted. I then took my leave, having fixed to return in five days, on the 6th Germinal. I apologized for pressing him thus, which I assured him I should not do in a business of my own private concern, and so we parted. And now is it not extremely provoking that, in a business of such magnitude, seven days have been lost? The papers are lying in the Minister's hands, ready and finished, and nothing to do but to send for them, yet they are not got. Well! if ever I get to be a Citizen Director, or a Citizen Minister, I hope I shall do better than that: I am in a rage;—hell! hell! " Fury, revenge, disdain, and indignation tear my swoln breast, whilst passions, like the winds, rise up to heaven, and put out all the stars!" As I have nothing to add more outrageous, I will here change the subject.

Went to see Othello; not translated, but only

*taken* from the English. Poor Shakspeare! I felt for him. The French tragedy is a pitiful performance, filled with false sentiment; the Moor whines most abominably, and Iago is a person of a very pretty morality: the author apologizes for softening the villany of the latter character, as well as for saving the life of Desdemona and substituting a happy termination in place of the sublime and terrible conclusion of the English tragedy, by saying that the humanity of the French nation, and their morality, would be shocked by such exhibitions! "Marry come up, indeed! People's ears are sometimes the nicest part about them." I admire a nation that will guillotine sixty people a day for months, (men, women, and children,) and cannot bear the catastrophe of a dramatic exhibition! Yet certainly the author knows best, and I have had occasion repeatedly to observe, that the French are more struck with any little incident of tenderness on the stage, a thousand times, than the English,— which is strange. In short, the French *are* a humane people when they are not mad, and I like them with all their faults, and the guillotine at the head of them, better, a thousand times, than the English. And I like the Irish better than either; and as no one can doubt my impartiality, I expect my opinion will be received with proper respect and deference by all whom it may concern. I have nothing to add. Upon farther recollection, I *have* something to add. In the course of the conversation, on my desiring Clarke to count upon all the opposition which the Irish aristocracy, whether Protestant or Catholic, could give, he said he believed I was in the right; for that, since he saw me last, he had read over a variety of memorials on the subject of Irish affairs, which had been given in to the French Government for forty years back, and they all supported my opinion as to that point. I answered, I was glad of it, but begged him not to build much on any papers beyond a very recent date; that the changes, even in France, were not much greater than in Ireland since 1789; that what was true of her ten or even seven years ago, was not true now; of which there could not be a stronger instance than this, that if the French had landed during the last war, the Dissenters, to a man, and even the Catholics, would have opposed them—but then France was under the yoke which she had since broken; that all the changes in the sentiments of the Irish people flowed from the Revolution in France, which they had watched very diligently, and that being the case, he would, I hope, find reason to believe that my opinion on the influence of the nobles and clergy was founded in fact. I then went on to observe that, about one hundred years ago, Louis the XIVth had an opportunity of separating Ireland from England, during the war between James II. and William III.; that, partly by his own miserable policy and partly by the interested views of his Minister, Louvois, he contented himself with feeding the war by little and little, until the opportunity was lost, and that France had reason to regret it ever since; for, if Ireland had been made independent then, the navy of England would never have grown to what it is at this day. He said " that was very true ;" and added, " that even in the last war, when the volunteers were in force, and a rupture between England and Ireland seemed likely, it was proposed in the French Council to offer assistance to Ireland, and overruled by the interest of Count De Vergennes, then Prime Minister, who received for that service a considerable bribe from England, and that he was informed of this by a principal agent in paying the money." So, it seems, we had a narrow escape of obtaining our independence fifteen years ago. It is better as it is, for then we were not united amongst ourselves, and I am not clear that the first use we should have made of our liberty would not have been to have begun cutting each other's throats: so out of evil comes good. I do not like this story of Vergennes, of the truth of which I do not doubt. How, if the devil should put it into any one's head here to serve us so this time! Pitt is as cunning as hell, and he has money enough, and we have nothing here but assignats: I do not like it at all. However, it is idle speculating on what I cannot prevent. I can answer for myself, at least: I will do my duty. But, to return: Clarke asked me, " had I thought of subsisting the French troops after the landing, in case the Executive decided in favour of the measure?" I answered, I had not thought in detail on the subject, but there was one infallible mode which presented itself, which was, requisition in kind of all things necessary: adding, that he might be sure, whoever wanted, the army should not want, and especially our allies, if we were so fortunate as to obtain their assistance. He asked me, "might not that disgust the people of property in Ireland? I answered, the revolution was not to be made for the people of property; but as to those of them who were our friends, the spirit of enthusiasm would induce them to much greater sacrifices; and as to those who were our enemies, it was fit that they should suffer: and I referred him, for a proof of what sacrifices the enthusiasm of a revolution would lead to, to his own experience of what had happened in France, and to what I knew had been the case in America, where, during the contest for their liberties, it was a scandal to enjoy the luxuries and almost the conveniences of life, insomuch that people of the first properties and situations went in old and tattered clothes. He admitted this, but observed that this enthusiasm would subside in time, as was already the case in France. I agreed with him; but observed, that I hoped our revolution, if attempted, would be completed long before the spirit of enthusiasm had cooled. I do not recollect any other circumstances material in our conversation.

22. I have worked this day like a horse. In the morning I called on Madgett to tell him that Carnot wanted the memorials, and begged him to expedite them. He boggled a good deal, and I got almost angry; however, I am growing so much of a states-

man, that I did not let him see it. It would be a most extraordinary thing, indeed, if one of the Executive Directory could not command a paper of this kind out of the pocket of Citizen Madgett. I resolved, however, not to contest the point, but quietly make a copy of the two memorials, and give them myself to Clarke. It is only the trouble, and I have nothing else to do, and it is very good business for me, and I do not understand people being idle and giving themselves airs, and wanting to make revolutions, whilst they are grumbling at the trouble of writing a few sheets of paper. I therefore dropped the business of the memorials, and Madgett then told me that he sets off to-morrow on a pilgrimage to root out the Irish prisoners of war, and especially Mr. Wm. Browne, who is to be sent to Ireland if he can be found out, or if he has not long since been discharged; that he means to go to Versailles, Compiegne, and Guise, and propagate the faith amongst the Irish soldiers and seamen. This is his favourite scheme, and is, in my mind, not to mince the matter, d——d nonsense. What are five hundred or one thousand Irishmen, more or less, to the success of the business? Nothing. And then there is the risk of the affair taking wind. I do not like it at all; but I surmise the real truth to be, that it is a small matter of job, (*à l'Irlandaise,*) and that there is some cash to be touched, &c. Madgett's scheme is just like my countryman's, who got on horseback in the packet, in order to make more haste. He is always hunting for maps, and then he thinks he is making revolutions. I believe he is very sincere in the business, but he does to be sure, at times, pester me confoundedly. With regard to Mr. *William Browne*, I wish to God, if he be still in France, that Madgett may be able to find him. And yet I dread his going to Ireland. If he be caught there, his life is gone; and, though I am willing to hazard my own, I have some doubts as to his. If Madgett proposes it to him, he will go, *bon gré, mal gré.* Well, let him! If he escapes, and Ireland is freed, she will reward him, and he will deserve it. He would, certainly, be the fittest person to go from hence, as he is known to all my confidential friends; and I could communicate with him, and he with them, much better than any stranger whatsoever. On the whole, if he is found, he must go, and I hope God Almighty will protect him, poor fellow! for I love him most affectionately. Perhaps, whilst I am writing this, he may be at Princeton, with Matty and the children. I have sent one brother already to Ireland on this business. It is pretty early to entrust a matter of high treason to a boy of fourteen. However, I have no doubt of him; and, if we succeed, I hope to see him yet a flag officer in the Irish navy. Well, I have made great sacrifices in this business. But, to return. Madgett tells me that the Minister is quite satisfied as to my having seen Carnot, and that he would be very glad if I would take an opportunity to insinuate artfully to him that Prieur de la Marne would be a very acceptable person in Ireland, (which I dare say he would, as his name is well known there,) and which

I may fairly do, as I am here the representative of the Irish people; so I am accredited. I will certainly mention Prieur to Carnot, as the Minister desires it; and I recollect Rowan told me in Philadelphia that when he was leaving Brest on his way to Paris, after his escape from Ireland, Prieur, who was then Deputy on Mission, shook hands with him, observing that he hoped they should land in Ireland together. It is not impossible that they may meet there. So, I am to become an *intrigant*, I find, and to procure appointments for ex-deputies and I know not what. " Hey day, what doings, what doings are here !" It is very laughable to think of the Minister of Foreign Affairs desiring me to recommend a member of the National Convention to the Executive Directory of France. Having done with Madgett, I returned home, and set doggedly to copying my two memorials; finished the first, and made a practicable breach in the second ; then wrote the eight foregoing pages in my journal, and now it is ten o'clock at night, and I am as tired as a dog, and my fingers are cramped, and I cannot see out of my eyes. Tomorrow I will finish my second memorial ; I expect time enough to go to the Luxembourg and give it either to Carnot or Clarke. " Business, business, said I, Mr. Secretary, must be done." I have quoted that once already, but a good thing cannot be done too often, and it is a choice quotation, and I caught it from P. P., who quotes better than any body, except my dearest love. I am but a fool to them, only I make sometimes a lucky hit. Oh Lord ! Oh Lord !

what wise memorandums I am making, and I am as tired as a devil, for I have written nine hours to-day, which is more than I ever did in my life. " What do I not suffer, O Athenians, that you may speak well of me?" Pretty and modest, comparing myself by craft to Alexander the Great! Well, the vanity of some people is most unaccountable! When I get into this track of witty and facetious soliloquy, I know not how to leave off, for I always think I am chatting to my dearest life and love and the light of my eyes. Well, I will not begin another page, and that is flat.—After all, I *must* begin another page; for, with my nonsense, I had like to forget the most important part of the business. The Minister is in daily expectation of three millions of livres in specie, one million of which he destines for our expedition. If this be so, it looks like business at last. The moment he receives the money he will begin his preparations. But then, Clarke, who is certainly at the head of the military correspondence, knows nothing of all this. " I am lost in sensations of troubled emotions." What am I to think? " Hey ho, hey day! I know not what to do, or what to say!" I have made a very wise rule for myself, and I will keep it; that is, never to be elevated by appearances, and, indeed, to say the truth, I see as yet no great appearances to elevate me. Well, I am blind with sleep, and yet I am bound in honour to finish this page, as I have begun it. Now for a quotation.

" There's thirteen lines gone through, driblet by driblet,
" 'Tis done. Count how you will, I warrant there's fourteen."

23. Madgett sent for me this morning to tell me as usual, that every thing is going on well, but, for my part, I think every thing is going on very slowly. However, I did not say so, and he went on, that he was going express to look among the prisoners for Mr. Wm. Browne, by the Minister's directions, and, if he found him, he would be sent off instantly for Ireland, after I had given him his instructions. So that affair is settled, if Matthew is to be found. It is a perilous business, but he must take his chance, and, as he will have no papers, I hope he may come off clear. He then consulted me as to the old scheme, (which I am more and more satisfied is some kind of a job,) concerning debauching the Irish prisoners. His idea is, they should be put aboard privateers, and landed in different parts of Ireland, to prepare the people, though neither they nor the people were to be in the secret. How they are to communicate what they do not know, is not very clear; however, let that pass. I answered, I should be very glad to see them all in Ireland on a proper occasion, but conceived it would be hazarding the whole measure to part with one of them until the landing was effected, as the enemy might surmise something of the business, and take effectual measures to prevent it; that, as to preparing the people, he might take my word that they were sufficiently prepared already. This is the six-and-fiftieth time I have given my opinion on this head, yet he still returns to the charge. I know the Irish a little. The way to manage them is this: If they intend to use

the Irish prisoners, let them be marched down under other pretences to the port from whence the embarkation is to be made. When every thing else is ready, let them send in a large quantity of wine and brandy, a fiddle and some French *filles*, and then, when Pat's heart is a little soft with love and wine, send in two or three proper persons in regimentals, and with green cockades in their hats, to speak to them, of whom I will very gladly be one. I think, in that case, it would not be very hard to persuade him to take a trip once more to Ireland, just to see his people a little. At least, I am sure if this scheme does not answer, no other will. It may also be right to make the first man who offers, a captain on the spot, and one or two more, subalterns. To return. Madgett spoke to me again about Prieur, with great commendation (and I dare say justly,) of his talents and patriotism, adding, that he had come out of power as poor as Job, and literally drank water to save the expense of wine, which he could not afford. This, in a member of the late *Comité de Salut Public*, is strong presumptive proof of his honesty. He added, that Prieur was almost a stranger to him, but that it was the Minister's desire, and that I should use some little address in mentioning it to Carnot. I answered, I certainly would do my best, and if I succeeded, and that we went to Ireland together, I believed if Prieur continued to drink water it would be out of a preference for that liquor, for we would put him in a state to drink what he liked. I always keep up the idea, and in fact, it is my opinion, that liberal provision should be made, in case we succeed, for those Frenchmen who might be in high station in Ireland, as the Generals, Commissaires Civils, &c. I am sure it would be money well laid out, and agreeable to the native generosity of the Irish people. In fine, I should like Prieur very well, from what I have heard of him, and will certainly push that affair as far as it will go. Madgett then told me the Minister desired I should draw up such a memorial as I thought the French commander ought to publish on landing. That is not quite so easy. I wished to evade it, by saying the style of French eloquence was so different from ours that I doubted my abilities to do it. He answered, it was precisely for that reason it was necessary I should write it; that, when I had done, the Executive Directory would make such alterations and additions as they might see necessary; but the ground-work must be mine. I then said I would try, and we parted. He is to be seven or eight days on his tour, apostolizing among the Irish prisoners, which, once for all, as he is conducting it, I do not like. For the manifesto. I never in my life had less appetite for composition than just now. It is a serious business, and I have no assistance. I wish to God P. P. was here, or Gog.* What shall I do? I am in a d——d fright. Well, to-morrow we shall see. At present my idea is to make it as plain as a pikestaff; but how will the French like

---

* A conventional name for Mr. John Keogh.

that? They love metaphors; but I think, in the present case, I will stick to plain English. " Well, if we must, we must, and since 'tis so, the less that's said the better!" Apropos! I should have observed that I finished the copies of my two memorials, and left them at Clarke's bureau, with a note that I would call the day after but one.

24. Began my French manifesto. It drags a little heavy or so, but there is no remedy. I wish they would write it themselves.

25. At work in the morning at my manifesto. I think it begins to clear up a little. I find a strong disposition to be scurrilous against the English Government, which I will not check. I will write on, pell-mell, and correct it in cool blood, *if my blood will ever cool on that subject.* Went, at one o'clock, to Clarke:—D—— it, he has had my memorials, and never looked at them. Well! this is my first mortification: God knows I do not care if the memorials were sent to the devil, provided the *business* be once undertaken. It is not for the glory of General Clarke's admiration of my compositions that I am anxious. He apologized for the delay, by alleging the mutiplicity of other business; and perhaps he had reason; yet I think there are few affairs of more consequence than those of Ireland, if well understood. But how can they be understood, if they will not read the information that is offered them?—Clarke fixed with me to call on him the day but one after, at two o'clock. The delay, to be sure, is not great; nevertheless, I do not like it.

There was something too, in his manner, which was not quite to my taste; not but that he was extremely civil: perhaps it is all fancy, or that I was out of humour. Well, the 27th, I hope, we shall see, and till then let me work at my manifesto. Heigho! I have no great stomach for that business to-day; but it must be, and so *allons.* But first I will go gingerly, and dine alone in the Elysian fields. It is inconceivable the solitude I live in here. Sometimes, I am most dreadfully out of spirits, and it is no wonder. Losing the society of a family that I doat upon, and that loves me so dearly, and living in Paris, amongst utter strangers, like an absolute *Chartreux.* Well! "Had honest Sam Crowe been within hail—but what signifies palavering?" I will go to my dinner. Evening;—did no good.—" I cannot write this self-same manifesto," said I despairingly. No opera. Went to bed at eight o'clock.

26. At work at the manifesto like a vicious mule, kicking all the way. However, I am getting on, but I declare I know no more than my Lord Mayor, whether what I am writing is good, bad, or indifferent: "Fair and softly goes far in a day." I am going fair and softly, but I cannot say I go far in a day. I have been writing now five hours, without intermission, and I am surprised to find how little I have done; but I write two lines, and blot out three, so it is easy to see how I *get on.* Well! now I think it is time to go to my dinner. I am to dine with my friend Dupetit Thouars, who has, I am heartily glad to find, re-entered the service. He

has at present the rank of Commodore, and if the war continues some time longer, may probably become an Admiral. I hope and believe he will do his duty, though he is a d——d aristocrat; but then he hates the English cordially, and that covers a multitude of sins. Evening: Dupetit Thouars prevented by business; but, to make amends, left a very troublesome French boy, to keep me from being low-spirited, I suppose. Got rid of him as well as I could. At night sent for a bottle of Burgundy, intending to drink just one glass. Began to read (having opened my bottle) Memoirs of the reign of Louis XIV. After reading some time, found my passion at a particular circumstance kindled rather more than seemed necessary, as I flung the book from me with great indignation. Turned to my bottle, to take a glass to cool me—found, to my great astonishment, that it was empty.—Oh ho!—Got up and put every thing in its place, *exactly*—examined all my locks—saw that my door was fast, as there may be rogues in the hotel—peeped under my bed, lest the enemy should surprise me there. It is the part of a wise man to be cautious, and I found myself, just then, inclined to be extremely prudent. Having satisfied myself that all was safe, " I mounted the wall of my castle, as I called it, and having pulled the ladder up after me, I lay down in my hammock and slept contentedly." This is vilely misquoted, but no matter for that; it is just like one of P. P.'s quotations. Slept like a top all night.

27. On looking over my manifesto this morning, I begin to think it is sad trash. God forgive me if I judge uncharitably, but it seems to me to be pitiful stuff; at any rate, it certainly is not a French manifesto at all, and I foresaw in the outset the difficulty of writing in the character of a French general. If I were to compose a manifesto for the Irish Convention, and had good advisers, I might get on; but as to this affair, I see that I shall have to give it up for hard work, as they say in Galway. Went at two o'clock to General Clarke, and had a long conversation. He told me he had read my two memorials, and without flattery could assure me they were extremely well done, (that of course); that he had made, in consequence, a favourable report to Carnot, who endeavoured to read them also, but finding a difficulty in reading English manuscript, he (Clarke) was to translate them for him; that all he could at present tell me was, that the Executive was determined to send a person directly to Ireland, and that he had in consequence written to an ex-officer of the Irish Brigade to know if he would go, but that he declined on the score of ill health. I told him I was sorry for that, as a military man, if one could be found proper in other respects, would be what I should prefer. He asked me, did I myself know any person fit to go? I answered, I did not, as I had no acquaintance and industriously avoided having any, in France; that I did not know, however, but at that moment I had a brother lying in the prison at Guise. I then gave

him a short history of my brother Matthew's affair, concluding by saying that if he were yet in France, and no more proper person could be found, he might do. At the same time, I did not at all like to propose him; first, because it was a service of danger, in which I did not wish to hazard his life, and next, that I would avoid recommending a person so nearly connected with me to the French Government, lest I might appear to act on interested views. Clarke then, after some civilities in reply, asked me what I thought of some of the Irish priests yet remaining in France. I answered, that he knew my opinion as to priests of all kinds; that in Ireland they had acted, all along, execrably; that they hated the very name of the French Revolution, and that I feared, and indeed was sure, that if one was sent from France, he would immediately, from the *esprit de corps*, get in with his brethren in Ireland, who would misrepresent every thing to him; and, of course, that any information which he might collect would not be worth a farthing. I added, that the state of Ireland might be much better collected from the debates of their Parliament, even mutilated as he would find them in the English newspapers which I saw upon his table, than from the report of any individual just peeping into the country and returning, supposing that he were lucky enough to escape; and I observed that these debates furnished the very strongest evidence, because they were extorted from the mouth of the enemy, who was so interested to conceal the facts, and who *would* conceal them, if he were able. (This I had mentioned in a former conversation, but I thought it right to press it, and it seemed to strike Clarke very forcibly.) I then went on to observe, that I hoped, if the measure were adopted by the French Executive, they did not mean to delay it till the return of this emissary, if one were sent, especially as his business would be to give information in Ireland, not to bring any thence. Clarke answered, supposing the measure to be adopted, certainly not; that all preparations would be going on in the mean time; but I must see it would be necessary to send a person to apprize the people in Ireland. I replied, by all means, but that whoever we sent, he must carry no papers, nor speak to above four or five persons whom I would point out, for fear of hazarding a discovery, which might blast all; in which Clarke agreed. We then fell into discourse on the detail of the business, being in fact a kind of commentary, *viva voce,* on the memorials. I began by saying, that as I presumed the number of troops would not be above five or six thousand men, I hoped and expected they would be the best that France could spare us. Clarke replied, they would undoubtedly be sufficiently disciplined. I answered, it was not merely disciplined troops, but men who were accustomed to stand fire, that we wanted; some of the old battalions from Holland or the Rhine; for as to raw troops, we should soon have enough of them. Clarke answered, that he could not promise we should have the pick and choice of the French army, but that if any were sent, they would be brave troops, that would run on the enemy as soon as they saw them. I answered, as to the courage of the French army, it was sufficiently known, and I would venture to say, that wherever they would lead, the Irish would follow. (I see that we shall not get veterans, if we get any, which is bad; but we must do as we can.) I then said, at least as to the cannoniers, of which we had none, it would be indispensable they should be perfectly trained and disciplined; in which he agreed. I then came to the General; and said it would be of the greatest consequence, if the thing were possible, that he should be an officer of reputation, whose name might be known in Ireland, where names were things of weight. He replied, that it would not be easy to get an officer such as I described to undertake the enterprise with so small a force. (This I was all along afraid of.) I replied, none would, unless some dashing fighting fellow, with a good deal of enthusiasm in his character, adding, that Bournonville, whom I only knew by reputation and Camus's report, seemed to me to be precisely such a man as he wanted. Clarke replied, as to Bournonville, he was already appointed to the army in Holland, and it was not to be supposed he would quit the command of sixty thousand men, to go and command six thousand. I answered, he knew best; but my opinion was, there was more glory to be acquired in Ireland, even with that force, and also more profit, (if profit were any object), as he must suppose the Irish nation would amply reward those who were instrumental in establishing their liberties, adding, that we were generous even to prodigality. He said he was sure Bournonville would prefer his present situation. (So there is an end of that expectation, for which I am sorry.) Clarke then said there were some Irish officers yet remaining in France, who might go, and he mentioned Jennings, who used to call himself Baron de Kilmaine—God knows why! I answered, that in Ireland we had no great confidence in the officers of the old Irish Brigade, so many of whom had either deserted or betrayed the French cause; that, as to Jennings, he had had the misfortune to command after Custine, and had been obliged to break up the famous " Camp de Cæsar;" that, though this might probably have been no fault of his, it had made an impression, and, as he was at any rate not a fortunate general, I thought it would be better to have a Frenchman. This naturally introduced the Irish Brigade (Clarke had served for two years in Berwick's,) and I gave him an account of the various slights and mortifications they had undergone, both in England and Ireland; how they had been obliged to accept the King's pardon for high treason, for having been in the French service; how those who were able were obliged to pay the fees, and those who were not, to accept it *in forma pauperis*, a circumstance so excessively degrading, that nothing could be worse; how the Lord Lieutenant had applied on their behalf to the Catholic Committee, and had been refused; how the very mob despised them, as an instance of which, I mentioned the anecdote of the Etat Major intending to go to mass on Christmas day in grand costume, and how they were obliged to give it up for fear of being hustled by the populace, who had given Dr. Troy warning that they would treat them as crimps; with all which Clarke was exceedingly delighted. He spoke of O'Connell with respect, as a good parade officer to prepare troops for service, but as having no extent of genius for command. (He would do for us as Baron Steuben did in America; and if matters go forward, I for one will be for his being employed, for I know he hates England, and my poor friend Sweetman, whom I shall ever deeply regret, had an excellent opinion of him.) He also said that Colonel Moore was the best officer amongst them; and, as to all the others, they were to be sure brave men, but none of them of any reputation. We then returned to our own affairs. I said, we should want a few engineers. He asked me for what, since we had no fortifications. I replied, for field service, redoubts, &c. He replied, that was always done by the Adjutant-Generals. I then observed I had one thing to mention entirely personal; that I had exerted myself a good deal, risked my safety on more than one occasion, and had a very narrow escape with my life; that if this business went forward, I hoped and expected the French Government would allow me to take a part in the execution, and that I was sure, if he would excuse the vanity of the assertion, that I could be of material service; that I was willing to encounter danger as a soldier, but had a violent objection to being hanged as a traitor, and, consequently, desired a *commission in the French army;* that, as to the rank, that was indifferent to me, my only object being a certainty of being treated as a soldier, in case the fortune of war should throw me into the hands of the enemy, who I knew would otherwise show me no mercy; and that I hoped, under all the circumstances of the case, my request would not be considered unreasonable. He answered, that as to that, he could see no possibility of difficulty; that, undoubtedly, I had a claim at the least for so much, and he was sure it would be done, and in the manner most agreeable to my feelings. (So I am in hopes, if the business goes forward, that this affair will be settled.) We then began to chat, rather than talk seriously, and moot points of war. First, as to Dublin, I told him I did not expect, with the proposed force, that much could be done there at first; that its garrison was always at least five thousand strong, and that the Government, taking advantage of the momentary success of the coalesced despots, had disarmed the people, taken their cannon, and passed the gunpowder and convention bills, whose nature and operation I explained to him; that, however, if the landing were once effected, one of two things would happen,—either the Government would retain the garrison for their own security, (in which case there would be five thousand men idle on the part of the enemy,) or they would march them off to oppose us, in which case the people would rise and seize the capital; and I added, if they preferred the first measure, which I thought most likely, whenever we were strong enough to march southward (if we were, as I had no doubt we should be, superior in the field,) we could starve Dublin in a week, without striking a blow. I then mentioned the great advantages which would result from a diversion in Connaught, if possible, from the discontents prevailing in that province, and the strong line of defence which the Shannon affords; and this I pressed upon him as strongly as I could. He saw all the advantages of it as clearly as I did, for indeed they are self-evident, but I cannot say he gave me any violent hopes that it would be attempted in the first instance. (N. B. What is to hinder our doing it ourselves in a week, by way of Sligo? Mind this, and examine the map.) We then spoke of Cork, of which I know nothing. He tells me the harbour is admirably situated for defence against any attack by sea, but if you are superior at land, you can, by taking possession of a hill that supplies the town with water, force it to surrender without striking a blow. I then mentioned my scheme as to the Irish, now prisoners in France, and made him laugh immoderately at my mode of recruiting, which is, however, admirably adapted to the gentlemen whom I should have to address. Seeing that he was tickled with the business, I exerted myself, and made divers capital hits at the expense of poor Pat, concerning

> " Women and wine, which compare so well,
> That they run in a perfect parallel,"

as the poet hath it. To be sure, it is vain to deny it, but the poor fellow is a little exposed on those two sides, and the foul fiend, who knows it right well, always judiciously chooses one or the other, or sometimes both, to defeat him. God knows, I have been buffeted by Satan, as well as another, in my time:

"With women and wine I defy every care."—(Sings.)

I would be glad to know what P. P. would say to my doctrine concerning the fallibility of poor Pat's judgment, when

"The wine looks red in the glass,
And the bright eyes of beauty are beaming."

Yes! yes! he is proof to all that, and so is P. P., and another person that shall be nameless. Well, we are all men, and so let me say no more about the matter. Clarke asked me, might they not serve us as the French prisoners did the British at Quiberon? I answered, there was this most material difference, that the French were brought back to fight against their country, and the Irish would be brought back to fight, not against their country, but against the English; and that I had no doubt but they would do their duty. I then begged him to keep me in Carnot's recollection, and having fixed to call on him regularly once a week, to see how things were going on, I took my leave—his last words being "I wish most sincerely, and I hope, the business will be seriously taken up by the Executive."

I like this day's business very well. I see I was wrong the day before yesterday, in thinking Clarke's manner cold. I fancy that it was myself that was out of temper, because, forsooth, he had not read my memorials. That was not unnatural on my side neither, but indeed, it was much more my anxiety about the business, than my *amour propre,* or any attachment to my own compositions. I hope I am above that, for I have a very pretty opinion of the purity of my motives. I have protested again and again, in these memorandums, that I am acting to the best of my judgment, (seeing that I have no advisers, which is a great loss,) and on the very fairest principles. Have I no selfish motives? Yes, I have. If I succeed here, I feel I shall have strong claims on the gratitude of my country: and as I love her, and as I think I shall be able to serve her, I shall certainly hope for some honourable station as a reward for the sacrifices I have already made and the dangers I have incurred, and those which I am ready and shall have to make and incur in the course of the business. Why not? If it were the case of any other person, I am sure I should have the same opinion. I hope (but I am not sure) my country is my first object; at least she is my second. If there be one before her, as I believe there is, it is my dearest life and love, the light of my eyes, and spirit of my existence. I wish more than for any thing on earth to place her in a splendid situation. There is none so elevated that she would not adorn, and that she does not deserve; and I believe that not I only, but every one who knows her, will agree as to that. Truth is truth she is my first object. But would I sacrifice the interests of Ireland to her elevation? No, that I would not; and if I could, she would despise me; and, if she were to despise me, I would go hang myself like Judas. Well, there is no regulator for the human heart like the certainty of possessing the affections of an amiable woman, and, if so, what unspeakable good fortune do I not enjoy. Well! I do love my wife dearly, and that is the God's truth of it; and she is a thousand times too good for me, and I am not very bad neither; but then she is so infinitely better, that it throws my great merit into the shade. For all that I have said of her and myself here, I will be judged by Whitley Stokes, and Peter Burrows, and P. P., who are three fair men; and now I have done this day's journal, and shall only observe, on looking over it, that I think I am as pretty a negotiator as a man would wish to see of a summer's day. But then this d——d manifesto sticks in my stomach!

28. Went to the Opera, as usual, like a fine gentleman. I always go to that theatre, because, as yet, I understand music better than French. *Panurge.* Superb spectacle. Lays, the best singer of the men; Madame Maillard of the women;— Madame Pontriel extremely pretty, though with something foolish in the expression of her countenance; Mademoiselle Gavaudan, an excellent comic actress; Defresne an admirable actor, and sings tolerably; all the others middling enough. Dancers:—

Vestris certainly the first, then Nivelon, Deshayes, Goyon, &c. Females: Clotilde, a fine figure with an infinity of grace and execution; but wants, as the French tell me, the *à plomb,* as they call it, that is, immobility of posture after executing a difficult passage. For my part I did not observe it till it was pointed out to me, but now I am beginning to grow something of a judge myself; Perignon and Chevigny, admirable dancers, and of merit so exactly equal that I know not which to prefer. They are both ordinary at once in face and figure, but manage themselves with such dexterity that nothing can appear more graceful than they do in all their movements. Duchemin pretty, and dances very well. Milliere as ugly as mortal sin, but a most charming dancer; I believe I like her the best. The Parisians prefer Chevigny. Nothing could be executed with more taste, or I may say more classically, than the Pas Russe was to night by Nivelon and Milliere. Once for all, the King's Theatre in the Haymarket is no better than a barn of strollers beside the *Theatre des Arts,* as to scenery, machinery, dresses, and decorations; but in revenge, their singers (being Italians,) are far before the French, who, on the other hand, excel the Italians, and all other nations, in their dances. It is impossible to conceive any thing in its kind more perfect than a grand ballet at the Opera of Paris; and, indeed, in all their theatres there is an attention paid to the preservation of costume, even in the minutest points, very far beyond the English theatres, where I have myself seen Macbeth (a Scottish chief of eight centuries ago,) dressed in a very spruce vest of scarlet regimentals, and a bag wig, in which he need not be ashamed to show his face at St. James's; and where, to this hour, Hamlet the Dane, the son of Horwendillus, is exhibited (even by Kemble, from whom I should expect better things,) in a fine black velvet full-trimmed suit, with the ribbon of the order of the Elephant over his shoulder! where King John is habited after the fashion of 1160, and his antagonist, King Philip, confronts him in a cocked hat and feather, and a coat and waistcoat of the last court fashion. These absurdities the eye is never shocked with in France, and they are as attentive to the appearance of the meanest domestic as of the hero of the piece. All the minutiæ of the scene are equally correct; for example, in a Grecian tragedy they would not introduce a pair of handsome plated candlesticks. They have carefully studied the antique, and whatever is graceful among the moderns, and profited accordingly. I believe I have now said enough of the Opera, to which the French are devoted *à la folie*. All the theatres are as full every night as they can hold, and I have never seen an instance of what we call in England a bad or even a middling house.

"My time, oh ye muses, was happily spent,
When Phœbe went with me wherever I went."

29. Am I not to be sincerely pitied here? I do not know a soul; I speak the language with

great difficulty; I live in taverns, which I detest; I cannot be always reading, and I find, by experience, that when one reads perforce, there is not much either of profit or pleasure in it, from which I infer, philosophically, that the nature of man is adapted to liberty, and that all restraint beyond what is necessary ——. O Lord! oh Lord! metaphysics! —I return to my apartment, which is, notwithstanding, a very neat one, as if I was returning to gaol, and finally I go to bed at night as if I were mounting the guillotine. I do lead a dog's life of it here, that is the truth of it: my sole resource is the opera.

30. Went to-day to the Church of St. Roch, to the *Fête de la Jeunesse;* all the youth of the district who have attained the age of sixteen were to present themselves before the municipality and receive their arms, and those who had arrived at twenty-one were to be enrolled in the list of citizens, in order to ascertain their right of voting in the assemblies. The church was decorated with the national colours, and a statue of Liberty, with an altar blazing before her. At the foot of the statue the municipality were seated, and the sides of the church were filled with a crowd of spectators, the parents and friends of the young men, leaving a space vacant in the centre for the Etat Major of the sections composing the district, the National Guards under arms, the officers of the sections, and, finally, the young men who were to be presented. The guard was

mounted by veterans of the troops of the line, and there was a great pile of muskets and of sabres before the municipality. When the procession arrived, the names of the two classes were enrolled, and, in the mean time, the veterans distributed the arms amongst the parents, friends and mistresses of the young men. When the enrolment was finished, an officer pronounced a short address to the youths of sixteen, on the duty which they owed to their country, and the honour of bearing arms in her defence, to which they were about to be admitted. They ran amongst the crowd of spectators and received their firelocks and sabres, some from their fathers, some from their mothers, and many, I could observe, from their lovers. When they were armed, their parents and mistresses embraced them, and they returned to their station. It is impossible to conceive any thing more interesting than the spectacle was at that moment; the pride and pleasure in the countenance of the parents; the *fierté* of the young soldiers, and, above all, the expression in the features of so many young females, many of them beautiful, and all interesting, from the occasion. I was in an enthusiasm. I do not wonder at the miracles which the French army has wrought in the contest for their liberties. When I looked at the spectacle before me, and recalled to mind the gangs of wretched recruits I had seen in Ireland, marching in their fetters, and handcuffed, I was no longer surprised at any thing; yet the poor Irish are a brave people; and I think it would not be impossible to bring them up to the enthusiasm of the French; at least if we have an opportunity we will try. I am more and more satisfied of the powerful effect of public spectacles, properly directed, in the course of a revolution. I should have observed that, during the ceremony, all the civic hymns were chanted, accompanied by a full band, and joined in the chorusses by the young men. I wish my dearest love had heard the burst of " *Aux armes, Citoyens!* " It is impossible to conceive the effect of that immortal hymn, unless by those who have heard it at a festival in France; it is absolute enchantment. This was a good day.

31. Blank! Not knowing what to do, I stroll about the book-stalls, and pick up military books dog cheap. If I had money to spare, I could make up a famous French library for a trifle. There are very expensive editions just now, if one chooses to lay out money in fine types, paper, and binding; but there are also most excellent editions of excellent works for half nothing. The ordinary price I pay for a duodecimo, bound, is fifty francs in assignats, which at the present rate of the louis, is about two pence. Mary, I know, will laugh at my collection of Etats Militaires, as she calls them; no matter for that: " By Cot's providinch they may be yused some time or other." I laugh at them myself sometimes, but I am tempted because they are bargains, in spite of Poor Richard, who says, " Never buy what you don't want, because it is a bargain. I have known many a man ruined by *buying bargains.*"

April 1796.

1. Lounged about "cheapening old authors at a stall." Saw a superb battalion of infantry and a squadron of cavalry inspected at the Tuileries by a general officer. The French are very fine troops, such of them as I have seen; they are all of the right military age, with scarcely any old men past service or boys not grown up to it. They are not very correct in their evolutions, not near equal to the English, and much less, as I suppose, to the Germans. This has a little shaken my faith in the force of discipline, for they have certainly beaten both British and Germans like dogs; but, after the spectacles which I see daily, why need I wonder at that? The *Fête de la Jeunesse*, for example, of yesterday, explains it at once. Discipline will not stand against such enthusiasm as I was a witness to, and, I may say, as I felt myself. I remember P. P. was always of that opinion too, though I doubted it, which shows the superiority of his judgment, and his more accurate knowledge of the human character. If we go on in Ireland, we must move heaven and earth to create the same spirit of enthusiasm which I see here; and, from my observation of the Irish character, which so nearly resembles the French, I think it very possible. The devil of it is, that poor Pat is a little given to drink, and the French are very sober. We must rectify that as well as we can; he is a good man that has no fault, and I have a sort of sympathetic feeling which makes me the

more indulgent on this score. Quere. Would it have a good effect to explode corporal punishment altogether in the Irish army, and substitute a discharge with infamy for great faults, and confinement and hard diet for lesser ones? I believe there is no corporal punishment in the French army, and I would wish to create a spirit in our soldiers, a high point of honour, like that of the French. When one of their Generals, (Marshal Richelieu) was besieging a town,* he was tormented with the drunkenness of his army. He gave out, in orders, that any soldier who was seen drunk should not be suffered to mount the assault, and there was not a man to be seen in liquor afterwards. Drunkenness then induced a suspicion of cowardice, which kept them effectually sober. It is a choice anecdote, and pregnant with circumstances. To return. There is a great latitude in dress allowed both to the French officers and soldiers, which has demolished, or at least much circumscribed, another of my prejudices; for I was, on that score, a great Martinet. I fancy truth may lie between P. P.'s opinion and mine, so let us compound as follows: If there be a high point of honour, and a spirit of ardent enthusiasm, then discipline (I mean that discipline which makes men machines,) may be, in a great degree, suffered to relax, and *a fortiori*, the minutiæ of dress, to be neglected; but if that point of honour and spirit of enthusiasm do not exist, their absence must be

---

* Port Mahon, in Minorca.

supplied by the force of discipline, and then, as part of the system, even the article of dress becomes of some importance. The French cavalry are armed only with sabres and pistols, without carbines. I am glad of that, for I always thought carbines useless. The fire of infantry seems to me to have very little effect in comparison of the noise it makes, and the fire of cavalry I am sure is nonsense. The *arme blanche* is the system of the French, and I believe for the Irish; at least if our affair goes forward, it will be what I shall recommend—for poor Pat is very furious and savage, and the tactics of every nation ought to be adapted to the national character. Platooning at forty yards distance may answer very well to the English and German phlegm, but as we have rather more animal spirits, I vote for the bayonet. I do not love playing at long bullets. To conclude, I wish to study the character of the French soldiers, and, if possible, to create the same spirit in Ireland, and, in a word, to make the French army our model instead of the Prussian. I think P. P. will allow that this is candid in me, after all the disputes he and I have had on the subject of discipline. In the afternoon went, for the first time, to the *Conseil des Cinq Cens* (the French House of Commons). It is certainly the first assembly in Europe, and the worst accommodated; the room is mean, dirty, and ill-contrived; the system of speaking from a tribune in itself bad, and rendered worse by placing the tribune at the feet of the President, (to whom the orator's back is turned) at the upper end of a very oblong room, so that those at the lower end cannot possibly hear half of what is said. They are likewise very disorderly, which I wonder at the more as they have had now six years' experience of public assemblies; but it is the same spirit of impetuosity that makes them redoubtable in the field and disorderly in the senate. As to their appearance, it was extremely plain. Nobody was what I would call dressed: many without powder, in pantaloons and boots. From the figure of the room and the appearance of the assembly, they put me strongly in mind of my old masters, the General Committee, at their famous meetings in Back-lane. The resemblance was very striking, with this difference, that I must say the General Committee looked more like gentlemen, and were ten times more regular and orderly, or, in a word, like a legislative body. They were only on business of course, and, as I found nobody to point out to me the most celebrated members, I did not remain above half an hour. On the whole, they looked more like their countrymen who broke into the Roman Senate, than like the Senators assembled in their ivory chairs to receive them; nor can I say, as the Ambassador of Pyrrhus did of the Senators of Rome, that they looked like an assembly of demigods. But it is very little matter what they look like. They have humbled all Europe thus far, with their blue pantaloons and unpowdered locks, and that is the main point; the rest is of little consequence.

2. Went-to day to Clarke, at the Luxembourg. He tells me that he has been hunting in vain for a proper person to go to Ireland; that he had a Frenchman tampered with, who was educated from a child in England, and spoke the language perfectly. That at first he agreed to go; but afterwards, on learning the penalties of the English law against high treason, his heart failed him and he declined. This is bad. However, there is no remedy. Clarke went on to tell me that if the measure were pursued (without saying whether it would or not), the Executive were determined to employ me in the French service in a military capacity; and that I might depend on finding every thing of that kind settled to my satisfaction. I answered, that as to my own personal feelings, I had nothing more to demand. He then wished I would give him a short plan for a system of *Chouannerie* in Ireland, particularly in Munster, for he would tell me frankly, the Government had a design, before any thing more serious was attempted, to turn in a parcel of renegadoes, (or, as he said, blackguards,) into Ireland, in order to distress and embarrass the Government there, and distract them in their motions. I answered, I was sorry to hear it. That if a measure of this kind was adopted with a view to prepare the minds of the people, it was unnecessary, for they were already sufficiently prepared. That it would only produce local insurrections, which would soon be suppressed, because the army (including the militia) would in that case, to a certainty, support the

Government, and every man of any property, even those who wished for the independence of their country, would do the same, from the dread of indiscriminate plunder, which would be too likely to ensue from such a measure as he described: that there was another thing very much to be apprehended in that case, which, if I were Minister of England, I should not hesitate one moment about, and in which the Parliaments of both countries would instantly concur, viz. to pass an act repealing those clauses which enact that the militia shall only serve in their own country, and directly to shift the militia of Ireland into England, and replace them by the English militia, which would serve to awe both countries, and most materially embarrass us. That, if all this were so, and these insurrections suppressed, their inevitable effect (grounded upon all historical experience) would be to strengthen the existing Government. That England would avail herself of such an opportunity to reduce Ireland again to that state of subjection (or even a worse one) she had suffered in 1782, and would bind her hand and foot, so as to make all future exertion impossible; in which she would be supported by the whole Irish aristocracy, who compose the Legislature, and who would sacrifice every thing to their own security. That, if France had nothing in view but to distress England for the moment, undoubtedly what he mentioned, however ruinous to Ireland, might have that effect; but if the Republic went on more enlarged views and sounder policy, she ought not for a moment to give consideration to the scheme. That, if the main force were once landed, undoubtedly it would be right to set Ireland in a blaze at the four corners, and burn out the English Government, but that I was satisfied it would be ruinous to make the measure he described precede the landing. Finally, I repeated that, as to myself, I was ready to be one of ten men, if the French Government were determined to send no more. I also begged him to remember that I gave this, with all due deference, as my fixed opinion on a point which I had considered, in consequence of an idea of the same kind having been started to me by Madgett, from the Minister. Clarke resumed by saying that, as to my being sent, it was not the idea of the French Government to risk my safety in that stage of the business. That the objections I had urged were of considerable weight, and that he would give them serious reflection. He then desired to see me in four or five days, and, after giving my address, which he demanded, I took my leave. (*Vide* Journal of March 22 and 23, on this subject, which, I am sorry to see, has got ground amongst them.) This conversation explains what Madgett (who is returned from his mission) told me this morning; namely, that he has got fifty-one Irish prisoners who would fight, blood to the knees, against England, and that he thought it would be very serviceable if they were dispersed through the country. I referred him, for my opinion, to our former conversations on that head; that I thought, undoubtedly, if the business were once begun, the wider the flame was spread, the better; but that the grand blow of the landing near Belfast should precede all others, and that being once effected, as many more as he pleased. I see, clearly, that my opinion will not be followed; and I fear it will be found to be so much the worse. I have, however, discharged my conscience. I cannot blame France for wishing to retaliate on England the abominations of La Vendée and the Chouans, but it is hard that it should be at the expense of poor Ireland. It will be she and not England that will suffer, and the English will be glad of it; for they hate us next to the French. If these ragamuffins are smuggled into the country, local insurrections will ensue; the militia will obey their officers; the bravest of our poor peasants will stand to be cut down; and of those who run away, numbers will be hanged and many more sent aboard the fleet, to fight the battles of England; and the Government will be so much the stronger:—not to mention the mischief which will be unprofitably done, even to the aristocracy. I dislike all this very much, if I could help myself, but I fear I shall not be able to prevent it. At all events, I have given my opinions honestly. Poor Pat! I fear he is just now in bad neighbourhood. Madgett tells me that Mr. W. Browne left Guise with his passport eight months ago. So there is an end of that business. I hope in God he is, by this, safe with the girls at Princeton. How happy shall we be if ever we have the good fortune to meet again! I suffer a great deal in this business; however, " 'Tis but in vain for soldiers to complain."

3. Called on Magdett this morning, by appointment. He is always full of *good news!* He tells me the marine force will be seventeen ships of war, great and small, with arms, artillery, &c. for 50,000 men; that many of the officers are already named, but he believes not the general-in-chief. All this is very good, but " Would I could see it, quoth blind Hugh." We then came to my commission in the service of the Republic. He asked me, as I was here the representative of the Irish people, would I not feel it beneath the dignity of that character to accept of a commission — for, as to the French Government, they would give me any rank I pleased to demand. I answered, that I considered the station of a French officer was one that would reflect honour on any one who filled it; that, consequently, on that score I could have no possible objection; that, besides, my object was to insure protection in case any of the infinite varieties of accident incidental to the fortune of war should throw me into the hands of the enemy; that, as to rank, it was indifferent to me, as I did not doubt but as soon as things were a little reduced into order in Ireland, I should obtain such a station in that service as they might think I merited; that, in the mean time, I should wish to be of the family of the general-in-chief, as I could be of use there (speaking a little French,) to interpret between him and the natives; unless the Government here

Portuguese to the Irish, by way of keeping the secret. D——n him sempiternally! What the devil brought him across me?—Dinner with Madgett: after dinner began my remarks on Fitzsimons, and, after relating the anecdote of the Portuguese despatches written in English, told him plump, I would not hazard the safety of my friends in Ireland, nor of the measure, by communicating with such an eternal blockhead. Madgett, at first, seemed inclined to make some defence for him; but the cause was too bad, and I was too determined, so he gave him up, and assured me he should not be sent; and there the matter rests; but I think I will go to-morrow to the Minister, and tell him a piece of my mind touching this said Mr. Fitzsimons. I must leave nothing to chance. I cannot conceive how Prieur could be mistaken in him. The fellow was fawning on me too; but I was as cold as ice and stiff as a Spaniard, and would not understand the broadest hints. Hang him! I have taken up too much of my paper about him and his " Portuguese written in English!" Is it not strange, however, that Prieur and De la Croix and Madgett, should be satisfied to let him pass on a business of such magnitude? I think I must go to the Minister, and make it *a point* that he shall be stopped. At all events, I will not communicate with him, "that's flat." After dinner walked for two hours in the Tuileries with Sullivan, talking red-hot Irish politics. Sullivan is a good lad, and I like him very well. Bed early.

4. Called on Madgett at nine o'clock, in order

most terribly provoking?—for it seems to be a thing settled, that he shall go. What am I to do in this cursed dilemma, and how came Madgett not to interfere in time? I objected all along to priests, as the worst of all possible agents, and here is one who is the worst of all possible priests. How the devil can I communicate with such an ass? It is impossible to conceive any thing more vulgar, ignorant, and stupid. If he goes to Ireland, the people there will suppose that we are laughing at them, to send such a fellow. What will Gog think? Yes, Gog will open his heart very readily to Mr. Fitzsimons! I am in such a rage I know not how to leave off abusing him. Well, I am to dine to-day with Madgett, and please the Lord I will tell him a piece of my mind. Perhaps I may be able to put a spoke in Mr. Fitzsimons's wheel, if it be not (as I fear it is) too late. To give a specimen of his talents (because he amuses me): There happened to be some Portuguese despatches taken aboard a vessel going to Brazil. Sullivan, Madgett's nephew, was carrying them to the office to be translated, and Mr. Fitzsimons made the following remark: " You will have fine fun, making out what these Portuguese fellows say: are all those papers, pray, WROTE *in English?*" The despatches of the Portuguese Ministry to the Governor of Rio Janeiro, *written in English!* Oh Lord! Oh Lord! I thought I should have choked, endeavouring to smother the irresistible propensity I felt to laugh in his face. Yes, he is a pretty devil of an agent. I suppose he will talk

all: he asked me then had I no person myself to recommend? I told him I knew not a soul in Paris. He then desired me to look for a proper person, (which I shall not do; for, in the first place, I know nobody, and, in the next, I will not make myself responsible by a recommendation;) for it was absolutely necessary, he said, that the Government should be informed of the actual state of things in Ireland. He then asked me, had I not seen General Clarke? I told him I had, by the orders of Carnot. Well, said he, I suppose he told you that the affair is in train, that preparations are making, " *et j'espere que ça ira.*" I told him I was very happy to hear it from him, and took my leave. This short conversation took place in the court of his hotel, where I met him coming out of his bureau. From the Minister, I went to Clarke, whom I saw for two minutes, he being engaged with a General officer and his Aid-de-Camp. I gave him my reasons, and he told me the plan was given up, which I am very glad to hear. He also said he had not been yet able to find a proper person to go to Ireland. I then mentioned that I had been with the Minister about Fitzsimons; that he was utterly incapable, and that I mentioned it to him, lest he might be taken by surprise as to his appointment; he then desired me to call upon him every three or four days, and so we parted. I am heartily glad the system of *Chouannerie* is knocked on the head, and I hope it is partly owing to my representations against it. I am now absolutely idle for three or four days, and I am truly weary of this life. " Fie upon 't, I want work!" Well, if ever I get to Ireland I shall have work enough, to make amends for this. Strolled, as usual, to the Champs Elysées, and dined alone. Delicious weather, and all the world diverting themselves except me. " Poor moralist, and what art thou? A solitary fly." I declare I am as much alone here as if I were in the deserts of Arabia, and that is hard in such a city as Paris. In the evening, *Comedie Italienne;* no great things. The opera is the only spectacle for me. Bed at ten. "Well, God's blessings be about the man," quoth Sancho Panza, "who first invented sleep; it wraps a man all round like his cloak."

5, 6, 7. Blank! Blank! Blank! This is sad!

8. Strolled to the *Palais de Justice* (the Westminster Hall of Paris), because I have a sneaking kindness for the profession of the law, of which I was so distinguished a member in my own country. Saw a man tried for stealing a plank; he told his story very judiciously, and he had a counsel who made a very good defence for him, and spoke extremely well. I understood every word of his speech, which I think is evidence that it was a good one. The jury made a respectable appearance. They retired to consider of their verdict, but I did not stay for the event. I suppose, from what I heard, the man was acquitted. The judge charged them with great moderation, and exactly in the language of the English law: told them it was their verdict, and not his; that the point for them to consider

was the intention of the culprit, as the fact was admitted; that if they believed he had no criminal intent, but acted merely through ignorance, they were bound to acquit him:—all which I liked very well. I did not think they had so much notion of criminal law in France; but it was because I grounded my opinion on that consummation of all iniquities and horror, the Revolutionary tribunal. The judges, five in number, were dressed in black, *à la Vandyck*, with hats decorated with the national feathers, and a tri-colour ribbon round their necks, like the collar of the orders of knighthood in England, to which were suspended the fasces and axes in silver, the emblem of their functions. The public accuser, or attorney-general, was habited pretty much after the same fashion: the lawyers had no discrimination of dress, which shows their good sense. It is the same in America; the judges alone are distinguished by their habits, and they are not disguised by that most preposterous and absurd of all human inventions, the long full-bottomed wig. Altogether, the appearance of the French *tribunal criminel*, and the manner in which the trial was conducted, pleased me extremely. Certainly, every justice was done to the prisoner. I was astonished at the purity of his diction, and politeness of his manner, in a short discussion he had with the public accuser, who, on his part, showed great lenity and candour. I am afraid an Irish thief would hardly conduct himself with the same talents, or, at least, the same manners; but let that pass. Poor Pat is not to be despised because he is not as polished as a Frenchman, and besides, who knows what we may make of him yet? He has very pretty capabilities. Went in the evening to see the *Deserteur*, at the *Theatre des Italiens*. Disappointed. A very poor performance; I speak as to the actors, for the piece itself is inimitable. Even Chenard, who, in general, is admirable, was very indifferent in Montauciel. His manner was dry and hard. The fact is, the French do not know how to represent a man drunk, which is owing to a defect in their education, for, as they never drink hard, they have no archetypes, so they form some vague notions of the manner in which a drunken man walks and speaks, but this is all from the imagination, and the perfection of acting is to copy nature. If Chenard had the great advantage to spend two or three afternoons with P. P. and another person, who shall be nameless, I think it might very much enlarge and improve his ideas as to the manner of acting Montauciel. By-the-by, the character of Montauciel, which is so inimitably characteristic of the French soldier, in the original, is miserably disguised on the English theatre; they have carefully preserved, and, I must say, improved his drunkenness, which is but a subordinate and accidental trait in France, and they have suffered his gaiety, his *fierté,* his carelessness of manner, and his high spirit, totally to evaporate. There is no character on earth more appropriate or better discriminated than that of a French dragoon, as I have myself had one or two opportunities of observing. In that view, Montauciel is inimitably drawn. Skirmish, the Montauciel of England, is nothing but a drunkard: take away his bottle, and you take his existence. Montauciel can maintain himself without it. But, I believe there is enough of criticism for the present, and, besides, I am sleepy.

9. Sullivan called on me this morning, with an English paper of the 31st March, (ten days ago,) in which is an article on Ireland, wherein mention is made of Sir Edward Bellew, of Bellewstown, being arrested, as connected with the Defenders. This surprises me, for he is a confirmed aristocrat, and he and all his family have been so devoted to the Government, as even to have the meanness of opposing the Catholics. Such is the gratitude of the Irish Government! But this piece of news is accompanied by another, which gives *me* the most sincere anxiety on every possible account, public or private: it is the arrest of John Keogh. Poor fellow! this is no place to write his panegyric. I have not received such a shock this long time. If we lose him, I know not where to look for a man to supply his place. I have differed from him at one time, but his services to Ireland have been eminent indeed, more especially to the Catholics; and, in all probability, they will prove his ruin; for, from the state of his health, confinement in the unwholesome air of a prison will be to him death as certain as the guillotine. I am inexpressibly concerned on his account. That infernal Government of Ireland! A long time have they been on the watch for his de-

struction, and I am sure they will stick at no means, however atrocious, to accomplish their ends. I can scarcely promise myself ever to see him again, and I can sincerely say that one of the greatest pleasures which I anticipated in case of our success, was the society of Mount Jerome, where I have spent many happy days, and some of them serviceable to the country. It was there that he and I used to frame our papers and manifestoes. It was there we drew up the Petition and Vindication of the Catholics, which produced such powerful effects both in England and Ireland. I very much fear we shall never labour together again for the good of our native country. I am sure he has been too wise and too cautious to put himself in their power; but what wisdom or caution is proof against forged and suborned testimony, which I know they will never stick at procuring? and in the state affairs are now in Ireland, any evidence will be received. Well, a day will come for all this. If we cannot prevent his fall, at least I hope we shall be able to revenge it; and I, for one, if it be twenty years hence, promise not to forget it. My heart is hardening hourly, and I satisfy myself now at once on points which would have staggered me twelve months ago. The Irish aristocracy are putting themselves into a state of nature with the people, and let them take the consequences. They show no mercy, and they deserve none. If ever I have the power, I will most heartily concur in making them a dreadful example. I am to meet Madgett on this business to-day;

but, see the consequences of delay! We have already lost, perhaps, the two most useful men in Ireland in their respective departments, Sweetman and Keogh. Unhappy is the man or the nation whose destiny depends on the will of another! This blow has deranged my system terribly. The Government here insist on sending somebody to Ireland. Keogh was the very principal person whom such a messenger ought to see: he is confined in a prison. I observe, in the same paper, that several other persons have been obliged to abscond, to avoid imprisonment. I have no doubt but that the most active and useful of my friends are of the number. This is a gloomy day. What if this indiscriminate persecution were to provoke a general rising, as in 1641? The thing is not impossible. Oh! France! France! what do you not deserve to suffer, if you permit this crisis to escape you! Poor Ireland! Well, it does not signify whining or croaking, and I am sworn never to despair; but the slowness of the people here, if they really have the means to act, is beyond all human suffering; if they have not, we must submit; but it is dreadful to think of it. Dined to-day in the Champs Elysées with Madgett and a person of the name of Aherne, a physician, who is to be sent to Ireland. Explained to him my sentiments as to the conduct he should adopt there, and particularly cautioned him against writing a syllable, or carrying a single scrape of a pen with him; pointed out to him the persons whom he is to see and speak to, at the same time that I fear many of the most useful are now either in prison or concealing themselves. This comes of delays; but that is no fault of mine. I like Aherne very well; he seems a cool man with good republican sentiments. He has been already employed in Scotland. Apropos, of Scotland: There is some scheme going on there, as I collected from hints which dropped from him and Madgett; but what it is I know not, nor did I inquire. My opinion is, that nothing will ever be done there, unless we first begin in Ireland. If we succeed, John Bull will have rather a troublesome neighbour of us. We shall be within eighteen miles of him. Aherne is to call on me to-morrow morning, in order to talk over the business of his mission at length, and I am to give him some memorandums, which I will advise him to commit to memory, and then burn them, by all means. I should have observed in its place, that I went at 12 o'clock to Clarke, and brought him the newspaper containing the account of Keogh's arrest, with a translation of the article in French for Carnot, which I got Sullivan to make. Clarke was just going off to the Directory, so I had hardly time to speak a word to him. I wished to speak to Carnot myself, and I could see Clarke was not at all desirous that I should have an opportunity. D——n such pitiful, jealous vanity! Every man here must do every thing himself. I have found this unworthy sentiment in every one of them, except Carnot. First, the Minister is disobliged because I go to Carnot; then Madgett would be huffed, if he dared, because I go to Clarke; and now Clarke, truly, wants to thrust himself between me and his principal. Please God, he shall not, though! If I want to see Carnot, I will see him, or I will be refused. I am to call on Clarke again tomorrow at one. I think I will then, with all possible deference and politeness, give him to understand my opinion on this point, which, as they manage it, is most excessively provoking, especially at a period when every minute is precious, and my anxiety is so great. Madgett tells me the Minister has been superseded in this business these fifteen days, and that it has been given entirely into the hands of Carnot. I am most heartily glad of that, because he is given to organizing a little. He is the man I want; and I hope the measure being given to his management, is partly, at least, if not entirely, owing to my going directly to himself, and to the discourse we had together, *malgré* my execrable jargon, which is neither French nor English. If that be so, as I hope it is, I may say that, in this instance, I have deserved well of my country: I hope I shall deserve better yet. *Nous verrons.*

10. Aherne called on me this morning, and I gave him a list of the persons he is to see, viz. Gog, Magog,* P. P., C. Teeling, R. S——, and S. Neilson; Oliver Bond, J. J. M'Nevin; with a quere as to J. P. and T. A. Emmet. I also gave him some trifling anecdotes, known only to ourselves, which will satisfy them that he has seen and conversed with me.

* Mr. R. M'Cormick.

When we had done I went to Clarke, who was for the first time denied to me; however I caught him, coming out of his bureau. He seemed, and probably was, in a great hurry. He said he had shown the newspapers to Carnot, who was very sorry the gentleman was arrested; but what could he do? I looked at him very earnestly, and repeated, "What could he do!" I then shrugged up my shoulders, and repeated twice in the French, "*Mauvaise augure.*" "No," replied Clarke, "you must not look on it in that light—you must not infer any thing from thence." We then walked on towards the Directory, whither he was going; and I pressed him, if the business were at all attempted, on the necessity of not losing a moment. He interrupted me, by asking, "How do you know that we *are* losing a moment?" I replied, that was enough; and so we parted. I am to see him again in a few days. From all this I infer, (for I ask him no questions,) that preparations are actually going forward somewhere, and, indeed, I have it indirectly from other quarters, which I am heartily sorry for—not that the business is going on, but that they talk so much about it. I wish they would be as reserved to others as Clarke is to me. But what do I care for his reserve? let them once do the business, and treat me as they like.

11. Sullivan called on me this morning, (for it is he who brings my secondary intelligence,) to tell me that D'Albarade, the late Minister of the Marine, is to command in the naval department of our

expedition, and that a confidential person told him yesterday he might look for good news soon for his country, as there was something at that moment doing for her in Holland, by which I presume that it is there preparations are making. I am glad of that. I mentioned Holland myself to Carnot, Clarke, and the Minister. By-the-by, the Minister is on the eve of being turned out, but as the business is now in the hands of Carnot himself, I am in hopes that will make no difference as to us. I do not glory at all in the present aspect of things.

12. Blank! How my life stagnates just now:— Well, " 'tis but in vain."

13. Aherne called on me this morning, to tell me that yesterday he saw Clarke, to whom he was introduced by Ysabeau, one of the *chefs de bureau* under the Minister of Foreign Affairs. He seems egregiously disgusted with both of them, and especially with Clarke, who I find has been talking sad stuff. They did not conclude any thing; but he collected from them, that the idea was, that he should go to Ireland, and one or two persons come from that country to *insense* the French Government on the state of affairs. Aherne mentioned the loss of time this would produce, and also that I was on the spot, ready and competent to give them every information. Clarke replied, after speaking handsomely of my abilities, that I had now been several months out of the country, and things might have changed since my departure; he also observed, that I seemed so earnest in the business, that my zeal might pro-

bably make me heighten the picture a little, without any intention of deceiving the French Government. To which Aherne replied, that all I had advanced was supported by the recent accounts in the papers, relative to Irish affairs. Clarke, however, did not seem satisfied, and so the affair rested. As to Ysabeau, who knows not one syllable with regard to the situation of Ireland, he has thrust himself into the business, and is to frame the instructions of Aherne. How he will contrive to adapt them to a subject of which he is totally ignorant, is more than I can possibly conceive. This is most intolerably provoking. Here is the liberty of Ireland shuffled back and forward between two French *commis*, one of whom is under gross prejudices and the other absolutely ignorant. What is to be done? As to me, how shall I satisfy Clarke that I am not the dupe of my own enthusiasm in the cause, supposing he is gracious enough to give me credit for being sincere? The more earnestness I show to convince him, the more enthusiasm I manifest; so here I am in an unfortunate circle.—By-the-by, Clarke is just as competent to regulate this affair as I am to be made Lord Chancellor of England, and for my fitness for that station, I appeal to all who ever knew me, in the capacity of a lawyer. I have not forgotten his nonsense, about gaining over some of the Irish aristocracy to our side, to begin with; such as Lord Ormond, for example; neither have I forgotten his asking me, might we not make something of Fitzgibbon? Good God! is it not enough to set one mad, to be obliged to listen and keep my temper, not to say my countenance, at such execrable trash? And yet the fate of Ireland is in a certain degree in this man's hands. Well, well, wretched, I again repeat it, is the nation whose independence hangs on the will of another. Clarke has also some doubts, as to my report on the influence of the Irish priests, whom he dreads a good deal; and this is founded on his own observation, in a visit he paid to Ireland in the year 1789. That is to say, a Frenchman just peeps into the country for an instant, seven years ago, and then, in the heat of the revolution, sets up his opinion against mine, who have been on the spot, who have attentively studied and been confidentially employed, and to whom nothing relating to Catholic affairs could possibly be a secret. That is reasonable and modest in my friend Clarke. He likewise catechised Aherne, as to the chance of our preferring monarchy for our form of Government, in case of a successful revolution; adding that, in such a case, we should, of course, consult the French Government in our choice. This is selling the bear's skin with a vengeance. I wonder does he seriously think that, if we succeeded, we should come post to Paris to consult him, General Clarke, a handsome smooth-faced young man, as to what we should do. I can assure him we should not. When he spoke to me on this head, he was more reasonable, for he said it was indifferent to the French Republic what form of Government we adopted, provided we secured our independence. It seems now he is more sanguine; but I, for one, will never be accessory to subjecting my country to the control of France, merely to get rid of that of England. We are able enough to take care of ourselves, if we were once afloat; or if we are not, we deserve to sink. So much for Clarke. As to his *confrère*, the other *commis*, Ysabeau, who has got into this business God knows how! (for I do not,) it is still more provoking. Aherne tells me he is a blockhead; but if he had ever such talents, how the devil can he give instructions on a subject of which he is utterly ignorant? I suppose he will hardly be inspired on the occasion. Well, poor Ireland, poor Ireland! here you are, at the mercy of two clerks, utterly incapable, supposing them honest; if they be not, (and who knows?) it is still worse. Aherne is gone to Ysabeau, to whom, by-the-by, Madgett gave in a draft of instructions, which he never showed me, (I know not why,) and which Ysabeau never condescended to read. I will stop to see what this conversation will produce. * * * * *

*Ysabeau is turned out!* A pretty time they choose to intrust him with the secret. Is not this folly incredible? Aherne saw the Minister himself, and spoke his opinion without reserve of Clarke, whom he thinks not honest. I do not know; I remember he told me in our first conversation, he was related to Lord Cahir and the Butler family, in Ireland. Lord Cahir is married to Fitzgibbon's niece. Will this explain his anxiety about the aristocracy, and his wish to hook in Lord Ormond, the head of the Butlers, and the monstrous extravagance of his questions about Fitzgibbon? It has a very odd appearance. If he should turn out a scoundrel, I will see what is fit for me to do; and if it is necessary to punish him personally, I *will* do it; for I begin to dislike him mortally. It seems he told Aherne, that the latter should apprize the people in Ireland to be on the look-out for assistance in September, or it might be November next (six or seven months!) and this he qualified by saying, " unless something should happen in the course of the campaign to prevent it;" a pretty general exception. When Aherne told this to the Minister, he seemed astonished; for the fact is, he is utterly unacquainted with the business. He, therefore, got rid of it, by giving Aherne a few queries in writing on the subject of Ireland, the answers to which are already in my memorial; but it was merely to gain time, and he said he would see Clarke himself, and let Aherne know the result to-morrow at one o'clock, and then give him his final instructions. Altogether, things cannot look worse. If Clarke be not honest, we are blown up. I have determined as to what I will do myself; I will first learn the result of the Minister's conversation with Aherne to-morrow, and what Clarke has said to him; I will then go to Clarke myself, and have an explanation with him, and I will insist upon being, in a certain degree, informed of what is going forward, which hitherto I have not done; in short, I will endeavour to bring him to something definite. If I find that impossible, I will write to Carnot my opinion fully, as well of the mode of doing business here in general, as of Clarke's conduct in particular, without the least reserve, and the grounds on which I found that opinion. I will likewise demand, that all my future communications be directly with himself, and state that I shall look on the rejection of this request as a symptom that the measure is abandoned. And if General Clarke is offended at all this, let him take his remedy. I suspect most violently that he is secretly counteracting the business, to save his noble connexions in Ireland; and if so, I should be heartily glad to have an opportunity to punish him personally. After all, it is possible he may be innocent, and I will not proceed but upon good grounds, such as will satisfy my conscience. Aherne is *acharné* against him, and so is Sullivan: I am much cooler than either of them. Aherne will denounce him again to the Minister, especially for what he said as to our consulting France relative to the choice of a monarch, which is, to be sure, most unaccountable in Clarke. Sullivan will set Prieur and Laignelot on his back. For my part, I know nobody, and of course I have not the power if I had the wish to intrigue against him, which I disdain to do. If I find him, or have satisfactory reasons to suspect him, to be a traitor in the business, I will denounce him at once to Carnot, and let him then act as he pleases. Aherne and Sullivan, who know the *pavé* better than I do, are satisfied he is betraying us. For my part, I am not convinced, though I see appearances strong against him. I will wait for further proof; and if I am once decided, I will then do what is right. Let us see what the next three or four days will produce, and in the mean time do nothing rashly. Dined at Aherne's, with Madgett and Sullivan. Choice Champaign—get half tipsy, partly with rage and vexation at the prospect before me. Have I risked my life, ruined my prospects, left my family and deserted my country, to be baffled by a scoundrel at last? If he prove one, woe be to him!

14. Breakfast with Aherne and Sullivan. They still hold their opinion as to Clarke. I will wait for further evidence. Aherne is to see the Minister to-day, and that will be one step towards demonstration. Agreed to dine together. Dinner—Aherne could not see the Minister: so nothing is done.

15. Went with Aherne to the Minister, and met with a most gracious reception. He had seen Clarke, to whom the military part of the business had been intrusted, and who assured him that preparations were actually making in the interior of Holland. With regard to Aherne, he said his instructions would be ready in three or four days. Then we shall see something of the matter. I mentioned to him the arrest of Keogh, and the embarrassment it must produce in our affairs. He observed, it would only inflame the people's minds the more. I answered, as to them they had been sufficiently inflamed already; but the embarrassment which I saw was in the imprisonment of him and others, inas-

much as they could be of such service in framing a provisional government. I observed, likewise, and begged him to remember, that the very men I had pointed out as my friends, and as the proper persons to speak to in Ireland, were the very people now imprisoned and persecuted by the British Government. I also took the opportunity to apologize for not seeing him oftener; said that I knew the value of his time too well to take it up in visits of ceremony, and we parted the best friends in the world; he assuring me that in every part of the business wherein he was engaged, I might depend on his utmost exertions. I must now wait till I see Aherne's instructions.

18. Called on Clarke, who is very reserved of late. Let him be! He had nothing to tell me of our expedition, but said they had some scheme of introducing *Chouannerie* in England, and desired I would write a paper fit to be distributed, in case of a landing on that scheme being effected. I told him I could not do it; that I did not know the grievances of England, and could not write in the character of a Frenchman. He said he was sure I could if I would try. So to get rid of the business, I said I would make the attempt, but won't. He is plaguy fond of *Chouannerie*.

20. This being the 1st Floreal, I left the *Hotel des Etrangers*, where I have been fleeced like ten thousand devils, and removed to the house where Aherne lodges, where I hope I shall live cheaper and more comfortably. Went with Aherne, at one o'clock, to

the Minister's, in order to see after his instructions. At last there is a prospect of something like business. The Minister read the draft of the instructions, in which there is a great deal of trash mixed with some good sense. Only think of one of the articles, wherein they say that if Ireland continues devoted to the house of Stuart, one of that family can be found who will be agreeable to all parties! Who the devil is this Pretender *in petto?* It is all one to us, however, for we will have nothing to do with him. I made one or two observations on the instructions, to the Minister; he acted very fairly; for he gave them to me, and desired me to make what observations struck me; and as to Aherne, he said that he must only be guided by such of them as might apply to the state of things he found there, and disregard those that did not; all which is candid. I see the instructions are written by Clarke, for I find in them his trash about monarchy, the noblesse, and clergy. There is one thing, however, which reconciles me to all this absurdity, which is, that the French Government promise us 10,000 men and 20,000 stand of arms; with that force I have not the shadow of doubt of our success. It is to be escorted by nine sail of the line, (Dutch, I believe,) and three frigates, and will be ready about the middle or towards the end of May, which is not more than six weeks off. If this be so—but let me not be sanguine. Went to Madgett to communicate this good news, and fixed to dine together, (Aherne, he, and I,) in the Champs Elysées. Dined accordingly; drank rather enough.

Walked out and saw the French soldiery dancing in groups, under the trees, with their wives and mistresses. Judge whether, in the humour I was in, with near two bottles of Burgundy in my head, I did not enjoy the spectacle. How often did I wish for my dearest love! Returned to the Restaurateur, and indeed drank off another bottle, which made three, and returned home in a state of considerable elevation, having several delightful visions before my eyes. Well, "Wine does wonders, does wonders every day." Bed: slept like a top.

21. Walked about Paris, diverting myself innocently. "I 'gin to be a-weary of the Sun!" I wish I could see once more the green sod of Ireland; yet Paris is delightful: but then "home is home." Well, who knows? I may be there yet.

22. Copied Aherne's instructions, and wrote my observations, which are very short. I barely mention what is necessary, and for the rest I say all is right; and that when he arrives in Ireland, I have no doubt but the people there will execute every part of them which circumstances will admit. Gave them to Madgett to translate. Went to Clarke to apprize him of my having changed my lodging: asked him, had he any news for me? He answered not. I replied that hitherto he had not found me very pressing for information; but that, nevertheless, I expected, when the time came, I should be properly apprized of every thing. He replied, "Certainly." I also said that, as to my own affairs, which I had scarcely mentioned, I hoped and expected that the

request which I had suggested once already to him, of being employed in the expedition, as an officer in the French service, would not be refused. He answered, I might depend upon that. I then mentioned the old subject of the necessity of losing no time: to which he replied, with an air of great significance, that, if the affair was undertaken, it would be within two years at any rate. He is a puppy, that is the truth of it. This good-humoured irony, I dare say, he thought extremely diplomatic; but I can assure him he acts the statesman very poorly. He is much fitter to figure away at Ranelagh than in a *bureau diplomatique,* for he is a handsome lad. I then mentioned Pichegru to him, observing that any old woman would make an Ambassador for Sweden, where they are sending him, whereas our expedition required a man of great talents and military reputation. He replied he was sure Pichegru would not undertake it. I said, I was not so sure of that; that if glory was an object with him, as doubtless it was, the dismemberment of the empire of England, the destruction of her power, and the establishment of a new republic in Europe of 4,500,000 people, were not ordinary occurrences. That if he was a man to be influenced by interested considerations, there was no doubt but, in case of our success, he would be rewarded by Ireland to the utmost extent of his wishes, as well as every person who was instrumental in effectuating her emancipation. This hint I threw out for the citizen Clarke himself. He made some vague indefinite answer, which signified nothing; so I dropped the subject, and shall not renew it with him: but I have a little scheme on that score, which a few days may develope. He then attacked me about his proclamation for *Chouannising* England. I replied that I had done nothing in it, and that if he would permit me to give my opinion, the measure was unwise and impracticable; that the peasantry of England were not at all in a situation which rendered it likely they would take any part in such a business, for several reasons, which I enumerated: that perhaps in Scotland, (which, however, I was not sure of,) it might do; but in England, never. He pressed me, however, to write the manifesto. I replied, as before, that I did not know their grievances, and would much rather write one for Ireland, which I did know. He desired me to do that also, and without loss of time. I promised him I would; and so we parted. He is a strange fellow. Does he know that the Minister has told me every thing that he is apprized of, relative to the business: and, if so, why all this prodigious reserve on his part? I suppose he has heard that secrecy is a necessary quality in a great statesman, and so he is acting this part, to impress me with an idea of his diplomatic talents. He is very much out, I can tell him. Standing as I do here, I confess I do not see the policy of concealing the measure from me, more especially when I hear it directly from the Minister, and indirectly, which I am very sorry for, from a dozen different quarters. Well, let him go to the dogs; though he is a pretty gentleman. I believe I am at least as much interested in the success of the measure as he is, and perhaps a little more. Confound him, I do not like him.

24. Called on Madgett to get my observations, which I gave him to translate. He tells me he has them not. Hell and the devil! Sure he has not lost them. It would be a pretty paper to set afloat just now in Paris, where there are, for aught I know, a thousand English spies. If it be gone, I do not know what may be the consequence; perhaps the blowing up of the whole expedition. Left Madgett in a rage, which I could scarcely conceal. *Evening*—he has found the papers. *Ah, je respire.* If he had lost them, I should never have forgiven him. Get Sullivan to translate them. To-morrow we go to the Minister's. The French have begun the campaign by a splendid victory in Italy; the negotiations between Wickham and Barthelemi have produced nothing, and the cry is now "*Guerre aux Anglais.*" All this is very good. *Theatre de la République:* Macbeth, by Ducis, much better than his Othello. Talma, in Macbeth; a most excellent actor. Lady Macbeth by Madame Vestris: very good, had I not seen Mrs. Siddons, before whom all the actresses here vanish. A good ridiculous farce, supported entirely by Dugazon, who represents five different characters. "Affairs look so well in the North, that it is impossible to displease me."

25. Went with Aherne to the Minister's, and gave him my observations, which he read, and liked

very well. He struck out, in consequence, all the stuff about royalty, &c. and returned the instructions to Aherne, in order to his copying them; but kept my observations, to show them to Carnot. He tells me Aherne will be despatched in a few days, and that he has every reason to think the expedition will be ready by the latter end of May. I begin to speak French like a Nabob. I astonished the Minister to-day with the volubility of my diction. On leaving De la Croix, who, by-the-by, has had a narrow chance of being turned out, but is now, I fancy, pretty safe, I met Sullivan, who gave me an English paper, with the quarters of the army in Ireland for this year; I was very glad to get it. I see but nine regiments of dragoons, and two of troops of the line; the rest all fencibles or militia: there is to be a camp of about 2,500 men in the North; and 2000 near Dublin, which with the garrison will make about 6,500 men. The whole force is about 30,000 men, as I guessed; but I am sure not above 20,000 effective. I have not the least doubt of success, if we can land with 10,000 French. Apropos of the French. Two days after the victory mentioned in my journal of yesterday, (called the affair of Montenotte,) they had a second action, at Millesimo, with the Austrian and Sardinian armies, whom they utterly defeated, taking every thing that was takeable, including one Lieutenant General, and God knows how many officers, colours, cannon, standards, and stores, together with 8,500 men; a pretty moderate victory, being the second in two days. I give up discipline for ever, after this, *provided always*, that we can raise such a spirit of enthusiasm, which I hope and believe is very possible, among the Irish. The French General is Buonaparte, a Corsican. Two French generals were killed at the head of their columns, and a third desperately wounded, leaping with seven grenadiers into the Austrian works; but, as I have often told P. P. " we are certainly the bravest nation in Europe." I cannot recall the names of the English generals who have fallen in this war, *within*, or, indeed, *without*, the enemy's lines. There was only one killed, Mansel, and he was an Irishman. This piece of news will wonderfully regale John Bull, especially coming close on the heels of a second loan of 7,500,000l. which he has cunningly borrowed from himself, in order to put down French principles, and preserve the regular Governments of Europe. The regular Government of Sardinia (which island is in open revolt) is in a hopeful way after the last battle. *The Atheists* are now within fifteen leagues of Turin, and only one strong place in their way; besides that, they creep into your strong places like cats. Ah! John! thou art a deep one. I declare I am in as pleasant a humour as a man could wish to see of a summer's day. One thing I wish to remark here, because it may be of use: If we have any generals killed, leaping in or out of trenches, their families must always be adopted by the Republic. I know nothing, judging by my own feelings, so likely to make men fight with enthusiasm, as the consciousness that their wives and children, in case of their falling in the public service, will become the objects of national gratitude. I like my new lodging very well, and especially I like being rid of that infernal extorting mansion, *L'Hotel des Etrangers, Rue Vivienne.* The villains have hardly left me one louis.

26. Wrote a short memorial on the force and disposition of the army in Ireland, as it appears in the English papers, and gave it to Sullivan to translate. I think it is very prettily done, which is not the case with all my productions. I will give it to the Minister to-morrow. Went in the evening to the theatre; Mademoiselle Ferlon a good actress, and pretty.

27. Sullivan brought me my memorial admirably translated. Went at one o'clock to the Minister's, where I met Aherne. The Minister tells us the Directory is just now occupied by very important business, but in two or three days will be disengaged, and then Aherne will receive his final instructions and be despatched; he also told me, that matters were so arranged, and combinations made, that in a month every thing would be ready. All this is excellent; but I am sworn never to believe it till I see it. What makes these notes valuable (that is to say, to myself and to my dearest life and love) is, that they are a faithful transcript of all that passes in my mind, of my hopes and fears, my doubts and expectations, in this important business. The Minister also said, he would instantly have a

copy made of my remarks, and have them given to Carnot; by which I see, or suppose at least, that the business is entirely in his hands, of which I am sincerely glad, for he is the man I have all along wished to fix my claws in. By-the-by, I must see the aforesaid organizer shortly, to wit, in three or four days, because I meditate a little stroke of politics (being my first); let us see how it will succeed! I intend artfully to insinuate a thing or two to him. I want, likewise, to sound him about Pichegru. As he is a "shallow Pomona," I foresee I shall overreach him. This day's paper gives an account of a third victory by the Army of Italy. It seems they were too confident on the two former ones, which induced Beaulieu, the Austrian General, though twice beaten, to make the attack with the *élite* of his army, with which he surprised the French right wing; and it was not without the most vigorous efforts of the remainder of the army, that he was at length repulsed, which, however, he was effectually, leaving 2,500 men in prisoners only. The French loss must have been severe. In the three battles, four generals have fallen, and three are desperately wounded; very like the British generals in Flanders, as I have already remarked with great wit and severity. The idea of attacking the French after being twice defeated, does Beaulieu's talents great honour; and had it not been for the invincible valour of the French soldiery, it seems very likely that he would have succeeded. As it was, it was a work of great difficulty to repulse him, the battle continuing from daybreak to three in the afternoon. Went in the evening to the *Theatre Feydeau.* Here are the veterans of the French stage : it is the Drury Lane of Paris. Molé is an excellent actor; in manner, age, voice, figure, and talents, he puts me strongly in mind of King. Mademoiselle Contat is a delicious woman; she is the Miss Farren of the *Rue Feydeau,* and in all respects just such another actress. She is forty years of age, and certainly does not appear to be above twenty-five. She has been the mistress of the whole French *ci-devant* nobility, and of course has no great devotion to the Revolution; yet she lives now, I am told, with Legendre the Deputy, who was, and for aught I know, is, a butcher in Paris. I confess I am so much of an aristocrat, that I do not glory in that circumstance. It is a scandalous fact, but I am afraid too true, that many deputies have availed themselves of their situation to secure the possession of beautiful women, who submit to their embraces to secure their protection. If so, it is abominable; I do not like to see the Republic pimp for Legendre. But people here mind these things much less than I do; for, on this topic, I have perhaps extravagant notions of delicacy and refinement, and their manners here are horribly dissolute, by all I can learn. Well, give me my own countrywomen, after all; they are the *materiel* to make wives and mothers. If I wanted a mistress, I would go to Paris or London. Protection! Legendre's protection! I like no protection but the protection of the law; that protects all. I find I am growing angry on this subject, so I will quit it. May be I am jealous of Legendre. Oh Lord! Oh Lord! Jealous indeed! Marry come up. Well, I am sleepy now, so I will go to bed, and Mademoiselle Contat may do the same, if she pleases.

28, 29. Blank! Blank! Is not this cruel; but what can I do? I have not lost one minute by my negligence since my arrival in Paris; well, that is some comfort, however. Madgett tells me peace is as good as concluded with the King of Sardinia, and that these late victories will give him a plausible excuse for cutting out of the party like the King of Spain. He tells me also that a revolution is organized in Piedmont and Sardinia; so that it is highly probable the poor *Roi des marmottes* may go and keep company with the Stadtholder: a pretty dialogue they would have in meeting! Voltaire's supper of the six kings, (was it six?) seems likely to be realized. But it is sad that I must be writing of revolutions in Piedmont and Sardinia, instead of ―――. Well! "'Tis but in vain," &c.

30. Called on Clarke again; he is a sad puppy, and I am fairly tired of him. Our dialogue is always the same. "Well, General Clarke, I have called to know if you have any thing to tell me."—"Not a word."—"Well, I hope when there is any thing going forward, you will let me know." Two or three words of common-place discourse follow, and so I take my leave, as ignorant as a horse. I confess I cannot fathom General Clarke's policy in

keeping me so totally in the dark. Moreover, to-day he was not over civil; for he spoke to me *en passant* in the porter's ante-chamber, being, as he said, in a hurry. If he was in twice as great a hurry, he might have spoken to me in his cabinet. I will not forget it to him, that I can tell him. I once filled a station as honourable as his, and I hope yet perhaps to fill one far above it; and if I do, I must not give myself airs like General Clarke. The puppy! I am as angry as the devil. One thing, however, I will do; as I have given him, by Carnot's orders, all the directions in my power, and as he will tell me nothing in return, but, on the contrary, evidently shows a disposition to avoid me, I will not call on him any more; I will very gingerly demand an audience of Carnot himself, and see what that will produce. This is sad! "I am as melancholy as a gib cat, or a lugged bear," and I cannot help myself.

## May 1796.

1. Blank! Thinking of my interview with Carnot; I declare I am literally tired of my life.

2. Went to the Luxembourg; saw Rewbell giving audience in his costume; wrote a note desiring to see Carnot, and was admitted; he recollected me perfectly. I began by saying, fluently enough, that in pursuance of his orders I had been several times with General Clarke, and had given him all the information I was possessed of, as well verbally as by memorials and

other papers. He said he knew I had. I then observed that, considering General Clarke as in an official situation, I had avoided pressing him to give me any information in return; but that, at present, when I learned directly from the Minister, and indirectly from many other quarters, that preparations were in a considerable degree of forwardness for the expedition, I hoped, when he considered the efforts I had made, the risks I had run, the dangers I had escaped, in endeavouring to lay the state of Ireland before the French Government, as well as the situation I had once the honour to fill in my own country, that he would not consider me unreasonably importunate in requesting him to give me such information as he might deem proper, as to the state of the expedition, supposing it were to take place. He replied, my request was not at all unreasonable; but that, before measures were finally determined upon, it would be necessary that the French Government should be satisfied as to the actual state of things in Ireland; and for that purpose a person should be sent to observe every thing, and make his report accordingly; for, if the people there were amicable to the French Republic, the attempt might be made, but if not, it would require a considerable force to conquer the country. This was a staggering blow to me, to find myself no farther advanced at the end of three months, than I was at my first audience. However, I recollected myself, and said, that undoubtedly the French Government was in the right to expect every possible information as to the actual state of the country; but that I begged leave to observe, there were few individuals more competent from their situation to give them that information than myself,—much more so than any stranger they might send, who would just slide into the country for a moment, and return, if he were lucky enough to escape; that, as to all I had advanced, I hoped he would find my assertions confirmed by the English Gazettes; that, nevertheless, if he doubted my information, or supposed that affairs might be altered since my departure from Ireland, and so thought it necessary to send a confidential person, I begged him to remember that the time was precious, and that there was not one moment to lose. He said he understood that I could not go myself. I answered I was too well known in that country to be there four-and-twenty hours, without being discovered and seized; that, consequently, I was the most unfit person in the world; but I took the opportunity to repeat that, if the expedition were undertaken, I hoped to be permitted to bear a part in its execution. He replied that the French Government would, in that case, certainly avail themselves of my courage and talents *(profiter de votre courage et de vos talens.)* But still he did not say whether the expedition would take place or not, though this was the second push I made at him on that head. When I saw he would not give me any definite information, I observed that there was a subject on which I had received such positive instructions on leaving Ireland, that I considered myself bound to mention it to him; and that was relative to the General who might be appointed to the command; that it was our wish, if possible, it should be Pichegru; that if he had remained at the head of the army of the Rhine, I probably should not have mentioned him; but that at present, when he was not employed in any military function, I hoped I was not irregular in praying him (Carnot) to turn his thoughts on Pichegru for that command; supposing, as before, that the expedition was to take place. Carnot replied, that undoubtedly Pichegru was an officer of consummate talents, but, at the same time, there were many generals not inferior to him in abilities (*aussi forts que lui.*) I replied, I was satisfied the Republic abounded with excellent officers; but that, in my country, the prejudice as to Pichegru's character was so strong, that I rated him equal to an army of 20,000 men, as to the effect his appointment would have on both parties in Ireland. He replied, that he would give every consideration to what I said on the subject, and that, at any rate, I had done perfectly right in suggesting Pichegru to the notice of the Directory. I then observed, that, as to Pichegru himself, I thought the appointment would add a new lustre to his former glory; that, if he desired fame, the assisting in creating a free Republic of 4,500,000 people, was an object of no ordinary magnitude; and if he was studious of his interest, which I did not suppose, he might rely on the gratitude of my country in its fullest extent, as might every person who should be instrumental in establishing her liberties. Just at this moment, General Clarke entered, and I cannot say that he seemed highly delighted at the *rencontre*. I took my leave of Carnot, and went over to speak to him. I told him in substance our conversation as above written, and when I mentioned Pichegru, he said, "Pichegru! Oh, he won't accept it." I said I was sorry for it. He then asked me if I had finished his proclamation for *Chouannising* England? I told him I found it impossible; but that I would finish the one I had begun for Ireland, whose grievances I knew, and with whose local circumstances I was acquainted; of both of which, with regard to England, I was utterly ignorant. He desired me then to finish that one, and bring it to him, without loss of time. I said I would in the course of four or five days, and took my leave. So! "I have got much by my intended expostulation," as Sir Peter Teazle says. In the first place, I am utterly ignorant whether there is any design to attempt the expedition or not; I put it twice to Carnot, and could extract no answer. My belief is, that as yet there is no one step taken in the business, and that, in fact, the expedition will not be undertaken. What signifies what the minister says? he is on the eve of being turned out every day, and is at this moment at open war with the Directory. They want him to resign, and he will not, but says they may dismiss him if they please. (By-the-by, the Directory are too fond of changing their ministers, which shows either want of judgment in forming their choice, or want of steadiness in adhering to it.) They are of course not very likely just now to trust him with their designs. I therefore must regard all he says, and Madgett from him, as of no authority whatsoever; and that being the case, it is impossible things can wear a more frosty appearance for our hopes. I am pretty sure Carnot has never read one line of my memorials, but has taken them on the report of Clarke; and God only knows what that report may have been. I cannot get it out of my head that that fellow is betraying the cause, or at least doing every thing in his power to thwart and oppose it; and what can I possibly do to prevent him? Absolutely nothing! That is hard; I fear all my exertions and sacrifices, and hopes, will come to nothing at last. Well, if it should be so, I hope I shall be able to bear it; but it is cruel. I begin now to think of my family and cottage again. I fancy it will be my lot at last to bury them and myself in the back-woods of America. My poor little boys! I had almost begun to entertain hopes of being able to rescue them from that obscurity, and above all things, to place my wife and our dear Maria in a situation more worthy of them: but, if I cannot, I must submit; it is at least no fault of mine; I think I have left nothing on my part undone, or untried, or unhazarded. If I have to go back to the woods, I must see and inveigle P. P. out with me, otherwise I shall be in great solitude. Perhaps Mr. William Browne is at home before me: at home! And is that to be our home after all? Well, if it must, it must. From this day, I will gradually diminish the little hope I had begun to form. I suppose another month at most will decide our fate, and if that decision be adverse, I will then try the justice and generosity of the French Government, in my own particular case. If they make me compensation, so; if they do not, I have nothing to do but to submit, and return in the first vessel to America. At least I shall be sure of tranquillity and happiness in the bosom of my family, especially if I can catch P. P. and Mr. William Browne. I will now wait to see what they will do with Aherne. If they despatch him promptly, the business may yet revive. If they delay him, or send a person of Clarke's choosing, I shall look on it as utterly desperate, and take my measures accordingly.

3—7. What signifies my making daily journals when I have nothing to say? The Directory gives me no business, and I am not in spirits to write good nonsense, and am tired of saying blank! blank! This day wrote an artful letter to Clarke, to see if I can list him, on the score of his interest:—it is also his duty. This is sad work, but what can I do? *Il faut hurler avec les loups.* I engage him 1000*l.* a-year for his life, if we succeed, and I rely on the nation to make good my engagement.

9. Saw Clarke; he told me that, if he gave me no information, it was because he was not permitted; that I might rely on receiving it, as soon as it was necessary I should be informed; and that I might also depend on it, that, *if the expedition was undertaken,* every thing should be made as agreeable to

me, personally, as I could desire. All this is civil, however; but still it is not what I want to come at. I told him, as usual, that I did not mean to press him, and would wait, in submission, for the determination of the Directory. I then asked him, had he read my letter? He said he had; but, as to any idea of reward, he was in the service of France, and it must be to her he should look for compensation. I replied, certainly it was just that France should reward him, but that did not preclude Ireland also from manifesting her gratitude; that he might rely on it, every individual in France who was instrumental in establishing our independence would be amply rewarded at the conclusion of the war. He replied, " We should not have the means; we had no money; and besides that, he did not much count on the gratitude of nations." To this I answered, that it was true we had little or no money, but that we had abundance of means besides: and as to the gratitude of nations, I did not think quite so humbly of it as he seemed to do; that America was an instance to the contrary, where every soldier and officer had been rewarded on the establishment of her independence, and where Lafayette had a provision of 80,000 acres of land, which was all he had to trust to at this moment on earth; and that I hoped we were as capable of gratitude as the Americans. I stopped there, and the discourse turned on the condition of Ireland. He asked me, had I finished the proclamation? I said not, but that I would bring it to him in two or three days at farthest. I then took my leave. On the whole I made no great way in this day's conversation; yet I was better pleased with Clarke, I do not know why, than I have been a long time past. He has got my memorandum on the number and disposition of the troops of Ireland. I also saw among his papers relating to the expedition, one, in the margin of which were the names of several towns in Holland and Dutch Flanders: what does that forebode? I cannot decypher, so let me go finish my proclamation: I have not looked at it since the 27th of April. I see I was in a wrong track, so I will begin on a new plan: *Courage, mon ami! allons!*

10. Madgett has got orders to find ten or a dozen intelligent prisoners, who are to be sent into England. Into England, of all places in the world! What can that mean? He tells me there is to be an expedition there, contemporary with ours, in order to cut out work for John Bull at home, and prevent his distracting his poor head too much about his Irish affairs. He tells me, also, that Hoche is to command in England. If that be so, it looks serious, but Madgett is so terribly sanguine that I know not what to think. I will say, for the present, in the language of the Gazette, " this news merits further confirmation." At work at my proclamation.

11. At work furiously at my proclamation; I like it better than my first attempt. Madgett is gone in search of his imps, whom he has orders to send off to Hoche as soon as he has found them. That looks a little serious, but still I am slow of

faith. This day the *Directoire Executif* has denounced a grand plot to massacre themselves, the legislative bodies, and the Etat Major of Paris, and to proclaim the constitution of 1793. Above forty persons have been arrested, and, at the head of them, Drouet, who stopped the King at Varennes in 1792, and has lain for three years in a dungeon in Austria, from whence he has returned not above six months. I am sorry for him, for I believe him a sincere republican; at the same time I would show no mercy to any man, whatever might be his past merits, who would endeavour, in the present position of France, to subvert the existing Government. If the plot had taken place, our business would have been in a hopeful way. I think, in my conscience, the French have, at this moment, an exceeding good form of Government, and such as every man of principle is bound to support. It might possibly be better, but the advantages which might result from an alteration are not such as to warrant any honest man in hazarding the consequences of another bloody revolution. The people of this turbulent city seem of the same way of thinking. I do not imagine, from all I can observe, that it would be easy, or, indeed possible, at present, to excite a serious insurrection in Paris. The Government is strong, the *enragés* are few, and the mass of the people seems disposed for tranquillity at any rate. As a friend to France and Ireland, and as an irreconcilable enemy to England, I am heartily glad of it, for I am not so completely *ultra-revolutionnaire* as some to whom I speak here. As an Irishman, I cannot but rejoice at the discovery of this complot. Had it succeeded, what would have become of us? Apropos! There is a law passed to-day, enjoining, amongst other things, all strangers to quit Paris in three days. I must apply to the Minister, and see what he says on that head.

12. Finished my memorial and gave it to Clarke. I should say, my proclamation. It is too long, but let Carnot cut it down as he pleases. Went to the Minister for permission to stay in Paris, *malgré la loi*. The Minister occupied: so I wrote him a short note, in very pretty French, which I left for him. In the evening the spectacle as usual. The French comedians are infinitely beyond the English. Even in the little theatres on the Boulevards, they perform admirably, and there is an attention to costume never seen in England. All the theatres too are pretty, and some magnificent. The opera, however, continues to stand first in my opinion. It is a charming spectacle, and I never go there without wishing for my dearest love. But matters are so uncertain here, that I labour to prevent myself wishing for any thing. I am a dog—I am a dog, and I lead a dog's life here, dancing attendance perpetually, and in constant suspense. I have, I know not why, foregone my usual amusements. Sad! sad! "Man delights not me, nor woman neither." What shall I do? the novelty of Paris is worn off, my anxiety about our affairs increases, and I get no satisfactory information. The devil puts it into my head some-

times that I am like Hannibal at the court of Prusias, supplicating his aid to enable Carthage to make war upon the Romans. There is a sort of analogy in the circumstances, excepting that I am not Hannibal, nor General Clarke, Prusias. Well, politics are fine things, *mais c'est quand on en est revenu.* I declare I wish our revolution was effected, and that I was set down once more quietly in the bosom of my family, and that is not very strange, for I doat upon them, and I am here like a fish out of water, and every thing frets me. Yet I admire the French, of all things; the men are agreeable and the women enchanting, and, if my mind were at ease, as it is not, I could make it out here very well, for some time longer, but as it is—— Well, I can't help myself, and so what signifies complaining. Let me write nonsense, and I cannot write good nonsense when I am not in spirits, and I am never in spirits now.—The French women are before the English, far and wide. They are incomparably well made, almost without exception. The English women have handsome faces; but, for figure and fashion, they do not approach the French; and then the latter walk so incomparably, and their language is so adapted to conversation, that they all appear to have wit. For their morality, it is, to be sure, "a nice morality, split my windpipe!" Paris, in that respect, beats London hollow, and that is a bold word, after what I have *seen* in London. Well, give me Ireland, after all, for women to make wives and mothers of. For " *casual fruition,*" go to London, or, indeed, rather to Paris; but if you wish to be happy, choose your companion at home. The more I see of this wide world, the more I prize the inestimable blessing I possess in my wife's affection, her virtues, her courage, her goodness of heart, her sweetness of temper; and, besides, she is very pretty, a circumstance which does not lessen her value in my eyes. What is she doing just now, and what would I give to be with her and the little *fanfans* for half an hour?

13. Called on the Minister, relative to the law enjoining all foreigners to quit Paris in three days. The Minister very civil; desires me to give myself no trouble, but in case the police should molest me, apply directly to himself or Carnot. This will do for the present. Dined with Madgett at the Champs Elysees, and drank like a fish.

14. Wrote a letter to Clarke, praying him to apply to Carnot for a written order for my stay, in case of accidents. Paris is growing more and more stupid on my hands, and this horrible suspense and delay kill me. There is a sad falling off in my journals, but it is not my fault.

15. Went to the Directory and saw Carnot, who desired me to write a short memorial desiring leave to stay, and bring it to him to-morrow. Saw Aherne; nothing done in his business. This is bad.

16. Delivered my memorial at the Luxembourg, and received directions to apply at the *Secretariat General* for a permission. Lounged in the evening to the *Theatre d'Emulation*, one of the little thea-

tres on the Boulevards: it was Easter Monday, and being a fête, the house was filled with the *bonne bourgeoisie*, all dressed out, and as gay and happy as possible. I was agreeably surprised to find the piece was the "School for Scandal," extremely well adapted to the French stage, and very well represented. It had an effect upon me which I cannot describe; I was alone, and it brought a thousand recollections into my mind. Shall I ever see the "School for Scandal" in an English theatre again? Well! that is the least of my grievances. The French comedians are incomparable, even in this little theatre of the Boulevards; they acted admirably, particularly Charles, Sir Oliver, and Lady Teazle; they excel in the management of their by-play, but they have one fault—in their soliloquies they always address themselves too much to the audience, with the expression as if they were telling them a secret. "The soliloquy always to the Pit; that is the rule." The civic airs were applauded with something like sincerity—a circumstance which I have not remarked for some time. On the whole I was very well amused. But how my life stagnates just now, when I have nothing to write of but the theatres of the Boulevards. Sad!

18. This day I had a tift with my lover Carnot. In signing the memorial which I delivered to him, I had written my name Theobald Wolfe Tone, *(dit James Smith.)* The permission was made out in the name of T. W. Tone, and of course was refused to me when I applied for it in the name of James Smith. I was therefore obliged, sore against my

will, to apply again to Carnot, who spoke very chuff about the trouble I gave him to write a second memorandum. I was horribly vexed, and told him civilly, but drily, that I was sorry for the mistake, but that it was not my fault. He then wrote a second note to the Secretary, so I suppose to-morrow it will be made out properly. Men in high station ought not to speak short to people who do not deserve it. I take that to be a very pretty political maxim, and so halt here for the present. I have not recovered my good humour yet.

20. Received at last my permission to stay in Paris. Only think of the folly of some people. The first permission, as I saw to-day, was for *Le citoyen Theobold Wolfe Tone, refugie Irlandais*. That was a pretty business to spread on a paper which was to be seen by the Lord knows how many clerks and *commis*, as well at the Luxembourg as at the Municipalité. Well, it was no fault of mine, as I told Citizen Carnot yesterday, and besides there is no harm done, for the paper is cancelled; so that affair is off my hands, and I have nothing to do but divert myself, for the Government here give me no business: " Fie upon this idle life! I want work." It seems the plot discovered by the Directory was dreadfully sanguinary. Amongst other features, all strangers were to present themselves, in order to their being imprisoned, *voluntarily, under pain of death*. If the fact be so, it seems I have had, among others, a very good escape; for in times of revolution, it is a short journey, sometimes, from the prison to that " undis-

covered country, from whose bourne no traveller returns." Things are better as they are, for France and for us. It is curious to observe how the enthusiasm of the Revolution is abated; even the immortal victories of the Army of Italy have not the smallest effect. I observe it particularly at the *spectacles*, where they sing (by order of the Executive,) " *les Chants Civiques*," every night, which are received with the utmost phlegm, and sometimes worse. Enthusiasm is a passion which will not last for six years of a war, which, however glorious beyond all historical example, has been attended with great individual suffering. I observe, too, the young men are the most disaffected part of the nation, which is caused by the dominion of the women, who are aristocrats without exception. This is very natural, and very bad. I did expect the rising generation would have been good republicans, but I cannot say that the fact has justified my anticipations. They sculk as much as possible from the requisition, which they evade by every means in their power. To see them in Paris they are a race of wretched Sybarites, yet these very young men, when they are forced at length to join the armies, see how they fight! This is a curious paradox. I believe if the Republic were to suffer a sudden reverse, for example, if Brunswick were once more at the passes of Argonne, the old spirit of France would revive; but, as it is, there is no enthusiasm here. There is, however, a good succedaneum in a well-organized Government, which, combined with the untameable courage of the armies, does the business sufficiently, as, I believe, General Beaulieu and the King of Sardinia can bear witness. It is very lucky the new Government was established before this absolute decline of public spirit. If the enthusiasm had failed before the present system was organized to supply its place, I know not what might have happened. At any rate, if the combined despots had, in that case, made any progress in France, it would only once more have roused the energy of 1792, and the two succeeding years, so that, at last, it would have come to the same thing. It is the successes of France which have abated her enthusiasm. I believe this is enough of politics for the present; I will only add, that, if I were in the place of the Directory, I would forbid the singing of all political airs at the spectacles, for a forced spirit is always a bad one.

21. This morning, on sallying out, the first thing I saw was an *affiche* of a vessel to sail in ten days for New York. This knocked me in the head for the whole day. I have been planning a thousand schemes. To-morrow, I will see Madgett, in order to take his opinion on one or two points. If I can do it with safety to my wife, and our dear, dear babies, I think I will settle in France.

22. Called on Madgett, and took a serious walk with him in the Tuilleries. I told him I had considered my situation maturely, and the result was, I felt a strong inclination to settle in France. That, by a rough calculation, I supposed I could command about 400 louis d'ors, with which I

could do very little in America, unless I went very far back; and then I should feel myself helpless, not being inured to labour, and servants not being to be had. That I conceived property would now be very cheap in France, and, therefore, begged his advice on two points. First, whether he apprehended, as I did not, that there was any danger of a counter-revolution, by which I meant the restoration of royalty, &c.; and next, whether it would be more advisable to purchase national or patrimonial property, with the small sum which I could command? Madgett replied, that, as to a counter-revolution, he did not well know what to say, more than that it was an event far from improbable. That the Government was in the most extreme distress for money; that the *mandats* had failed, and what would be substituted he could not pretend to guess; that the approvisionment of Paris was a work of immense difficulty, and if there once came an actual scarcity of food, it was impossible to say what might be the result from the fury of a starving and enraged populace; any one of them might take it into his head to cry *Vive le Roi*, and, perhaps, the whole mass adopt it; that Pitt was moving heaven, earth, and hell, to ruin the finances; that the louis was to-day at 10,500 francs; that things were driven now to that state, that a very few days must decide whether the Government could go on or not, and that, for himself, he wished he was fairly out of it. He added, that perhaps it would be better to purchase patrimonial property, and that, with the sum I mentioned, I might procure an estate of ten times the value, or 4000*l.* We then fixed to meet in three or four days, and, in the mean time, he is to make inquiries, and turn the matter in his thoughts. For my own part, whether it is that I am younger and more sanguine than Madgett, or less acquainted with circumstances, I have not the smallest apprehension of a counter-revolution. The present Government is one of extraordinary mildness, perhaps too much so, but if pressed by an invincible necessity, they must, and I have no doubt will, have recourse to stronger measures. But what decides me is the excellent spirit of the army. The mutiny among the *Legion de Police,* which now appears to have been a ramification of Babœuf's plot, was quelled in an instant by the other troops, and I see to-day a most excellent address to the Directory, from the privates and non-commissioned officers of the 3d dragoons, who form a part of their guard. Whilst the armies continue steady, I fear nothing. I believe I can lay out the little money I can command to more advantage here than in America, supposing only the half of what Madgett says to be true; besides, I am here *à portée* of Ireland. I need not recite over my reasons, but, as at present advised, I think I will write an order by this vessel to my love, to convert every thing possible into specie, to buy louis d'ors at the Bank of Philadelphia, and set off for Havre, with our family, in the first ship that sails. Good God! how happy shall I be if I can fix them in a comfortable cottage in France. For my schemes of ambition, I am almost worn out of hope; I act now without expectation, and merely that I may say nothing on my part has been left untried or undone. If there comes a peace, and I settle here, it will be but a step for P. P. to come and visit us, and to be sure we will not make him welcome, and there is no wine in France, &c. I feel my ancient propensities revive a little.

23, 24, 25, 26. After balancing, for four or five days, and turning the matter every way in my thoughts, I have taken my resolution, and written this day to my dearest love, to Rowan, and Dr. Reynolds, acquainting them with my determination to settle in France, and desiring them to make preparations for the departure of my family with all possible haste. It is a bold measure, but " *Audaces fortuna juvat.*" If my negotiation here succeeds, it will be best they should be in France; if it fails, still I am satisfied it is more advisable for us to settle here than in America. At all events, the die is cast. It is an epoch in my life. I have decided to the best of my judgment, and if I fail, I fail. I am weary of floating about at the mercy of events; let me fix myself, if possible, at last.

27. Paris has been in a sort of smothered fermentation for several days, and I suppose a very few more must bring matters to a crisis. Within a fortnight, all the assignats will be called in and exchanged against their value in mandats, which, in other words, is changing at once the whole currency.

The small assignats of 100 francs, and under, will be allowed to circulate for the conveniency of the poor. A hundred livres in assignats are worth to-day about two pence halfpenny; their nominal value is £4 3s. 4d. That is a pretty reasonable depreciation. For my part, who am neither financier nor *agioteur*, I do not pretend to understand the question, but I can clearly see it is no ordinary matter to annul, at one blow, the entire currency of a nation, and substitute another in its place; yet it has been done once already in the case of the assignats, which superseded gold and silver, as the mandats will, I have no doubt, supersede the assignats. Something or other must be done, or the finances here will tumble. I hope the Government will have firmness. They seem lately to have been assuming a higher tone, and I am glad of it; for I sometimes could not help thinking of King Log, when I saw them insulted with impunity. If they stand bold, the enemies of the Republic will be put down; but if they go back one step, or even fluctuate, in my mind, they are lost. It is certainly a most critical period. If the Government holds out till the 1st Messidor, which is now three weeks off, and if their new scheme of finance succeeds, to secure which nothing seems wanting but firmness on their part, the Republic will be established for ever. As it is, " we are walking on embers, covered with unfaithful dust." Courage! a few days will settle the business, and I doubt not, for my part, prosperously. *Vive la Republique!* Yesterday I had a visit from the *Com-*

missaire de Police of my section, by order of the *Bureau Central de Paris,* in order to bring me before my betters for remaining in town contrary to the law of the 21st Floréal, concerning strangers. However, "I jumped suddenly upon him and deprived him of the use of his weapon," by producing my permission to remain, signed Carnot, and countersigned Legarde, Secretary, on which he begged my pardon, dressed a *procès verbal* of the business, which I signed, and so we parted the best friends in the world. This visit is owing to some blunder in the *Bureau Central,* where I went the day after I received my permission, to have it viewed by the proper officer, who omitted, I suppose, to make the necessary entry. I am glad to find the Government serious in compelling strangers to leave Paris; they are a pest to France, speculating in her funds and ruining her currency. I am told there is an exception in favour of Americans. If I were the Government, I would not suffer one of *them* to remain for whom the Ambassador would not engage personally, because of the multitude of English agents and spies, who all pass here for Americans.

29. Went to the *Fête des Victoires,* which was celebrated to-day in the Champ de Mars. The Directory, the Ministers, the *Corps Diplomatique,* &c. all assisted, in grand costume. Incense was burning before the statue of Liberty, and the usual civic hymns were chanted, with two or three new ones, composed for the occasion, and alluding to the successes of the Army of Italy. It was a superb spec-

tacle, and the spirit of the people seemed much better than I expected, under all the circumstances of the case. There were about 6000 troops under arms, divided into fourteen battalions, representing the fourteen armies of the Republic, each of which received from the hands of Carnot, the President, a standard, and a garland of oak, the emblem of victory, which was borne by the handsomest grenadier of the corps. The troops made a very fine appearance, all young healthy men, fit for active service. I was placed at the foot of the altar, in the middle of my *brethren* of the *corps diplomatique*, but, for particular reasons, I chose to remain incognito. Altogether, I was exceedingly pleased with the exhibition, and the tears were running down my cheeks when Carnot presented the wreaths and standards to the soldiers. It was a spectacle worthy of a grand Republic, and I enjoyed it with transport. *Vive la République!*

JUNE 1796.

3. A faint ray of hope has broken to-day across the impenetrable gloom which has, for some time back, enveloped my prospects. I called on Clarke, *pro forma*, not expecting to find him, in which I was not disappointed. I found, however, a note, informing me that he had read my proclamation, (see May 12,) and liked it very well; that, however, it would be necessary to curtail it somewhat, and that he desired to see me for that purpose, any time after this day and to-morrow. It is the first time

he has desired to see me. Well, that is something. I wrote an answer immediately, appointing the 18th Prairial, (6th June,) by which I leave him, out of respect, one day clear. Will any thing come of this? I am glad Clarke likes my proclamation, which I found too long myself. I see he has a correct taste in these things. If the expedition takes place, it will be something to boast of to have written the proclamation. But let me not be " running before my horse to market." I have kept my hopes under a strict regimen all along, and latterly, God knows, on a very low diet. I will not let this little breeze tempt me to spread a deal of canvass, merely to have it to furl again. Things are, however, better to-day than they were yesterday.

4, 5. A French lover of mine, M. Dugas, took me to-day to Versailles in his cabriolet. It is a pleasant drive of twelve miles from Paris, the environs of which are certainly before those of London, but far inferior to those of Dublin, which are beautiful beyond description, owing to the two great features of the sea and the Wicklow Mountains. The chateau of Versailles is truly magnificent, and the gardens of vast extent, but of most tiresome uniformity; all in the old school, straight alleys, clipt hedges, round basins, marble statues, and systems of terraces. It is a detestable style. There are some admirable paintings still remaining, particularly one of Charles I. of England, by Vandyck, which has been engraved by Strange, and one of Charles XII. of Sweden, which is a striking resemblance of

Lord Landaff. All the furniture has been removed or sold, except a most magnificent cabinet, which belonged to Marie Antoinette, and in which she kept her jewels. Nothing can exceed the extravagant flattery displayed in the ceilings, which are all painted in allegories, alluding to the different events in the reign of Louis XIV. who is represented in them, one time as Hercules, another as Mars, and again as Jupiter; what makes it still better is, that all these paintings were executed by his order. I was particularly struck with one, where there is a group of four figures, Louis XIV. his brother Orleans, the Grand Condé, and Turenne, certainly not ordinary men. Portraits of illustrious characters are the kind of painting which I like best. There is also a good portrait of Mme. de Maintenon. It would take a week to examine the palace and gardens, and I did not remain much above an hour. I saw, however, enough to satisfy me that the King of France was magnificently lodged; but, for my part, I should die of the spleen in a week, if I were confined to the chateau de Versailles. It is the same with all the palaces I have ever seen, which are not many. Hampton Court, in England, is magnificent, but it would be lost in Versailles. From the Chateau we walked to Trianon, which is about half a mile distant. The pavilion is beautiful, viz.: the outside, which is all I saw, being built wholly of coloured marble. The gardens are like those of Versailles, equally monotonous, but less extensive. We then went to the Petit Trianon, the favourite retreat of

Antoinette. It is a most delicious spot, completely finished in the English style. After the dreary regularity of the two other gardens, I was enchanted, and even the French acknowledged the infinite superiority of taste manifested in laying out the grounds. Trianon would be beautiful in England, but in France it is like fairy ground. There have been some pretty frolics executed here. I could not help making many profound reflections whilst I walked through it, " *de vanitate mundi et fuga sæculi.*" I do not wonder the Queen regretted to fall from the station she once held. Altogether it made me melancholy.

6. Called this morning, by appointment, upon General Clarke. Found him more cordial in his manner than ordinary. He told me he had read my proclamation, and found it extremely well done; that, however, it would be necessary to curtail it considerably, for the first point in these compositions is to insure their being read, and, for that, it is necessary they should be short; that there would be a longer one prepared for those who studied politics, but that mine was destined for the people and soldiery. I thought there was good sense in all this, and I can safely say that, in all the public papers I have ever written, I am above the personal vanity of an author, as I believe Gog can witness. I therefore told him I would mince it *sans remorse.* He then told me I might rely on it, they had not lost sight either of the business itself, or of my share in it. We then talked for a few minutes of the gigantic

foreign affairs, told him this day, that the French were landed in Ireland to the number of 15,000 men; that they had been perfectly well received by the people, who were flocking about them in thousands when the despatches were sent off; that he had this from Beffroy, a member of the Cinq-cent, who had it directly from one of the Directory. All this is very circumstantial and precise, and, I confess, staggers me extremely. There must be something in it, or how would Beffroy and Grandjean come to think of Ireland at all? A frigate (the Atalante) has also certainly arrived at Brest, within these few days, after accompanying a fleet of transports, &c. After all, if it should be to Ireland! Madgett is as sure of it as of his existence, and is most terribly chagrined at its being kept a secret from him. For my part, the main point to me is that the landing be effected; my concern in the business is the least part of it. Yet, I should be mortified to the last excess not to bear some part. "*Quoi! les Français en Irlande—et Montauciel n'y est pas?*" "I am lost in sensations of troubled emotions." On the whole, I think it very unlikely that the report should be true, yet it is certainly possible; and there are strong circumstances in its favour. Among others, it is now a month since Madgett sent off fifteen Irish prisoners to Hoche, by Clarke's orders, who said they were intended for England, which, by-the-by, I did not believe. (See May 11th.) But then, why should the Directory conceal such a piece of good news from the public, and why should Clarke con-

ceal it from me? If the report be true, they have
not kept faith with me; for both Carnot and Clarke
assured me, if the expedition were undertaken, I
should be of the party, and Clarke repeated it in our
last conversation; and, I confess, it would give me
great pain to be left out of the business here, after
having laboured successfully thus far. Notwithstanding all that, I wish to God the report were
true. That is the main point; my interests are of
little consequence, and, besides, in the long run, the
truth will come out, and justice be done to all parties.
Madgett is a thousand times more enraged than I
am, though I think with less reason; for he has
neither done nor suffered as much in the business as
I. Once for all, I do not yet believe it. A very
few days must ascertain the truth or falsehood of
the report, and, in the mean time, I think I will
take no steps whatsoever.—The Directory have received to-day the news of two victories, one in Italy,
(being, I believe, the tenth, at least, this campaign,)
in which Beaulieu has been again totally routed before
Mantua, with loss of all his baggage, cannon, stores,
and his whole Etat Major prisoners. That, I think,
will settle the affair in Italy. The other is on the
Rhine, being the second (the first was gained two or
three days before, but I forgot to insert it): I have
not seen the details, but I learn it is a complete
victory. The Emperor is like to make a worthy
campaign of it. To be sure, the military exertions
of the French are beyond belief. Only think of the
Government maintaining fourteen armies, (nearly

1,000,000 of men,) absolutely without money or credit. It is inconceivable. It is true, Buonaparte has raised a little cash in Italy, for he has given notice to Citizen Carnot to draw on him for seven millions, at sight, payable at the Bank of Genoa. I wonder how John Bull would like to discount his bill. However, after all, here am I in Paris, at a most critical period, and in a state of anxiety which baffles all description, writing nonsensical memorandums. I wonder where is P. P.! If the French are in Ireland, I think I can give a guess. Confusion! "*Tête, ventre, sang— Mille bombes!*" Are the sans-culottes in Ireland, and I here? Oh Citizen Carnot, can it be that you have broken faith with me? "White cat, white cat, thou hast deceived me! and instantly he felt the scratch of a cat's paw on his hand." Well, if the worst comes to the worst, my friends in Ireland will not forget me.

12. Drank punch last night with Madgett. He is come off his confidence a little, as to the landing. "Goodman Verges speaks a little of the matter; an old man and his wits are not so blunt, as, heaven help me! I could desire they were." He does bore me, sometimes, most confoundedly. Moreover, I think I see by his discourse that he has his eye on the ambassadorship of Ireland, that is to be. He has not talents for that station; and, besides, age is beginning to make inroads on his faculties: yet Madgett is a good fellow, and has, undoubtedly, a strong claim on the gratitude of his country, if she

succeeds; but he is not to be her ambassador to the French Republic. His misfortune is, that he thinks it is he does every thing, and moves every thing, and knows every thing, and I can see that he knows no more of what is going forward than my boot; it is laughable enough to see him sometimes hiding his ignorance and want of importance under a veil of great mystery and reserve, in which I always indulge him by telling him, like a dog as I am, that I do not want to press on his official delicacy, &c. He tells me to-day, that, in consequence of a memorial which he gave in some months ago, containing what passed in the Privy Council of England, with his remarks thereon, Spain will have a fleet at sea, and will break with England in fifteen days. " Would I could see it, quoth blind Hugh." I have quoted that already, but no matter. *Nous verrons.* It would be a great point gained, if Spain would declare against the common enemy of the liberties of mankind.

14. Called on Clarke this morning, for want of other idleness. Saw him for two minutes, mentioned Madgett's report of the landing, adding, that I did not believe it. He assured me it was utterly unfounded. So there is an end of that business. I observed, it was dreadfully indiscreet in whoever had set it going. He agreed, but observed it was sometimes impossible to prevent the indiscretion of people. He also told me he had not yet had time to read my proclamation as cut down. I fixed to call on him the 1st Messidor, in four or five

days, and so we parted. Clarke was civil enough. I want to consult him as to what I am to do, concerning trade affairs. My finances are reduced to a state truly deplorable. I am worth to-day about thirteen louis-d'ors, which will not last me more than a month, and I must not let myself be run to the last sol. I might have been, perhaps, something more economical, but not much, all things considered. Paris is, after all, much more reasonable than Philadelphia, and I need not say, a million of times more pleasant. Yet it is absolutely impossible to lead a more comfortless life than I do here. It is dreary; it is pitiful. All my habitudes are domestic, and here am I, isolated in the midst of Paris, in which there is not a single soul interested in my well or ill being. At home or abroad, it is all one, and I cannot express how this sinks my spirits. I am as much in a desert, for all purposes of happiness, as if I were in the midst of Caffraria. The Opera is my only resource, and that will not do at all times. I always go alone, and have nobody to whom I can communicate the pleasure I sometimes feel, or the observations which strike me. After the friendship of P. P. and the inestimable happiness of my dearest love's society, judge how I feel here, where neither man nor woman cares if I were in the moon. The only thing that consoles me, and it is a powerful consolation, is the unparalleled success of the French arms. I think England must tumble, and, if so, we rise. I see, in the "Morning Chronicle," which I get from time to time from Sullivan, that the journey of Lady Bute to Madrid, where her husband is ambassador, is suspended until it is known what turn affairs will take in Spain. I see, likewise, that there is a camp forming at St. Roch, and a levy of 60,000 men ordered in that country. That looks warlike. It is certain that Beaulieu is flying before Buonaparte, who gives him no respite; that the French are making a progress nearly as rapid on the Rhine as in Italy; that the Austrian armies are in the greatest disorder, and utterly dispirited and sick of the war, a circumstance of the last importance; that the Emperor has sent Count Metternich to London, most probably to announce his determination to make peace instantly, and, if so, the battle will remain to be fought out between France and England. *Alors, nous verrons!* Madgett, (but he is no great authority, as appears from divers parts of these entertaining and instructive memorandums) always informs me that we are waiting on the Dutch. Carnot tells me nothing, Clarke nothing, and the Minister knows, I am sure, no more than Madgett. Nic. Frog, it is true, is always plaguy slow in his motions, yet he has contrived to steal a march on John Bull already. Would to God he were after stealing a second. My very soul is sick with expectation. I cannot think it possible but England must tumble, and I have the greatest faith in the talents of the Government here, and in their *acharnement* against the English. It is said to-day that two deputies from the Emperor are actually arrived incognito, to treat for a peace.

That young gentleman has made prodigious acquisitions in the French territory, in virtue of his alliance with John Bull. It is said, likewise, that Richery has sailed from Cadiz, with his seven sail, and twelve sail of Spanish ships of the line under Solano, but nobody knows where. If they fall in with the British, that will probably bring matters to a crisis; but John Bull will thrash them both at sea, to the end of time, if they do not inveigle Pat out of his hands. I wish to God Carnot was as sensible of this as I am. Well, here I am, and here I must remain, and I am as helpless as if I were alone, swimming for my life in the middle of the Atlantic.

15. Got a parcel of English newspapers from Sullivan. Strolled out into the fields, all alone, and lay down under a hedge to read them. Melancholy as ten thousand devils, and no wonder. I see the Americans have ratified the English treaty, after all, by a majority of fifty-one to forty-eight. The Dutch fleet which gave John Bull the slip, put into Teneriffe, March 26th, in bad condition, to look for provisions. It consists of two sixty-fours, one fifty gun ship, four frigates, and two sloops of war. They are bound for the Cape of Good Hope. I wish they were well there, and after driving the English out, but I fear it. Quere. Are the troops on board French or Dutch? Because, on that circumstance the event will probably turn.—I see Combe is returned for the city of London, and Fox is first, on the 7th June, for Westminster; he is opposed by Admiral Gardiner, who is within a dozen of him;

Horne Tooke is the third candidate, and is above one thousand behind both of them. Fox and Tooke made admirable speeches from the hustings. From the little I can observe, being nearly uninformed, the new Parliament will probably be as hollow with Pitt as the old; I mean the counties, for as to the boroughs, there is no doubt of them. There are three war members, for example, returned for the city of London. So best! The more warlike they continue the better. Reading these papers has left me as dull as ditch water, and I did not need that.

17. Called to-day for the first time, God knows when! on the Minister. He was busy and could not see me. That is no good sign, nor is it very bad; altogether, I do not much glory in it. The news to-day is, that the King of Naples has made his peace, paying 30,000,000 livres, *en numeraire*, and withdrawing his cavalry from Beaulieu, and five sail of the line from the British Admiral in the Mediterranean. That will strengthen the Emperor and John Bull prodigiously! This news is not confirmed; but if it has not yet happened, it soon must, for the petty Princes of Italy are, as the French say, "*en queue pour faire la paix.*" This is an excellent metaphor, taken from a crowd, who stand one behind another in order to be served in their turn, as the poor of Paris, for example, at the bakers. There cannot be a more ridiculous image.

19. Called on Clarke by appointment. Found his aid-de-camp copying my proclamation, as abridg-

ed. Clarke seemed glad to see me, and begged me to make a copy myself, as he wanted it immediately. I accordingly sat myself down at his desk, and he went about his lawful occasions. In about half an hour I had finished, and he returned. I told him in three words the position of my affairs; that I had gone on thus far entirely on my own means, and calculated I had about as much as would enable me to carry on the war another month, in which time I should be "*a sec*," as the French say; finally, I asked his advice on the premises. He answered me friendly enough; he said they must provide for me in the military line, for which I had expressed an inclination, and in the cavalry, where the pay was most considerable; but added, that the pay of all ranks were below their necessities. He then asked, had I ever served? I answered, no; that I had been a volunteer in the Belfast regiment, which I considered as no service, but was fond of a military life, and in case of any thing being done for Ireland, it would be the line I should adopt. He then said my not having served might make some difficulty, but that he would see about it, and let me know the result in three or four days, adding, that I might be sure something would be done. He then took me in his carriage to the Minister's, with whom he had business. On the way I told him it was extremely painful to me to apply to the Republic for any pecuniary assistance, but that circumstances compelled me; that I was not a man of expense, and that of course a moderate supply would satisfy me; and added, that being engaged here in the service of my country, any sum advanced to me was to be considered as advanced on her account, and as such to be repaid, with all other expenses, at the conclusion of the business. He laughed at this, and said we should have no money. I said that was true, or, at least, we should not have much; but we should have means, and I instanced the quantity of English property which would, in that event, be forfeited to the state, and assured him we should have enough to pay our debts of justice, of honour, and of gratitude. As to want of money, which I admitted to him, he seemed to dwell on it but little;—France had given, and was giving, a splendid example of what could be done, even without money, when a people were in earnest. The conversation then turned on the expedition. He said it would be absolutely necessary the General-in-chief should speak English. I said it would, undoubtedly, be convenient, but not absolutely necessary. He then observed it would be hard to find an Irishman qualified for the command. I answered we should prefer a Frenchman, on account of the effect it would produce on public opinion, and especially a General whose name had figured in the Gazettes. (This is a circumstance I never miss to suggest, when an opportunity offers.) He then mentioned three or four names of Irish Generals, Kilmaine, Harty, Lynch, and O'Keefe, with his opinion on their situation and talents in very few words. I repeated I would wish to see a French General at the head of the business, and that these officers might be employed under him. He seemed at length to be of my opinion. In the course of this discussion, I asked him why he might not command the expedition himself? He answered, that if he were to make the offer, he was sure the Directory would not accept it, as they could not spare him from the department where he was placed. This discourse brought us to the Minister's, where we parted, and I am to return in a few days; in the mean time he is to see into my affair, and let me know the result.—And now, what is to be the end of this? When I made the offer and request of being employed in a military capacity, I certainly limited it in my own mind to the expedition, but here it is generalized. If I were a single man, I should not hesitate an instant, as I look upon the situation of an officer in the service of the French Republic, to be the most honourable in the world; and besides, it is my passion. But when I think of my wife, and our three children, (and perhaps, by this time, a fourth,) depending on my life for their existence, it staggers my resolution, and I know not what to determine. I have written to her to come to France, and am I to leave her and them to chance, and go, perhaps, to be knocked on the head at the frontiers? If I were an officer it would be only my duty, and I should have no choice; but as it is——In the service of my own country I hope I should avoid no danger which came fairly in my way, and if I fell, I should leave my family to the public gratitude, which would, I have no doubt, preserve them from want; but here I have no such prospect. I am extremely embarrassed. I will take these four days to consider.—After all, if I should turn out a Captain of French dragoons, it would be droll. " It is a life I have desired; I will thrive." Assuredly, if I were single, I would embrace the offer on the instant; but my fears for my wife and my poor little babies perplex me in the extreme. This offer makes no part of my original system, nor does it come in the strict line of my duty. I declare I know no more what to determine than a horse. Certainly,

> " To give a young gentleman right education,
> The army 's the only good school in the nation."

But then, Matty; and——and the darlings. Well, something I must do, and that speedily; for, " money, money, money is your friend." What would I give that my family were here to-day! Well, " Let the world wag ;" I have four days yet to reflect. I fancy I will state my difficulties to Clarke and hear what he says. *Allons! Courage!*

20. To-day is my birth-day—I am thirty-three years old. At that age Alexander had conquered the world; and at that age Wolfe had completed his reputation, and expired in the arms of victory. Well, it is not my fault, if I am not as great a man as Alexander or Wolfe. I have as good dispositions for glory as either of them, but I labour under two small obstacles at least—want of talents and want

of opportunities; neither of which, I confess, I can help. *Allons! nous verrons.* If I succeed here, I may make some noise in the world yet: and, what is better, the cause to which I am devoted is so just, that I have not one circumstance to reproach myself with. I will endeavour to keep myself as pure as I can, as to the means; as to the end, it is sacred— the liberty and independence of my country first, the establishment of my wife, and of our darling babies, next; and last, I hope, a well-earned reputation. I am sure I am doing my very best here, as, indeed, I have endeavoured to do all along. " I am not idle, but the ebbs and flows of fortune's tide cannot be calculated." I will push every thing here as far as I can make it go. I have taken it into my head to-day that our expedition will not take place, if at all, until the winter, because of the Channel fleet. Howe is to have the command, with twenty-eight sail of the line, and they are moving heaven and earth to man them. I should not be surprised if our business was the cause of these great exertions. I cannot doubt but Pitt is informed of every thing which passes here, and, of course, of my arrival, obscure as I am. Perhaps it may be fear of Spain, with whom it seems likely the Republic is about to form a treaty of alliance. At all events, if the Channel fleet be once at sea, there is an end of our expedition for the summer, as I told the Minister long since. Well, there is no remedy but patience. John will thrash them all at sea to the end of time, whilst he is able to press poor Pat into the service;

and this is what I labour (God knows with what success!) to impress on them here. If we were independent in Ireland, all parties, friends and enemies, would soon feel the difference.

21. I walk almost every day to the Tuileries to see the guard relieved. There are about four hundred infantry and from fifty to eighty dragoons. The grenadiers attached to the national representation, are, I am satisfied, for appearance, and I have no doubt for courage, the first corps in Europe. I am more and more pleased with the French soldiery, notwithstanding the slovenliness, to speak out, of their manœuvres and dress. Every one wears what he pleases; it is enough if his coat be blue and his hat cocked, and even that I have seen dispensed with; the essential part is that they all seem in high health and spirits, young, active, and fit for immediate service. Their arms they keep in *tolerable* order, but there is nothing of that brilliant polish of arms and accoutrements, which I have seen in England. Their bayonets are too short, which is a fault, and their muskets are much lighter than ours. Their grenadiers are noble fellows, and, luckily, Jourdan has 22,000 of them in one corps on the Rhine. They are fond of ornamenting themselves, particularly with flowers. One scarce sees a sentinel without a little bouquet in his hat or breast, and most frequently in the barrel of his firelock. I like that, and I do not know why; but it pleases me. I believe I have a small prejudice in favour of the French, especially the army,

which is the flower of the nation. Their dragoons are fine fellows, but ill-mounted, which is a pity; both they and their horses are slovenly, like the infantry; but that does not prevent them from fighting like tigers, for the truth of which I appeal to the slaves of the despots, whom they are driving before them, (thank God!) in all quarters. It is said, to-day, the Emperor sent Commissaries to the Directory, to amuse them and gain time; but the Directory smoked the contrivance, and refused all suspension of arms. They were quite right. Beat him well, and he will negotiate in good earnest. *" Si vis pacem, para bellum."* John has been defeated in his first attempt this campaign in the West Indies. He sent 4,000 men to take Leogane, but it seems they came back without their errand. Much good may it do his poor heart, because I have a regard for him!

22. Bad news to-day. Jourdan has received a check, and, I fancy, a pretty serious one, which has compelled him to repass the Rhine, and Kleber to fall back on the Sieg. He says it is but an affair of posts; but an affair of posts would not lead to such consequences. We have lost men, cannon, ground, and character, which is worst of all. I fear this will force Moreau, whose advanced guard is under the walls of Manheim, to retreat also. Bad! Bad!— Well, " 'Tis but in vain for soldiers to complain." One thing, however, it will encourage John Bull in his warlike propensities, and the King will meet his new Parliament with the successes of the Emperor

in his mouth : so out of evil comes good. Madgett showed me to-day a private letter which he had just received, indirectly, from London, informing him that a rupture with Spain was looked upon there as inevitable, and that the Admiralty were actually issuing letters of marque against the Spaniards. I hope to God it is true! Clarke has likewise applied to him for the names of such persons as he would wish to be employed in our business, and Madgett concludes, from circumstances, that there will be two embarkations, one from Holland and one from Brittany. I do not, however, build much on Madgett's inferences, which he often takes up on very slight grounds.

23. Called on Clarke in the morning, and found him in high good humour. He tells me that he has mentioned my business to Carnot, and that within a month I may expect an appointment in the French army. This is glorious! He asked me, would I choose to serve in the cavalry or infantry? I said it was equal to me, and referred it to him to fix me in the most eligible situation. I fancy it will be in the cavalry, " for a Captain of horse never takes off his hat." He then told me that he was at liberty to acquaint me so far, as that the business, and even the time, were determined on by the Directory, and the manner only remained under discussion. There is good news at last.—I observed to him, after expressing the satisfaction I sincerely felt at this information, that I wished to remind him of the great advantages to be derived from the landing being

effected in the North, particularly from the circumstance of framing our first army *of the different religious persuasions,* which I pressed upon him, I believe, with success. I then asked him, if he had many Irish prisoners remaining, as I thought they might be usefully employed in case of the landing being effected. He laughed at this, and said, " I see you want to form your regiment." I said I should like very well to command two or three hundred of them, who might be formed into a corps of Hussars, to serve in the advanced guard of the army, not only as soldiers, which I knew they would, and with sufficient courage, but as *eclaireurs* to *insense* the country people. He seemed to relish this a good deal, and I went on to say that, in such case, they should be as an Irish corps in green jackets, with green feathers, and a green standard with the harp, surmounted by the cap of liberty. He bit at this, and made me draw a sketch of the device, and also a description, which he took down himself in French, from which I infer the standard will be made directly. All the world, (viz. Matty, and Mary, and P. P.) will laugh heartily at this council of war, because it savours of the *Etat Militaires,* and P. P. in his wisdom, will remind me of my famous button for the National Volunteers, which did such mischief in Ireland. " But I will jump suddenly upon him, and deprive him of the use of his weapon," by reminding him that I swore solemnly then, never to quit until I saw that button upon every soldier's coat in Ireland; in which declaration, " clenching a fist something less than the knuckle of an ox, Mr. Adams declared he would support me." After that, I think he will be reduced to a state of silent mortification, which will be truly deplorable. To return to Clarke: He desired to see me regularly every fifth morning; and assuring me again that he would charge himself with my business, we parted. I fancy, in the upshot, I shall be sent to Lisle to recruit, and, in that event, I will make " reeling Bacchus call on Love for aid;" or, in the language of the vulgar, I will attack Pat with women and wine, which defy every care; and, because I know he has an ear for music, I will also bring a fiddle with me. I understand John Doyle's Irish heroes, (the 87th,) are there to a man; and, as many of them are from Prosperous, in my own county, and many more from Glasmanogue, and not a few from Mutton Lane and Crooked Staff, I think I shall be able to make something of them. I will make, I hope, as good a colonel as John Doyle, though he is a brave man and a tolerable officer. Whilst I was with Clarke, Madgett called on him, and I stepped into the next room whilst he gave him audience. It was to recommend Aherne to be employed as a military man in this business. Clarke seemed, I thought, disinclined. He asked me, did I know Aherne? I answered, that I saw him merely officially by the Minister's orders, but that I knew nothing whatsoever to his prejudice, and that, as to Madgett, I had a very good opinion of him, and, of course, supposed he would not recommend an improper person; that, however, I could say nothing from myself for or against him, further than what I had mentioned. N. B. I do not wish to hurt Aherne, but I had rather he was not employed in Ireland *at first*, for he is *outré* and extravagant in his notions; he wants a total *bouleversement* of all property, and he has not talents to see the absurdity and mischief, not to say the impossibility, of this system, if system it may be called. I have a mind to stop his promotion, and believe I must do it. It would be terrible doctrine to commence with Ireland. I wish all possible justice to be done to Aherne, but I do not wish to see him in a station where he might do infinite mischief. I must think of this. I told Clarke I had written for my family, and was determined, at all events, to settle in France.

24. "I have now not fifty ducats in the world!" but, hang it, that does not signify: am I not going to be an officer in the French service? I believe I might have been a little more economical, but I am sure not much. I brought with me one hundred louis to France, and they will have lasted me just six months, by the time they are run out; after all, that is no great extravagance. Besides, "a fool and his money are soon parted." Poor Pat was never much noted for his discretion on that point, and I am in some things as arrant an Irishman as ever stood on the Pont Neuf. I think I have made as good a defence as the nature of the case will admit, and I leave it to all the world whether I am not

fairly excusable for any little *dédommagement* which I can lay hold on, seeing the sacrifices I have made thus far, the services which I hope I shall at last have rendered my country, and especially the dreary and tristful solitude to which I have devoted myself in Paris, where I have not formed a single connection but with the persons indispensably necessary to the success of our business.

25. There has been a d——d lie in circulation these two days, that the advanced guard of Buonaparte's army in Italy has been cut to pieces, to the number of fifteen thousand men; and there are scoundrels in Paris base enough to seem not sorry for it. However, to-day it is formally contradicted, by a letter of Buonaparte's just published, which bears date thirteen days later, and makes no allusion to any check whatsoever. My heart was sunk down to my heels at the bad news, and I was as melancholy as a cat; for I have every thing dear to me embarked on the fortune of the Republic, and I would as lief they would put ratsbane in my mouth as come croaking to me with their evil tidings. " I am now a little better, but very faint still." I wish I was after getting my brevet. Madgett tells me to-day he has orders from Clarke to find him some twenty-five recruits in fifteen days, to be sent after the first fifteen to Hoche; and, in our last conversation, Clarke told me they were not for Ireland. Where the devil are they for, then?

26. I go regularly every day to the Tuileries, at twelve o'clock, to see the guard relieved: it is one of

my greatest relaxations. I take pride in the French troops, though they are neither powdered nor varnished like those of the other states of Europe. I frequently find the tears gush into my eyes whilst I am looking at them. It is impossible to conceive a body of finer fellows than the guards of the legislative body,* who are, by the by, perfectly well dressed and appointed, in every respect. They are all handsome young men, six feet high, and well proportioned. They have, as I believe I have remarked already, the air of officers in soldiers' coats, and look as if they were set up by the dancing master rather than the drill sergeant. As to the courage of the French soldiery, I believe it is now pretty well understood in Europe: nevertheless, "one Englishman is always able to beat five Frenchmen;" which is very consoling to John Bull. I wonder what figure poor Pat will cut upon the sod. I fancy he will not be much amiss. Well, let me once see myself in Ireland, buckled to a long sabre, and with a green coat on my back, and a pair of swinging epaulets on my shoulders, "*Alors nous verrons, MM. de la Cabale.*" The Whig Club, I see, are taking up the condition of the labouring poor. They are getting frightened, and their guilty consciences will not let them sleep. I suppose they will act like the gentry of Meath, who, for fear of the Defenders, raised their workmen's wages from eight-pence to a shilling per day, but took care at

---

\* This corps was the nucleus of Napoleon's *Vieille Garde*.

the same time to raise the rent of their hovels, and the grass for their cows, in the same proportion, so that at the end of the year the wretched peasant was not a penny the richer. Such is the honesty of the Squirearchy of Ireland. No! no! it is we who will better the condition of the labouring poor, if ever we get into that country; it is we that will humble the pride of that execrable and contemptible corps, the country gentlemen of Ireland. I know not whether I most hate or despise them, the tyrants of the people and slaves of the Government. Well, I must not put myself in a passion about them. I have not, however, forgotten the attack made on my honour by Mr. Grattan, nor that intended on my life by Mr. G. Ponsonby. I fancy I shall stand as high one day as either of those illustrious whigs. If I do, I hope I shall act as becomes me. I am in a good humour to-day; I do not know why. Huzza, generally! *Vive la Republique!* Went in the evening to the *Theatre Feydeau*, to see the " Festin de Pierre." Incomparably well performed. I remember P. P. was delighted with Don Juan, who is the archetype, as he observed, of Lovelace. Fleury, who played the part, is an admirable actor. He is the Lewis of the Theatre Feydeau, but Lewis is not worthy to be his *valet de chambre.* D'Azincourt is the Sganarelle, and a most excellent one. I saw this piece already at the *Theatre de la République,* with Baptiste and Dugazon in the same characters. It is hard to say which is best. I believe I prefer Fleury to Baptiste, and Dugazon to D'Azincourt.

They are all four inimitable actors. The English comedians are beasts beside the French, but this I have already said a thousand times. I have likewise seen lately the "Barbier de Séville," with Fleury in Almaviva, D'Azincourt in Figaro, and Mlle. Lange in Rosine. It is not possible to conceive better acting. D'Azincourt is the true Figaro of Beaumarchais, and Mlle. Lange is a charming woman, who has ruined several young fellows, and one in particular, twice over. I have also seen at the *Theatre de la République*, " Robert, chef de Brigands," a translation of the Robbers of Schiller. It acts very well, and Baptiste is admirable in Robert. I am writing here like a *Muscadin*, (N. B. *Dandy*) about the theatres, and all that kind of thing. But what can I do? I must write something to amuse myself, and I have nothing more serious. When I have, I will not be found to neglect it for the spectacles. After all, give me the opera.

27. A sad rainy day, and I am not well, and the blue devils torment me. Hell! Hell! Allah! Allah! Allah! To-morrow I will go and see Clarke about my commission. Will it not be extraordinary to see me in the service of the Republic? That will console me for the exile I lie under from my native country. It is raining now like ten thousand devils.

28. Called on Clarke by appointment. I told him I had two things to mention: First, that as we had the Pope now in our grasp, I wished him to consider whether we might not artfully seduce him into writing to his legate, Dr. Troy, in order to secure,

at least the neutrality, if not the support, of the Irish Catholic clergy. He objected, that this would be recognizing the authority of the Pope, and said he was sure the Directory would make no public application of this sort; besides, that it would be making the matter known in Italy. I replied, that undoubtedly it was not a matter for an official application, but for private address; and, as to making it known, it need not be applied for until the last stage of the business; nevertheless, I merely threw it out as a hint for his consideration, without pressing it, as I expected no formidable opposition from the priests in Ireland. The other thing I had to mention was, that Madgett told me last night there was a person going to London officially, as commissary of prisoners, and pressed me very much to write to my friends by that opportunity: that I had only said I would think of it, as I did not consider myself at liberty to take such a step without his approbation. That I wished to know whether I should write or not, and, if I were to write, what line I should follow? That, if I were to allude to our business, I must beg him to give me such information as he might think fit to communicate, without at all wishing to press him on the subject. That, if I were not, I thought it best not to write at all, as I was in general disinclined to writing, even where it was necessary, and much more so in the present instance, where all I should have to say would be, that I was alive and well in Paris. Clarke answered, "As to that, your friends know it already." I replied, "Not that I knew of." He answered, " Ay, but I know it, but cannot tell you at present how." He then went on to tell me he did not see how to explain himself farther, " for," added he, "if I tell you ever so little, you will guess the rest." So it seems I am a cunning fox without knowing it. He gave me, however, to understand that he had a communication open with Ireland, and showed me a paper, asking me if I knew the handwriting. I did not. He then read a good deal. It stated very briefly, that fourteen of the counties, including the entire North, were completely organized for the purpose of throwing off the English yoke and establishing our independence; that, in the remaining eighteen, the organization was advancing rapidly, and that it was so arranged that the inferiors obeyed their leaders, without examining their orders, or even knowing who they were, as every one knew only the person immediately above him. That the militia were about 20,000 men, 17,000 of whom might be relied on; that there were about 12,000 regular troops, wretchedly bad ones, who would soon be settled in case the business were attempted. Clarke was going on, but stopped here suddenly, and said, laughing, " There is something there which I cannot read to you, or you will guess." I begged him to use his discretion without ceremony. He then asked me, did I know of this organization? I replied, that I could not, with truth, say positively I knew it, but that I had no manner of doubt of it; that it was now twelve months exactly since I left Ireland, in which time,

I was satisfied, much must have been done in that country, and that he would find in my memorials that such an organization was then begun, was rapidly spreading, and, I had no doubt, would soon embrace the whole people.—It is curious this coincidence between the paper he read me and those I have given here, though upon second thought, as truth is uniform, it would be still more extraordinary if they should vary. I am delighted beyond measure with the progress which has been made in Ireland since my banishment. I see they are advancing rapidly and safely. The paper also stated, as I had done, that we wanted arms, ammunition, and artillery; in short, it was as exact in all particulars, as if the same person had written all. This fixes my credit in France beyond a doubt. Clarke then said, as to my business, he was only waiting for letters from General Hoche, in order to settle it finally; that I should have a regiment of cavalry, and it was probable it might be arranged that day; that the marshalling of the forces intended for the expedition was entrusted to Hoche, by which I see we shall go from Brittany instead of Holland. All's one for that, provided we go at all. I returned Clarke my acknowledgments, and he went on, desiring me not to mention all this to Madgett, of whose discretion he had no opinion, (in which he is very right) but rather to train him off the scent, by appearing to think the business not likely to be attempted, which I promised I would take care to do. We had then some good-humoured laughing at Madgett, who is literally the greatest P. P. I ever saw. In fact, the " *Cinq*" are but five puppets, whom he dances, and Carnot, a soft youth, who never opens his mouth but to utter the words which he puts into it. He amuses me often by this, as I have already remarked in these wise and engaging memorandums. Clarke then said, he supposed they should see me again here as Ambassador. I replied, that if the business was undertaken, I was ready to serve my country, where and in what manner she thought I could be most useful; that, if my services were necessary in France, I should undoubtedly be highly honoured by the station, but I rather thought, from the circumstance of my being, perhaps, the only man so intimately connected with both Catholics and Dissenters, (from the station I held with the one, and the friendship which, I might say, the others bore me,) that I should be detained in Ireland, in order to cultivate and ensure that spirit of harmony and union so essential to the success of our affairs. I took this opportunity to mention to Clarke, that, on my departure, I should have a request to make to the Directory, viz. that, if they were satisfied with my conduct here, they would be pleased to signify it by a letter, addressed to me from the President, or a resolution, or such means as they might think proper, in order that I might have, on my return, a testimonial to show my countrymen that I had, to the best of my power, executed their instructions. Clarke said he was sure the Directory would readily accede to my request, which was but reasonable; and, in fact, I think so myself.

> " Such services rendered, such dangers incurred,
> He himself thinks he ought to be better preferred."

I have a fine spot of ground here, clear before me, for castle-building, but I will not be in too great a hurry to lay the first stone. I have not got my commission yet, and it will be quite time enough when I am Colonel to begin dreaming of being an Ambassador. " A Colonel of horse in the service of the Republic!" Is it not most curious? Well, after all, I begin to believe my adventures are a little extraordinary. Eighteen months ago, it was a million to one that I should be hanged as a traitor, and now I am like to enter the country in which I was not thought worthy to live, at the head of a regiment of horse. It is singular. P. P. used always to be foretelling great things, and I never believed him, yet a part of his prophecy seems likely to be verified. He said that I had more talents, and would make a greater figure than Plunkett or Burrowes. For the talents, " negatur," but for the figure, the devil puts it into my head sometimes that he was right. I am very well pleased with myself this morning, as I believe the track of these memorandums will prove. My name may be spoken of yet, and I trust there is nothing, thus far, attached to it of which I need be ashamed. If ever I come to be a great man, let me never forget two things :—The honour of my masters of the General

Committee, who refused to sacrifice me to the requisition of Mr. Grattan; and the friendship, I may say, of the whole town of Belfast, at the moment of my departure into exile. These are two instances of steadiness and spirit, under circumstances peculiarly trying, which do honour to them, to me, and to our common nature. I never will forget them. Affairs look rather well in the north to-day; Moreau has passed the Rhine on three points near Strasbourg, and I cannot foresee the consequences, for Madgett tells me he has organized a revolution in Swabia, and, if the poor Emperor Francis loses that, after Brabant and the Milanese, what will he do? To be sure, the French are going on miraculously this campaign. It must be Providence itself which guides them, for the common liberties of man. Surely, surely, our poor country cannot be fated to remain much longer in slavery to England. The Milanese have three Commissioners now in Paris to negotiate the establishment of a republic and the subversion of the Austrian tyranny. Well, poor Ireland has a sort of a Commissioner too, at Paris, on pretty much a like business. Oh! if the British were once chased from Ireland, as the Austrians from Milan! Well, who knows? But their d——d fleet torments me. As it is, we ourselves, miserable rascals that we are, are fighting the battles of the enemy, and riveting on our own fetters with our own hands. It is terrible! There is a report to-day that the Piedmontese are in open insurrection; that the King of

Sardinia has been forced to fly from Turin, and take refuge under the French flag at Coni, one of his ci-devant fortresses. It is by no means improbable. Thus all the world are emancipating themselves but Ireland, notwithstanding which, as I have always told P. P., " we are undoubtedly the bravest nation in Europe." I wish I could see a little more of it though. Well, perhaps I may by-and-by. "I hope to see a battle yet before I die." But, I am running on with nonsense. Let me return to General Clarke. I mentioned to him that it would be highly necessary somebody should be sent to Ireland without delay, to apprize the people there of what was going forward. He said he was surprised Aherne did not go. I answered, that he had not the means, the Government not having yet paid up his arrears. Clarke said, as to that, he knew nothing, but as to the sum necessary for his departure, he could have it at once. I observed, that it seemed to me highly indiscreet to trust a man so far as the Minister had trusted Aherne, even to giving him his instructions, and afterwards to break with him, in which Clarke concurred. And certainly it is strange conduct in De la Croix, though I am not sorry on the whole that Aherne does not go to Ireland. From an expression of Clarke, I am led to suppose it possible that he may be himself of the expedition. He has relations here in the French service, one of whom, at least, will go for Ireland; and he observed that he had some doubts how others of them, who remained in Ireland, would act; " but, I believe," added he, " when they see Elliot (his cousin) with me, they will most probably join us.". The words *with me*, struck me; but I did not ask him for any explanation. The thing will soon explain itself. He told me Moreau's plan for crossing the Rhine had been arranged six months back in the Directory, and the secret kept all the time. That is surprising. As for our business, it is what the French call " *Le secret de la Comedie ;*" but I cannot help that.

29. Madgett tells me to-day that he has heard from Duckett, who is, I understand, a great blackguard, (who has heard from a Mr. Morin, who is I know not what,) that there are to be two expeditions to Ireland, one from Flushing, commanded by General Macdonald, an Irishman, and the other from Brest, commanded by General Hoche. Madgett added that he had endeavoured to put Duckett off the scent, by saying he did not believe one word of the story, but that Duckett continued positive. The fact is, it seems likely enough to be the truth, and probably is so; but it is most terribly provoking to have the subject bandied about as table-talk by such a fellow as this Duckett, to whom, by-the-by, Charles De la Croix revealed in confidence all that he knew three months ago, for which he ought to be d——d : happily at present he knows nothing, as I believe; so I presume he will keep the secret. I took this opportunity to train off myself a little from Madgett, in consequence of the hint which Clarke gave me yesterday, by saying that I was weary, and sick of expectation, when I saw nothing done, and

that my belief was, nothing would be done; that I wished I had my family in France, and were settled quietly in some little spot, and well quit of the business. He exhorted me not to despair, at which I only shook my head significantly, like Lord Burleigh, and so we parted. I am to-day on my last five louis, which is a circumstance truly amusing. My regiment, if I get it, comes just in the nick of time. But hang money, I hate to think of it, and yet there is no doing without it, in this vale of tears. "*Effodiuntur opes, irritamenta malorum,*" as the learned Lilly saith in his grammar. If that be so, I shall soon be on the high road to virtue, for I am like to be shortly quit of all temptation to vice. But hang it for me, as I have said archly enough above. (Sings) " Oh money, money, money is your friend." —" Passion of my heart and life, I have a greater mind to cry." (Sings) " When as I sat in Babylon ; and a thousand vagrant posies," &c. &c. &c.

END OF VOL. I.

LONDON:
PRINTED BY S. AND R. BENTLEY, DORSET STREET.

CPSIA information can be obtained
at www.ICGtesting.com
Printed in the USA
LVHW080429201222
735535LV00004B/142

9 781357 412890